FELICE D. GORDON

After Winning
The Legacy of the New Jersey
Suffragists, 1920–1947

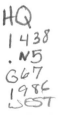 Rutgers University Press, New Brunswick, New Jersey

Winner of the New Jersey Historical Commission's
Alfred E. Driscoll Prize

Library of Congress Cataloging in Publication Data

Gordon, Felice D., 1932–
   After winning.
      Bibliography: p.
      Includes index.
      1. Feminists—New Jersey—History—20th cen-
tury.   2. Women social reformers—New Jersey—His-
tory—20th century.   3. Women—Suffrage—New
Jersey—History—20th century.   4. Women in poli-
tics—New Jersey—History—20th century.   I. Title.
HQ1438.N5G67   1986   324.6'2'09749   85–11745
ISBN 0–8135–1137–2

Title page illustration: Representatives of the Consumers' League of New Jersey, the New Jersey Women's Republican Club and other women's organizations look on
as Governor George S. Silzer signs the Night Work Bill
into law, March 21, 1923. From the Records of the Consumers' League of New Jersey. Courtesy of Department
of Special Collections and Archives, Rutgers University
Libraries.

For Alvin

Contents

Preface

THIS book began several years ago as an investigation into women's political activities in New Jersey in the fifty-year period after women won the vote. I planned to evaluate women's political role in this period as a reflection of their role and status in American society. While political scientists had studied women as voters, as political party members and officers, and as officeholders in the post–World War II era, and while historians had examined women's political role as an aspect of the suffrage movement, very little research had been done on women's political activities in the postsuffrage era at either the national or state levels. New Jersey, an urban, industrialized state, could serve as a test case to illuminate the experience of women in politics. Moreover, I believed that the findings would be a useful contribution to the history of women, for the involvement of women in the political arena challenged the traditional view that politics, a highly public activity, was properly reserved for men and that women's primary obligations were to the more private realm of home and family.

As I explored the varied aspects of women's political participation, I began with the New Jersey suffragists and their dramatic fight for the vote. Their organizational records, their personal papers, and the newspaper accounts of their activities brought them to life. I gradually began to feel that I knew the leaders almost on a personal basis, and I was somewhat in awe of them. They seemed to be a special breed of strong, dedicated, articulate women. Many of the same women who labored for years to put a state suffrage referendum on the ballot in 1915 were holding major leadership positions when the federal amendment was ratified in February 1920. And when the vote was achieved and incorporated into the federal constitution, the suffragists did not put aside their burdens of leadership but continued in a variety of ways to work for the social reform many had promised would occur and to press for the complete equality many had sought.

It was soon apparent that my original research objective was far too broad and unwieldy but that narrowing my focus to studying the activities of the New Jersey suffragist leaders both in the suffrage and postsuffrage periods would yield many of the answers I had sought about women and politics and would shed some light on the often asked but not satisfactorily answered question What happened to feminism after 1920?

I wish to express my gratitude to the many individuals who helped me bring this book to fruition. First, I want to thank Gerald N. Grob for his continual encouragement, for his careful reading and suggestions for changes in the original draft as well as his ready availability for consultation. My appreciation also goes to William L. O'Neill, particularly for his suggestion that I narrow my original broad focus to examine the activities of the suffragists after 1920; to Richard P. McCormick for his thoughtful comments and probing questions which helped immeasurably to shape my study; to Ruth B. Mandel, director of the Center for the American Woman and Politics, for her insights about the parallels between the experiences of the suffragists in politics in the 1920s and 1930s and those of women today. I am grateful to the New Jersey Historical Commission for awarding my manuscript the Alfred E. Driscoll Prize, which helped to make the publication of this book possible.

I am indebted to the staffs of various libraries whose facilities I used for my research. I particularly want to thank Edward Skipworth of Special Collections, Alexander Library, Rutgers University; Don Skemmer, Keeper of Manuscripts, New Jersey Historical Society and his successor Carl Lane; and Olga Mackaronis, executive secretary of the New Jersey State Federation of Women's Clubs.

My appreciation goes to Phyllis Marchand who provided a comprehensive index to a relatively complex text; and to June Traube for her painstaking labors typing the first and final drafts of the manuscript.

I want especially to thank my husband, Alvin, who not only gave me support and encouragement during the years I was engaged in researching and writing this book but was a most careful and constructive critic.

Abbreviations

AF of L	American Federation of Labor
CCCW	Committee on the Cause and Cure of War
CEDAW	Committee to Eliminate Discriminations Against Women
CFLE	Committee for Law Enforcement
CLNJ	Consumers' League of New Jersey
CU	Congressional Union for Woman Suffrage
LWV	League of Women Voters
NAWSA	National American Woman Suffrage Association
NCL	National Consumers' League
NJFBPWC	New Jersey Federation of Business and Professional Women's Clubs
NJLWV	New Jersey League of Women Voters
NJSFCWC	New Jersey State Federation of Colored Women's Clubs
NJSFWC (SFWC)	New Jersey State Federation of Women's Clubs
NJWCTU	New Jersey Woman's Christian Temperance Union
NJWP	New Jersey Woman's Party
NJWLC	New Jersey Women Lawyers' Club
NJWRC	New Jersey Women's Republican Club
NJWSA	New Jersey Woman Suffrage Association
NJWTUL	New Jersey Women's Trade Union League
NLWV	National League of Women Voters
NWP	National Woman's Party
OWLs	Organized Women Legislators
SC	State Council (State Council of New Jersey Republican Women)
SFWC	New Jersey State Federation of Women's Clubs
WCTU	Woman's Christian Temperance Union
WIL	Women's International League for Peace and Freedom
WJCC	Women's Joint Congressional Committee
WPU	Women's Political Union
WSRC	Women's State Republican Club

After Winning

Introduction

THE course of feminism in the United States after 1920 has yet to be fully examined by historians. Far more is known about women's activities on behalf of social reform and equal rights in the period preceding that date. Feminism as a vital movement was laid to rest, historians have said, with the winning of the vote, not to resurface for another forty or so years, in the 1960s. Or so it has seemed, based on the existing research. Indeed, the following composite portrait of feminists in general and suffragists in particular can be drawn from the studies of several historians—Eleanor Flexner, Aileen Kraditor, William O'Neill, Lois Banner, and William Chafe—who have focused primarily on the woman's movement at the national level:[1]

Unlike the suffragists of the nineteenth century, who demanded the vote because it was woman's natural right, their early twentieth century counterparts sought the ballot because of the good they thought it would accomplish. The twentieth century suffragists claimed that women, armed with the ballot, would end political bossism, dissolve the trusts, and secure the passage of laws that would improve society. As mothers and homemakers, they felt uniquely qualified to deal with social problems men had failed to solve. Much of society was, after all, an extension of the home. Emphasizing their traditional roles as guardians of the family, and not seeking the broad equal rights once demanded by the nineteenth century feminists, these suffragists gained a large following and ultimately won a victory for their cause with the passage of the Nineteenth Amendment. The suffragists thus made the ballot a panacea for society's ills, but having promised the millennium they were vulnerable to ridicule when they failed to achieve their objectives. Not only did a small percentage of women vote in the 1920s, but they voted much like their husbands. No woman's bloc appeared. The woman's movement, once held together by the drive for the suffrage, now splintered into numerous organizations. Those organizations that had existed before 1920 were now weakened by smaller memberships and a hostile, conservative climate. Moreover, younger women did not share their mothers' enthusiasm for social reform. Their concerns were personal. They embraced instead the social changes of their era: a new sexual freedom; a relaxed dress code; and opportunities to drink, smoke, and dance in public. The final blow to the hopes of the suffragists was delivered with the onset of the Depression in the 1930s. The concern with recovery ended any possibility that the reform efforts of the suffragists might be revived.

This portrait of the postsuffrage fate of feminism is just beginning to be challenged by historians who have posed new questions about women's experience in the 1920s and 1930s and taken a closer look at women's public activities in this era.[2] Did the suffragists retire from public life after the vote was attained, these historians have queried, or did they channel their efforts into other organizations? Did the suffragists make a concerted attempt to get into the parties? Have the post-1920 activities of women at the state and local levels been obscured by the tendency of historians to focus on the national scene? Why did the early hopes of the suffragists, so bright after winning the vote, that women would be an effective force for social reform and sexual equality dim as the years wore on? When there was failure, where did the responsibility lie?

This book is part of the recent historical effort to enlarge our understanding of the course of the suffrage movement and to fill the gap in women's history literature in the post-1920 period. It is a study of the postsuffrage activities of the New Jersey suffragist leaders who served on the boards of the major state suffrage organizations from 1910 to 1920 and carries forward that investigation until 1947, when a new state constitution was adopted. New Jersey had an active suffrage movement and is thus an appropriate state for an in-depth analysis. It is my contention that the experience of women in public life in New Jersey in these decades was not unique but was replicated in many ways in other urban, industrialized states. But before this can be said with certainty, numerous other state studies on this subject will have to be completed.

In 1910 the New Jersey suffrage movement was more than fifty years old. Beginning that year, paralleling developments in the suffrage movement nationwide, it gained new vitality and momentum. New suffrage groups were organized, and a dynamic new leadership in all suffrage organizations used arguments and aggressive strategies

that dramatically increased enrollments and heightened public awareness of the suffragists' demands. The suffragists' activities, previously
reported in the back pages of the woman's columns of the daily newspapers, began to receive major news coverage. No longer limiting
their efforts to camp meetings and parlor get-togethers, the suffragists made house-to-house canvasses in major cities; traveled in
colorfully decorated automobiles around the state, advertising their
slogans; and held mass rallies and parades. Throughout the ensuing
decade, equal franchise leagues and suffrage societies sought to
win men and women to their cause through press releases, public
speeches, broadsides, and pamphlets.

To answer the broad questions posed by this study, specific questions need to be asked about the suffrage and postsuffrage period:
What were the major New Jersey suffrage organizations, when were
they organized, and who were their leaders? Why did the suffragists
believe women should be given the vote? Who were the individuals
and what were the organizations that opposed woman suffrage? After
the suffrage was won, did the suffrage leaders continue as activists in
various organizations? Can the suffragists be described as reformers in
this period, or did they become disillusioned with reform? What were
they involved with ten years after winning the vote? Twenty years
later? From a national standpoint, historians have judged that the suffragists' successful campaign for the vote and their postsuffrage endeavors made little difference to the position of women. What of the
New Jersey suffrage movement? Was it overall a failure or a success?
Or is it valid to judge it in these terms? Did the suffragists have en-
during accomplishments?

The answers to these and other questions can be found in the
records of the New Jersey women's organizations the suffragists
joined, the papers of several suffragists, and the newspaper reports of
organized women's activities in the 1920s and 1930s. The records, papers, and reports tell a story similar to its national counterpart only
in its broadest outlines, for, looking closely at the details, that story is
far more complex. The historical record reveals the ultimate failure of
the suffragists to achieve political equality and equal rights in general
and, contrastingly, the strengthening of women's reform, nonpartisan organizations. This outcome, however, was far from certain in
the early years after the suffrage was won. In the early 1920s the possibility was strong that women could eventually move into political

life in increased numbers with real influence. Women's failure to win equal rights in the political arena and their solidified role as reformers—or Moral Prodders, as I call them—who chose to remain essentially outside the political system, was the gradual result of developments that spanned a period of approximately twenty-years. This study is an examination of those developments.

My characterization of suffragists as Moral Prodders and Equal Righters does not imply hard and fast categories. Rather, the terms serve to indicate the different directions women took as they assumed their new voting rights and the sex-role definitions that those directions embraced. The Moral Prodders emphasized women's special interests and moral qualities that they believed necessitated a separate political identity. The Equal Righters stressed women's basic similarity with men, which, they said, called for equal access to economic and political life. The point here is one of emphasis. Indeed, at times the lines were not that clearly drawn. The suffragists in the New Jersey League of Women Voters, for example, were the ideological soul mates of their counterparts in the other nonpartisan organizations, all of whom I have categorized as Moral Prodders; yet they could take a number of equal rights stands. Similarly, the suffragists and other women who chose to be active in the political parties, whom I have judged to be basically Equal Righters in outlook, could maintain that women had special moral virtues. And even the members of the Woman's Party (as Susan Becker points in her study of the national organization between the wars), who fought so adamantly for the Equal Rights Amendment and complete legal equality, could assert that their feminist goals were essential because of women's special, indeed superior, attributes.[3]

Almost all the suffragists I studied served on the executive boards of the major state suffrage organizations. A few exceptions were those women known to have served as presidents of large suffrage organizations in major cities, such as Elizabeth and Camden, and to have been active in the postsuffrage period. Other exceptions were women who held positions in the National American Woman Suffrage Association or who headed organizations that actively endorsed suffrage, such as the New Jersey Women's Trade Union League.

Whenever possible, I call the suffragists by their full given name, such as Caroline Wittpenn (or Mrs. Wittpenn) and not the name usually listed on the organization's letterhead, such as Mrs. Otto

Wittpenn. When at times I refer to a woman as a suffragist in the postsuffrage period, I am, of course, referring to the fact that she was a suffrage leader before 1920. On the other hand, my labeling of women as "nonsuffragists" or as "associates" or "fellow workers" of the suffragists does not necessarily mean that these women had been opposed to woman suffrage (while some of them were undoubtedly antis, or indifferent to the question, it is more likely that they either supported the suffrage drive or were too young to have participated in it) but that they had no known or active connections to the suffrage movement. Indeed, the "associates" are an ever-present part of this study. For while this book focusees on the suffragists, it is also about the many women without strong suffragist ties who joined the suffragists in the 1920s and 1930s in active involvement in public life.

CHAPTER ONE

The Demand for the Vote, 1857–1920

T wo events—one in 1857 and the other in 1858—could be said to have marked the unofficial beginning of the New Jersey suffrage movement. The first occurred on February 25, 1857, in the State House in Trenton, when the Special Committee on the Equality of Women's Rights of the Assembly Committee on Judiciary heard a petition from a group of Monmouth residents, led by one Harriet M. Lafetra, that stated "'men and women alike suffer many evils,' and [requested] a revision of the statutes of New Jersey so as to remove 'the various and grievious legal disabilities under which the *latter* are placed, and thereby establish the legal equality of women with men.'" The committee responded that it could not fulfill the petitioners' request. Although it agreed that "both men and women alike suffer many evils," it pointed out that revision of the state statutes would not only be "a task in comparison of which the labors of Hercules sink into insignificance" but would be contrary to the appropriate subordinate position of women to men. The first woman, Eve, it noted, had "introduced sin into the world." Although men sympathized with women, and even looked up to them as their superiors in many regards, the task of ruling matters of state and in family relations had forever gone rightly to men, ever since that fateful day in the Garden of Eden.[1]

The second event occurred in December 1858, when the tax collector in Orange received the following letter:

> Orange, N.J. December 18, 1858
>
> Mr. Mandeville, Tax Collector, Sir:
>
> Enclosed I return my tax bill, without paying it. My reason for doing so is, that women suffer taxation, and yet have no representation, which is not only unjust to one-half of the adult population, but is contrary to our theory of government. For years some women have been paying their taxes under protest, but still taxes are imposed, and representation is not granted. The only course now left us is to refuse to pay the tax. We know well what the immediate result of this refusal must be.

But we believe that when the attention of men is called to the wide difference between their theory of government and its practices, in this particular, they cannot fail to see the mistake they now make, by imposing taxes on women, while they refuse them the right of suffrage, and that the sense of justice which is in all good men, will lead them to correct it. Then shall we cheerfully pay our taxes—not till then.

Respectfully,

Lucy Stone[2]

The author of the letter was already a relatively well known woman's rights advocate. Her husband, Henry Brown Blackwell, was equally known as an outspoken abolitionist. Nine years after writing this letter she would help to found the New Jersey Woman Suffrage Association. Since her graduation from Oberlin College in 1847, Stone had been speaking, from church pulpits and on the lecture circuit of the Anti-Slavery Society, on behalf of woman's rights and black emancipation. In 1850 she was a participant in the first Woman's Rights Convention in Worcester, Massachusetts.[3]

Lucy Stone was a member of the first generation of notable woman suffragists, among whom where Elizabeth Cady Stanton, Lucretia Mott, and Susan B. Anthony. It was these women who argued, on the grounds that justice demanded it, for female suffrage; abolitionism; and a variety of legal, professional, and educational rights for women. Some of them were leading participants in the historic Seneca Falls Convention, held in upstate New York in 1848, whose Declaration of Sentiments modeled after the Declaration of Independence supported equality for women. They held annual woman's rights conventions between 1850 and the outbreak of the Civil War.[4]

In the antebellum period, suffragists felt that the lack of the vote was but one of many inequalities that women endured. Suffrage, moreover, was not given strong emphasis. As historian Eleanor Flexner notes, "The early woman's rights movement showed little interest in getting the vote; few felt its importance then as strongly as Mrs. Stanton. Of more immediate concern were the control of property, of earnings (not the same thing by any means), guardianship, divorce, opportunity for education and employment, lack of legal status (women still could not sue or bear witness), and the whole concept of female inferiority perpetuated by established religion."[5]

The suffragists were rejecting the Victorian idea that men and women had sharply delineated spheres of endeavor: men that of work, and women that of home and family. As several historians have recently observed, the Victorians, in the early nineteenth century, elaborated a cult of domesticity that described woman's world as a moral, serene haven from the pressures of business and commerce. The cult of domesticity made women the moral superiors of men but also denied them the political and civil rights that men took for granted. But the concept of woman's sphere also fostered women's growing sense that they shared a special outlook with one another. Paradoxically, it was women's belief that they had different concerns than men that forged what Nancy Cott has called "the bonds of womanhood," which ultimately made the early woman's rights movement possible.[6]

Stone was a prominent figure in a split that developed in the woman's rights movement shortly after the Civil War. The congressional decision to enforce the franchise of all black men, including the newly freed slaves, by constitutional amendment (the Fourteenth and Fifteenth amendments) and to ignore the demands of women for the ballot forced feminists to decide whether these amendments should have their support. In 1869 two national woman suffrage organizations came into being in large part over this question. The National Woman Suffrage Association, organized by Stanton and Anthony, opposed the amendments and pledged to work for a broad spectrum of equal rights for women. The American Woman Suffrage Association, founded by Stone and Henry Ward Beecher, accepted the amendments as a realistic first step and committed itself to winning the suffrage on a state-by-state basis.[7]

Suffrage had thus moved to a prominent place on the woman's rights agenda. The founding of the New Jersey Woman Suffrage Association (NJWSA) in 1867 was part of the movement to establish similar state associations throughout the country. The New Jersey suffrage movement, however, had a unique quality. While suffragists elsewhere worked to win the vote for women, the New Jersey suffragists insisted that they wanted only to regain what once had legally been theirs. They argued that women had been granted the right to vote by the Constitution of 1776 (which gave voting rights to "inhabitants" who met the property and residence requirements) and that they had been illegally deprived of that right by a new election law in 1807, which strictly limited the franchise to free white men.[8] This law was formally incorporated into the new state Constitution adopted in 1844. (Indeed, until it was withdrawn, women—primarily single women and widows—had exercised their right of suffrage.)[9]

The suffragists insisted that the law of 1807 was illegal and that its subsequent inclusion in the Constitution of 1844 was illegal as well since constitutional procedure, which provided that an amendment to the Constitution be passed "by a majority of both houses of two successive legislatures" and then "ratified by the people, at a special election," had been ignored. In the late 1860s delegations of suffragists presented a number of petitions to the legislature seeking restoration of their suffrage rights, and on at least two separate occasions they challenged the legality of the Constitution of 1844 by entering the polls and attempting, unsuccessfully, to vote with the male voters.[10]

These early suffragists wanted the vote for a variety of reasons. Justice demanded both that their rights be restored and that they not be taxed without representation. But the ballot meant more. It would give women the power to rectify many state laws that placed them in a position of "servitude and inferiority." These laws were enumerated by Stone in a pamphlet published by the state suffrage association in 1868 entitled "Reasons Why the Women of New Jersey Should Vote."[11] Stone's remarks embraced a new component of the suffragist argument, one that would become more prominent toward the end of the nineteenth century, not only in New Jersey, but throughout the nation. The early suffragists had focused on justice as the basis of their brief for woman's rights. Later suffragists retained that argument and added another: expediency. The "justice" argument rested on the doctrine of natural rights and the equality of all persons. The "expediency" argument sought to demonstrate what women could accomplish if given the vote. Stone's writings expressed both points of view.[12]

The vigorous suffrage activity that took place in the years immediately after the founding of the NJWSA was due in large part to the leadership of its founder. Suffrage societies were formed in numerous cities, including Newark, Paterson, Passaic, Camden, New Brunswick, Rahway, Morristown, and Vineland, and state conventions were called at irregular intervals. When the Blackwells left New

Jersey in 1870 for Stone's native state of Massachusetts, the suffrage groups lapsed into relative inactivity.[13]

There were several important exceptions to the suffragists' general failure to gain ground in the next two decades. First, a state law, passed in 1873, granted women the right to run for the position of school trustee. Second, another passed in 1887 enabled women residing in villages and country districts (but not in cities) to vote at school meetings. The latter law was interpreted to mean that women could vote for trustees as well as for appropriations. Between 1873 and 1895, fifty women served as school trustees. This grant of limited suffrage paralleled similar moves in other states: Kansas in 1861, Michigan and Minnesota in 1875. By 1890, nineteen states had granted full school suffrage.[14]

The third exception, which took place in the 1880s, was the decision of the New Jersey Woman's Christian Temperance Union to support the suffrage cause. The NJWCTU had been founded in 1874, the same year that the national body was organized in Cleveland. The founders believed that excessive consumption of alcohol was destructive to family life and particularly oppressive to women. Frances Willard, the national WCTU secretary-treasurer, first spoke publicly in favor of woman suffrage at the national convention in 1876, declaring that women needed the ballot to change the drinking laws and to effect a variety of other reforms. Willard pushed for the formal endorsement of suffrage and immediately tried to build support by speaking at various state WCTU conventions. The NJWCTU was slow to take up her challenge, but seven years later, following the lead of the national organization, it announced that it intended to support woman suffrage. In 1884 it established its Department of Franchise, with Theresa Walling Seabrook of Keyport, an ardent suffragist, as chairman.[15]

With the reorganization of the NJWSA in 1890, the suffrage movement gained new life. Eleven suffragists meeting in Orange adopted a new constitution and elected Judge John Whitehead president and Dr. Mary D. Hussey, an attorney, secretary-treasurer. Hussey and succeeding presidents in the next three years—the Reverend Antoinette Brown Blackwell in 1891, Amelia Dickinson Pope in 1892, and Florence Howe Hall in 1893—had been active suffragists for many years and knew the national leaders as well. Hussey's mother, a well-to-do

Quaker, had been in the state suffrage movement since the 1870s and had contributed generously to the suffrage cause. Hall's mother was Julia Ward Howe of Boston, a leader of the American Woman Suffrage Association and author of "The Battle Hymn of the Republic." Blackwell, who had the distinction of being the first woman ordained as a minister in the United States, participated in the first national Woman's Rights Convention. Hall's administration, lasting from 1893 to 1900, was the most influential. Local societies were established in Bayonne, Elizabeth, Plainfield, Westfield, Passaic, and Orange, and the association held its first public meetings.[16]

The organizational change and revitalization of the state suffrage movement in 1890 paralleled developments at the national level. That year the rift in the national suffrage movement was healed when the "National" and "American" wings merged and became the National American Woman Suffrage Association. All suffragists now agreed that the ballot was the most important item on the feminist agenda. The vote was essential, they argued, if women, from their perspective as wives and mothers, were to enact societal reforms. This more conservative argument, emphasizing women's unique nature and, indeed, more moral qualities rather than their innate similarity with men, would ultimately help to convince both men and women of the importance of placing the ballot in women's hands.[17]

One of the major objectives of the NJWSA in the 1890s was winning the vote, of course, but it had other concerns as well. It encouraged women to exercise their right of school suffrage, and they did so in greater numbers. But in 1894 a state supreme court decision (in an unrelated case) in effect declared the law of 1887 unconstitutional. In the opinion of the attorney general, this decision did not affect the right of women to vote for school appropriations. (Ironically, although women had lost the right to vote for school trustees, they could constitutionally hold that office, and continued to do so.) Immediately after the court decision, the suffragists embarked on a campaign to regain school suffrage. Their primary objective was to place a referendum on the ballot to grant women full school suffrage in cities, villages, and country districts through constitutional amendment.[18]

Also seeking to improve the legal status of women, NJWSA set up its Committee on Laws Relating to Women in 1894. The committee investigated "laws relating to Marriage, Divorce, and the guardianship of children, [and] the number and variety of official positions occupied by women in this State." The committee chairman, Mary Philbrook, a young attorney from Jersey City, advised women that they had an obligation to know their rights under the law as property holders and as citizens.[19]

By the 1890s women in New Jersey had advanced their legal and economic position in many areas, as they had elsewhere in the nation. Women, both single and married, could acquire property, sue and be sued, and retain earnings and wages in their own name. Women also held positions on a few state boards. Nevertheless, glaring inequalities still remained. The differences in the dower and curtesy interest, the rights of wife and husband to inherit their spouse's real estate had not changed. The husband remained the guardian of the child. There were no colleges for women in the state, nor did the major universities, such as Princeton and Rutgers, accept them. Although women could enter most professions, they were not eligible for entrance to the bar until 1895, when the legislature passed a law making that possible.[20]

The full acceptance of women into the legal profession occurred because of Philbrook's celebrated challenge in 1894. Philbrook received her training in law by serving several apprenticeships in various law offices in Hoboken and Newark. In February 1894, at the age of twenty-two, she applied to the court for admission to the bar examination, knowing full well that she was the first woman in the state to do so. Her employer made the application (which had been written by Philbrook) in her behalf. "The admission of women to the bar," the application read, "is a question not of taste, propriety or politeness, but of civil right. Certain qualifications may be required, but sex should not be made one of these conditions." The practice of law, it continued, "involve[d] the right to earn a livelihood and to acquire property," which was guaranteed to all citizens of New Jersey by the state constitution. The court was impressed with the applicant but found that it could not grant the motion until the legislature passed a law allowing women to apply to the bar. Aided by the lobbying efforts of the NJWSA and the support of leading Jersey City citizens, Philbrook succeeded in persuading the legislature to pass the necessary legislation in January 1895. She passed the examinations in June and was sworn in that same month.[21]

By 1897 the suffragists had high hopes that their efforts to regain school suffrage would be realized. In March the legislature had passed the resolution a second time as required by law, and a special election was called for September. Other women's organizations, such as the New Jersey State Federation of Women's Clubs (SFWC), the WCTU, and the Working Girls' Societies joined the suffragists in the campaign that spring and summer. The defeat of the referendum by a margin of approximately 10,000 votes out of a total of approximately 140,000 votes came as a bitter disappointment.[22]

With the issue of school suffrage shelved for the immediate future, the state association settled in for a decade of modest activity. Over the next ten years, the state board met a few times a year, and total membership remained essentially unchanged. Nevertheless, the situation did not return to the drift that characterized the 1870s and 1880s, for the organizational structure remained in place. Most important, the public was becoming aware that woman suffrage was an issue that was alive and active.[23]

In the years between 1896 and 1910 the national suffrage movement entered what has been dubbed "the doldrums," for no additional states granted women the vote. As of 1910 women voted only in four sparsely populated states: Colorado, Idaho, Wyoming, and Utah. Women gained the vote in Colorado in 1893 and Idaho in 1896 after successful amendment campaigns. Wyoming and Utah had already granted women the vote as territories at the time they were admitted to the Union. Unexpectedly, in 1910 a successful referendum campaign in the state of Washington ended the period of quiescence. Other successes followed: California in 1911 and Oregon, Kansas, and Arizona in 1913.[24]

New Jersey had its doldrums too. Between 1905 and 1908 the state suffrage association was leaderless and there were no drives for legislative action. With the election of Clara Laddey to the presidency in 1908, the NJWSA entered a second period of revitalization. In 1910 Laddey named Lillian Ford Feickert, of Plainfield, then thirty-two years old, as enrollment chairman. Under Feickert's aggressive direction the association grew dramatically. By 1912, when Feickert assumed the presidency, the NJWSA consisted of twenty-eight leagues and had a membership of twelve hundred.[25]

In this period of renewed activity, new suffrage groups were being organized. The first, the Equality League of Self-Supporting Women (subsequently renamed the Women's Political Union), was founded in Newark in 1908. It affiliated with and modeled itself after the more militant New York Equality League, which had been organized a year earlier. A small, centralized organization made up of business and professional women, it consciously shunned the woman's club image and focused on its immediate political objective: to win Republican and Democratic party endorsement of a suffrage amendment to the state constitution.[26] The second suffrage group, the Equal Franchise Society of New Jersey, was founded in 1910 at Castle Point, Hoboken. The society was similar to the NJWSA in method and ideology but allied with the New York Equal Franchise League. Local societies were quickly established throughout the state. And the third, the New Jersey Men's League for Equal Suffrage, was established that same year in Newark by several prominent New Jersey businessmen and religious leaders, many of whom were married to active suffragists. Within a year the league was able to announce that its membership was drawn from "nearly every county in the State and has at least one member of Congress on its rolls."[27]

By 1910, then, there were four state suffrage organizations, and a number of men had declared their willingness to work for the cause. Forming a joint legislative committee toward the end of 1911, these organizations began to plot a course to bring a suffrage amendment referendum before the New Jersey voters. The effort formally began in January 1912 when a resolution was first introduced in the Senate; it ended three years later when the resolution finally passed both houses of two successive legislatures. In these intervening years the suffragists experienced failure and frustration, yet the idea of equal suffrage continued to gain support. Of critical importance to their ultimate success, in 1913 both Republican and Democratic party platforms included endorsements of a suffrage referendum.

Their opponents were mobilizing too. Early in 1914, as passage appeared promising, two "anti" groups were formed, one female, the other male. The New Jersey Association Opposed to Woman Suffrage, which had a female membership, grew rapidly. Within a year the association reported that it had fifteen local leagues and a total membership of eighteen thousand. The Men's Anti-Suffrage League of New Jersey, a far smaller organization, boasted a membership of prominent individuals, including members of the clergy. Its president was Colonel William Libbey, a member of the Princeton University faculty, and its luminaries included former Governor Edward C. Stokes, a former judge, and a former state senator.[28]

Suffragists and antis sought to persuade the legislature to support their respective positions. Each time the legislature held hearings and voted on the measure, hundreds of women (and men) from around the state, representing both groups, streamed into the state capitol to demonstrate and filled the assembly galleries to cheer their spokesmen. By February 1915 the suffragists had won the first round. The legislature passed the amendment with only four negative votes in the senate and by unanimous vote in the assembly. A special election was set for October 19. The suffragists now had to woo the male voters of the state in the second round that was about to begin.[29]

While the New Jersey suffragists directed most of their efforts toward their goal of winning the suffrage through the state route, they did not neglect the alternate, less promising avenue: enfranchisement through a federal amendment. The credit for reinvigorating this relatively dormant approach went to a new group of national suffragists that emerged in 1913 and to their leader, Alice Paul, a Quaker from Moorestown, New Jersey. Paul was a graduate of Swarthmore College. Between 1907 and 1910 pursuing graduate study in England in social work, sociology, and economics, she joined the Pankhurst suffragists and participated in several protest demonstrations, including one that marched on Parliament. She was arrested on several occasions. Paul was impressed by the effectiveness of these tactics in publicizing the suffragists demands. Not long after her return to the United States in 1912, she and Lucy Burns, a suffragist she had met in England, began to formulate plans to lead a similar movement dedicated to the passage of a federal suffrage amendment. A year later Paul accepted the chairmanship of the Congressional Committee of the National American Woman Suffrage Association (NAWSA) and named Lucy Burns vice chairman. The committee opened its headquarters in Washington, D.C., and immediately began a national campaign to win the Congress and President Woodrow Wilson to its cause.[30]

A central aspect of the NAWSA committee plan (the committee now called itself the Congressional Union for Woman Suffrage) was sending a series of state delegations to meet with the president. On

November 15, 1913, a New Jersey delegation (the fourth in the series) of seventy-three women from the NJWSA, the Women's Political Union (WPU), the Equal Franchise Society, and the Women's Trade Union League arrived in Washington. The president received the suffragists and promised that he would give the idea of a federal suffrage amendment his consideration. His vaguely worded response was at least an improvement over his earlier statement that he was too busy with tariff and currency matters to think about woman suffrage.[31] Moving President Wilson toward support of suffrage had double significance for the New Jersey suffragists, for the president was not only a national leader but a voting resident of New Jersey. His endorsement would stimulate congressional action, but of more immediate importance, it would be of considerable assistance to the state referendum campaign. Wilson's endorsement was a prize the suffragists determined to win.

As far as the Congressional Union (CU) was concerned, such visits were only the beginning of the effort to influence the White House and the Congress. It soon became clear that its single-minded devotion to a federal amendment was in conflict with the parent body's state-by-state approach. By 1914 the CU had separated from NAWSA and became an independent entity.[32] The CU did not form a state branch in New Jersey until 1916, when the national organization renamed itself the Woman's Party. Until then, all New Jersey activity was directed through the national organization. By 1915 the CU was ready to participate with other suffragists in New Jersey's referendum campaign, but it did so with reservations. It maintained that winning the suffrage in each state was a tedious and undemocratic process. "There is no reason whatever why the women of New Jersey should be subjected to this laborious and costly process of converting the male population of the entire State," it observed.[33]

Toward the end of 1911, a third path to winning woman suffrage—the legal one—was taken by Mary Philbrook, who made headlines for the second time in her young career. Philbrook chose to make a formal legal challenge of the exclusion of women from the suffrage in New Jersey, and her challenge became the much publicized *Carpenter v. Cornish*, heard by the state supreme court in April 1912. The origins of the case began on Election Day in 1911, when Harriet Carpenter, a Newark teacher, accompanied by Philbrook, attempted to register in an election district of Passaic Township. When Carpenter was refused, Philbrook asked that the incident be noted in the register, thereby establishing a basis for a court suit.[34]

In her argument before the court, Philbrook claimed that women had been illegally deprived of their voting rights by the Constitution of 1844 and that they had been granted those rights by the Constitution of 1776. The court disagreed with the plaintiff. The Constitution of 1776 in no way conferred the right to vote upon women because it used the term "inhabitants," it noted. The Constitution was referring to "a certain class of inhabitants" who were similarly privileged by laws which preceded the Constitution of 1776, which did not include women. Furthermore, the court found, the Constitution of 1844 was legally drawn and limited the right to vote to males over twenty-one years of age.[35]

Philbrook later admitted that she had had little hope that her suit would be won. She had undertaken the appeal because "it was giving the cause great publicity and support." Although she could have brought her appeal to a higher court, she chose not to do so, since the suffragists' movement to amend the state constitution seemed close to success.[36]

The suffragists were well aware that it was the male voters of the state who would have to be convinced that women should be granted the vote. Over the past few years they had lobbied in the state legislature and recruited women into their organizations. But now their publicity and propaganda largely sought to persuade men that the time for woman suffrage was at hand. Through mass meetings, parades, and press releases—with posters, banners, and ribbon-bedecked touring automobiles—the suffragists sought to enter the public consciousness. By 1914 the NJWSA had opened headquarters in Plainfield and the WPU in Newark; out of both flowed a constant stream of broadsides and pamphlets. The NJWSA and WPU memberships were "22,000 and 4,000 respectively." By the spring of 1915 the suffragists were preparing to embark on their most important campaign. The four major suffrage organizations formed the Cooperative Committee to coordinate innumerable details and the Committee of One Hundred to raise the funds to make the publicity possible. The antis were readying a similar efffort.[37]

The referendum campaign was more than a matter of state interest. That fall, voters were being asked to decide on similar referenda in three other major industrial states: Pennsylvania, New York, and Massachusetts. Only one other industrial state, Illinois, had granted women the vote, but there women had received only partial—presidential—suffrage. New Jersey's election came before all the others and thus became a test case of current voter opinion. The campaign was carefully followed in national magazines and newspapers.[38]

Between April and October 1915 the suffragists remained in the public eye. Their views at that time are of particular importance to this study, for they were to shape the direction the suffragists took in the years after 1920. More than reasoned explanations as to why women should have the ballot, these views reflected the attitudes the suffragists held about women's proper social role. Well before 1915 suffragist argument had evolved from one which emphasized justice as the reason for granting women the vote to one that spoke of justice and expediency as well. By the early twentieth century, the suffragists were listing new benefits woman suffrage would bring. The vote would not only improve women's legal status, as the suffragists of the 1890s had argued, but it would eliminate the evils that accompanied modern industrial life. Clara Laddey, NJWSA president, in her address to the association's twenty-first annual convention in 1911, listed these evils: "child labor, sweat shops, the social evil, intemperance, dishonesty in office, cruelty and injustice."[39]

By the time of the referendum campaign, suffragists were pointing out that the record proved that numerous social benefits accrued from granting women the ballot. They compared the full suffrage states with nonsuffrage states and observed that the record of the former was superior in the passage of the Eight Hour Law for working women, of laws "regulating child labor, making fathers and mothers equal guardians of their children," passing "mothers' pension laws, laws giving teachers equal pay for equal work, [and] laws raising the age of consent for girls." They made similar comparisons on a global scale to show that the death rate of babies was radically lower in those nations that had woman suffrage. New Zealand, the first country to grant women the vote, the suffragists noted, had the lowest infant death rate in the world, and the next four ranking countries also had woman suffrage. The United States, by comparison, ranked only eighth.[40]

Most suffragists were middle class women who were not members of the paid labor force. Their concerns about industrial law were on behalf of another class of women who had their sympathy. The working women in the suffrage ranks, on the other hand, maintained that they would personally benefit from the vote. They held that if women won the vote, they would pass laws that mandated an eight-hour day and prohibited industrial homework. The appointment of factory inspectors and labor commissioners would be other benefits. Trade union organization was not enough, one of their representatives observed; "the lack of direct political influence is one of the great reasons that women are underpaid and in many cases work longer hours than men."[41]

The underlying reason woman suffrage would result in social reform, the suffragists claimed, was that women had a different point of view from men. They were more concerned about matters related to the home and family. Through various organizations they had pressed for pure food laws and laws regulating highway billboards, motion pictures, and prostitution. They had special concerns about prison reform, hospital care, child labor, and working women. It was a mistake, they believed, to think that men could represent women in these matters. By virtue of their sex, men could not appreciate the implications of numerous matters related to the security and moral well-being of family life. What is striking about this twentieth century expediency argument is how much it resembles the nineteenth century doctrine of separate spheres. True, the modern suffragists no longer referred to woman's piety and submissiveness, as did their Victorian predecessors, but their emphasis on women's prime concerns with home and family and their celebration of woman's moral superiority over men reechoed the cult of domesticity elaborated earlier. Paradoxically, the suffragists were calling for political equality in words that negated the meaning of true equality.

While the suffragists went to greater lengths to demonstrate what women would accomplish if given the vote, they did not neglect the justice argument. Women were entitled to vote for the identical reasons that men voted, a WPU broadside argued. Women were taxpayers, citizens, and human beings. Furthermore, a NJWSA broadside noted, women were considered free and responsible human beings in the eyes of the law. If women broke the law, they were expected to pay the penalty, just as any man. Contract default, theft, murder, failure to pay taxes, forgery—all had to be acknowledged by the woman guilty of these transgressions. Is a man arrested in her place; does a man serve her prison term, sit in the electric chair for her, or make restitution for tax default? it asked. "WHO REPRESENTS HER?" "Why is it that the only place in the world where man wants to represent woman is at the polls?"[42] All the suffragists at one time or another referred to justice *and* expediency as the basis for their argument. The CU, however, stressed justice as its rationale. Although it supported the referendum campaign, it continued to hammer away at the need for a federal amendment. Equal suffrage, the *Suffragist* (a CU publication) observed more than once, was "a fundamental of democracy" and the "main issue in national politics." Its attainment would bring "political equality" and "political freedom."[43]

Historian Aileen Kraditor's observation that the distinction between the suffrage argument based on justice and that based on expediency was one of seeing women as similar to men on the one hand and as different from men on the other, provides an apt analysis of the New Jersey suffragist argument. When the suffragists used justice as their rationale, they were saying that women were equally human and were therefore entitled to equal rights and opportunities. When they argued that expediency required the vote, they stressed the differences and noted the special viewpoint of women. The suffragists could thus state, as part of the same argument, that women were both like men and different. In the postsuffrage era, most of these suffragists emphasized one point of view at the expense of the other, but a substantial number had great difficulty reconciling these two conflicting positions.[44]

Expediency was the foundation of the antisuffrage position, but the arguments employed were different. In their literature, the antis tried to demonstrate that men were managing the affairs of government as well as possible and that conditions would measurably deteriorate if women voted. The publicity of the Men's Anti-Suffrage League emphasized the superiority of men in the governmental realm. Men, it maintained, were experienced in business matters and had the power to back up lawmaking, while women did not. Woman suffrage would bring inexperience and weakness into government life. Political bosses would increase their power as the number of "well-meaning but misinformed" voters increased. The antis declared that they were not saying that women were men's inferior but rather that women had their special sphere of responsibility in which they excelled: the home and its related institutions, "the church, the school, and the hospital." The female antis emphasized that women would lose their special moral role if they were granted the suffrage. The similarity of suffrage and antisuffrage argument was striking in this case. Both groups could celebrate the spiritual and moral excellence of womanhood in support of their opposite positions.

Just as the suffragists made comparisons between the suffrage and nonsuffrage states to show that suffrage had brought about social improvement, the antis averred that the opposite had occurred. The best child labor laws and laws for working women, they maintained, could be found in the nonsuffrage states. In the suffrage states, on the other hand, suffrage had accomplished little but double the vote. Finally, the antis argued that it was a mere 20 percent of the women of New Jersey who wanted the vote, as evidenced by the number of enrolled suffragists. The majority of women were well satisfied with things as they were. Suffragism, moreover, could be equated with radicalism, socialism, and anti-Christianism. Support of socialism or feminism would "[help] to lay the axe at the tap-root of Christian civilization," they warned.[45]

As the fall election approached, prominent New Jersey individuals took sides. The antis had the support of leading politicians. Governor James Fielder, a Democrat, revealed that he opposed woman suffrage. David Baird, Republican leader in southern New Jersey, and James Nugent, chairman of the Essex County Democratic organization, were the most vocal anti politicians. In addition, the *New York Times* reported that "some of the most prominent women in New Jersey have enlisted for the fight on woman suffrage," including the widow of President Grover Cleveland, and "Mrs. Garrett A. Hobart, of Paterson, the wealthy widow of a former vice-president of the United States." The suffragists had an impressive group of adherents too. Among them were Thomas A. Edison, U.S. Senator William Hughes, congressmen, ex-Governor John Franklin Fort, state senators, assemblymen, and mayors, and prominent newspaper editors.[46]

Two weeks before Election Day, the suffragists won a stunning victory when President Wilson came out in favor of woman suffrage. But the President was careful to state that his endorsement was made "as a citizen of New Jersey" and not as the leader of the Democratic party. There was jubilation in the suffragist camp and predictions of a certain election victory. Journalists, however, were more cynical in their reaction, observing that given the forthcoming presidential election, Wilson did not want to antagonize women in the suffrage states. The president had moved closer to supporting the suffragists' goals by endorsing suffrage through the state route, but he had not budged from his opposition to a federal amendment.[47]

Two hoped-for endorsements failed to materialize. Although the General Federation of Women's Clubs had endorsed suffrage in 1914, and the state federations in the three campaign states of New York, Massachusetts, and Pennsylvania had done so by 1915, the New Jersey State Federation of Women's Clubs (SFWC) continued to defeat suffrage resolutions submitted at state conventions. (A fuller discussion of the SFWC can be found in Chapter 3.) The New Jersey American Federation of Labor also voted against endorsement, a loss for the suffragists, for the New Jersey AF of L had supported suffrage in 1913.[48]

All four referenda were defeated that fall. Massachusetts voters delivered the heaviest defeat to their amendment, while suffragists made their best showing in Pennsylvania. In New Jersey, the amendment was defeated by 51,108 votes out of a total of 317,672 cast. The suffragists assuaged their bitter disappointment with the fact that 42 percent of the electorate had voted in favor of the amendment. In a series of postmortem evaluations, they laid the blame for the defeat on a number of factors, but the most plausible explanation appeared to be that given by several newspapers and magazines: there were simply not enough male voters who were convinced that women should be granted the vote. With one exception—rural Ocean County—every county in the state had turned down the amendment proposal. Even Essex County, where the suffragists were particularly active, had voted against the amendment by a considerable margin.[49]

The referendum defeat, and those that followed in New York, Pennsylvania, and Massachusetts, initially appeared to be a serious setback for the entire suffrage movement. But late 1915 marked a major turning point for the movement in New Jersey and for the national movement as well. State amendment efforts were thereafter de-emphasized, and a new drive began for a federal amendment. Only days after their defeat, the New Jersey suffragists began to make plans for a new campaign. There was no preparation for another referendum, since the Constitution precluded another vote before five years had passed. The CU, which had been moving in this direction all along, saw the outcome of the New Jersey election as further proof that the state-by-state approach was faulty; and NAWSA, under the leadership of Carrie Chapman Catt, its new president, now shifted its full attention to the federal amendment. Catt had just led the New York Woman Suffrage Association's referendum campaign and had proved herself to be an excellent organizer. Nine months after assuming the presidency in December 1915, she revealed her "winning plan" to enroll the thirty-six state suffrage associations in a carefully orchestrated campaign to win passage and ratification of a federal amendment in approximately six years.

Although both national suffrage organizations were now working for identical goals, their methods were radically different. The CU began to work in earnest to fulfill Alice Paul's original objective, which was to hold the party in power responsible if it failed to endorse the suffrage amendment. In June 1916 it organized the National Woman's Party (NWP), with membership open to the voting women in the twelve states with full or presidential suffrage. The immediate aim of the new organization was the defeat of Democratic candidates in the fall election, especially the president.

NAWSA, on the other hand, rejected the idea that Democrats should be singled out for defeat whether or not they were sympathetic to woman suffrage, and it still hoped to win President Wilson's support. Meanwhile, male and female voters were weighing other issues. One of the main issues of the election of 1916 was government policy toward the war in Europe. Wilson pledged neutrality. When the Democrats won the election and carried ten of the twelve suffrage states, it appeared that many suffragists and their male allies had failed to be convinced by the WP argument.[50]

By the middle of 1917 several developments had considerably altered and strengthened the structure of the state suffrage movement. The first was the consolidation of the major suffrage organizations. In December 1915 the Equal Franchise Society voted to disband and to merge with the NJWSA. Eight months later the WPU voted to do the same. Those individual branches of the WPU that chose to remain intact were free to do so. The largest of these was the Newark

WPU, which had a substantial membership and remained a viable group until 1920.[51]

The NJWSA was now the major suffrage organization in the state, with a combined membership of over fifty thousand. Lillian Feickert, who continued to be reelected to the presidency at annual conventions, had emerged as the most prominent figure in the New Jersey suffrage movement. As she crisscrossed the state addressing various suffrage groups, she gained increasing press coverage, attention, and respect. "She came here last night," reported the *Paterson Morning Call*, on Feickert's address to that city's suffrage organization, "and those of us who heard her went away with the impression that Mrs. Feickert was aggressive, a campaigner, a politician, a fighter, and an extremely practical woman, all rolled into one."[52]

The second development, the establishment of a state branch of the CU, with headquarters in Newark, took place in early 1916. The New Jersey CU president was Alison Turnbull Hopkins (Mrs. J. A. H. Hopkins, as she preferred to be known) of Morristown, whose husband had been a prominent state leader of the Progressive party. The formation of the state organization was a result of a decision by the national CU to create geographical sections made up of state branches in the nonsuffrage states. The New Jersey CU, which became the New Jersey branch of the Woman's Party in early 1917, remained a relatively small organization. A number of its leaders, however, were involved in NWP activities. Two, Hopkins and Julia Hurlbut of Morristown, organization vice president, were among the NWP women who picketed the White House and suffered arrest and imprisonment that June.[53]

The NWP began to picket the White House on January 10, 1917, demanding passage of the federal suffrage amendment. Its leadership declared that its other, less militant, tactics had proved ineffective. The steady flow of delegations to see congressmen, senators, and the president had not yielded concrete results, it noted, nor had efforts to defeat Democratic candidates. The arrests began on June 22. Hopkins and Hurlbut spent three days in prison and were then pardoned. Other NWP women who manned the picket lines throughout the summer and into the fall were less fortunate. Sentences of thirty days, sixty days, and even six months were meted out. Alice Paul was in jail from October 20 until her release on November 28, when all of the NWP prisoners were pardoned and arrests came to an end.[54]

The picketing effectively focused national attention on the suffragists' demands, but it also brought new dissension in suffragist ranks. The NJWSA, like NAWSA, immediately disavowed the pickets. Moreover, after the United States entered the war on April 7, an overwhelming majority of its membership found the NWP decision to continue picketing a government at war totally unsupportable. Indeed the association was convinced that the NJWP (like the NWP) was basically lukewarm about the war effort and publicly accused it of lack of patriotism. "As you know," Feickert observed in a memorandum that fall, "their total membership in the State is very small, and chiefly made up of disgruntled women who left this Association because they did not approve of our doing war work."[55]

The third development, the endorsement of woman suffrage by the New Jersey State Federation of Women's Clubs (SFWC), took place at the federation's spring convention in 1917. The clubwomen were bowing to the inevitable, for by 1916, the state federations in thirty-five states had endorsed suffrage. The assumption of the presidency by Agnes Anne Schermerhorn, a staunch suffragist who had been chairman of the federation's legislative department for the previous two years, also helped push the clubwomen toward endorsement of suffrage. Under her leadership, the SFWC voted in favor of a resolution in May 1918 that requested the president to "use his influence as leader of his party" to pressure Democratic senators to vote for the federal amendment, and "[urged] upon the Senate the immediate passage of this amendment as a war measure."[56]

Lastly, at its fall convention in 1917, the NJWSA voted to accept the New Jersey State Federation of Colored Women's Clubs as an affiliate. Following the affiliation vote, two NJSFCWC officers became members of the NJWSA state board. The federation had been founded in 1915, in Trenton, to bring together thirty black societies of the WCTU, "the object being to consider plans for arousing greater interest in the Temperance movement and colored people of New Jersey." Its president and founder was the Reverend Florence Randolph of Jersey City. Its parent organization was the National Association of Colored Women, founded in 1896, which merged two national organizations founded a year earlier, the National Federation of Afro-

American Women and the National League of Colored Women. The black women's club movement had its origins in self-help efforts in slavery days and in the years immediately following the Civil War. More formally institutionalized in the 1890s, the various clubs worked in the ensuing years to improve their schools and communities and actively fought lynching and racial prejudice. By 1914 the National Association of Colored Women "represented over 50,000 black women in 28 state federations and over a thousand clubs."[57]

The affiliation of black clubwomen and the endorsement of the SFWC swelled the number of organized women who were now committed to support the suffrage movement. While membership figures of the NJSFCWC in 1917 are not known, six thousand women joined the black federation by 1919. By 1917 the membership of the SFWC was twenty thousand. The organized suffragists numbered a probable several hundred in the NJWP, and the NJWSA had a membership of one hundred thousand.[58]

By 1918 the outlook for the New Jersey suffrage movement seemed measurably brighter. The entry of the United States into the World War proved an important aid. The war was ostensibly being fought to make the world safe for democracy, and the suffragists sought to sway the unconvinced that the democratic aims of the war were incompatible with the powerlessness of American women. As suffragists involved themselves in war work alongside other women, they pointed to the incongruity of the refusal to grant the vote. These were strong arguments, and their logic brought new converts to the suffrage movement.

Several key political figures now lent their support to the suffrage cause. The war undoubtedly swayed many politicians, but, as historian John D. Buenker points out, there was also evidence that, by 1918, New Jersey political leaders were gradually adjusting to the idea of woman suffrage, as they were in other urban, industrial states. In particular, Buenker notes, the urban Democratic political machines in the nation, always staunch opponents of woman suffrage, no longer saw voting women as a threat to their interests. The voting record of women in the suffrage states proved to them that women voted like their husbands and not as a bloc.[59] The differences in the New Jersey political picture between the 1915 referendum campaign and 1918 point up the shift in sentiment. In 1915 Governor James

Fielder, a Democrat, was a known, if not highly vocal, antisuffragist. By 1918 Governor Walter E. Edge, a Republican, had clearly stated his approval of the federal amendment, and both United States senators, Joseph Frelinghuysen, a Republican, and William Hughes, a Democrat, favored suffrage as well. But the most important evidence that support of the federal amendment had become politically acceptable, not only in New Jersey, but throughout the nation, was the announcement on January 9, 1918, that President Wilson favored the amendment's passage. The long-sought endorsement came on the eve of the vote on the measure by the House of Representatives. The House finally passed the federal amendment on January 10 by a vote of 274 to 136.

This political support was far from unanimous, however. Members of New Jersey's congressional delegation were among those casting a negative vote, along with congressmen from other industrial states. Two influential county political leaders, David Baird and James Nugent, continued their opposition. Both Nugent and Frank Hague, the new mayor of Jersey City and leader of the Hudson County Democrats, were instrumental in defeating a suffrage plank in the Democratic platform adopted in October 1918.

Equally important to the suffrage cause, there was mounting evidence that more New Jersey women were supporting the movement with each passing day. The membership total of 120,000 cited by the NJWSA could not be lightly disregarded, and when the large membership of the SFWC swelled the ranks of suffrage supporters, the antis claim that the overwhelming majority of New Jersey women did not want the vote was discredited.[60]

In the past the NJWSA had criticized the Women's Party for its militancy, but it now entered a militant phase of its own. For the first time, the NJWSA and the WP had similar tactics as well as goals, as they both worked to defeat political candidates. In the fall of 1918, an election was conducted to fill the unexpired term of U.S. Senator Hughes, who had died the previous February. The opponents were former State Senator David Baird, Republican, from Camden County, and State Senator Charles O'Connor Hennessy, Democrat, from Bergen County. Baird, the interim appointee, was a declared antisuffragist. Hennessy, on the other hand, had been an overt friend of suffrage since the 1915 campaign, when he had lent his name to its published list of supporters.[61] The suffragists considered Baird's defeat essential to the immediate welfare of the entire suffrage movement. The NJWSA and the WP began their separate campaigns five weeks before Election Day, declaring that a vote for Hennessy was a vote for suffrage. The NJWSA also organized the Essex County Political Campaign Committee to work for the defeat of the twelve Nugent-approved Democratic Assembly candidates, all known antisuffragists, and for the election of the Republican candidates, all of whom favored the federal amendment.[62]

The New Jersey Association Opposed to Woman Suffrage once again sought to counter suffragist efforts, claiming that antisuffragist women were in the majority and attempting to equate suffragism with pacifism. "Don't forget that every dollar given to defeat woman suffrage is a dollar toward winning the war," it admonished its membership. But the outcome of the election proved the power of the political organizations rather than the effectiveness of "anti" propaganda. Baird was elected, "though he ran 9,000 votes behind the rest of the ticket," and the entire Nugent slate won. Baird held office only a few months, for his term ended the following March. To the advantage of the suffrage cause, however, former Governor Walter E. Edge, the full-term senatorial candidate, also won the election.[63]

The suffragists opposed an antisuffrage candidate again in September 1919, when a primary race for the Democratic gubernatorial nomination was fought between State Senator Edward I. Edwards, of Hudson County, and James Nugent. Edwards announced that he favored woman suffrage and if elected would work to have New Jersey ratify the federal amendment. The NJWSA decision to work for Edwards's nomination, which was successful, and then for his election was made on suffrage grounds alone. His Republican opponent, Newton Bugbee, indicated that he preferred a voter referendum on the federal amendment to a ratification vote by the state legislature. The Democrats now had a suffrage plank through Edwards's influence, and the Republicans had none. "We shall do all we can to insure the election of Mr. Edwards in conformity with our rule to stand by our friends," Feickert declared on October 1. "We shall support Republicans as well as Democrats in this campaign and shall continue to be non-partisan, while enthusiastic in support of those in both parties who have and are aiding the cause of woman suffrage."[64]

The election of Edwards was undoubtedly due to many factors, but the suffragists could rightfully feel that their support had been influential. Feickert's policy—"stand by our friends"—was repeated many times in the future in her leadership capacity in the postsuffrage period. The results of the 1919 campaign sustained her future belief that organized women could effectively influence political events. In these political campaigns the suffragists had demonstrated that women could organize to support candidates and to defeat others. The political parties in the state would note that and remember it when women finally won the franchise.

On June 4, 1919, the Senate at long last passed the federal amendment. The suffragists next step was to assure the ratification of the amendment by the state legislature. The New Jersey Suffrage Ratification Committee was formed in July with Feickert as chairman. Cooperating organizations were the NJWSA, the SFWC, the SFCWC, the WCTU, and the State Organization for Public Health Nursing. There were also cooperating groups of business and professional women.[65]

While the NJWSA ratification effort initially sought to convince the legislature as a group that it should ratify the amendment, the WP strategy was more detailed. Its leadership analyzed the probable voting positions of each legislator and concluded that the outcome for ratification was not bright. In September the NWP sent one of its national organizers to work with the state leaders who were lobbying in Trenton, a tactic it had used in other states. Together, the national and state WP successfully sought out legislators in each house who would agree to organize support for the amendment.[66]

The legislature began formal consideration of the amendment in January 1920. In spite of the prestigious support being given to the ratification effort, approval was by no means assured. The senate passed it on February 2 by a vote of eighteen to two, but in the assembly there were last ditch efforts to have the amendment ratified by a referendum instead of by the legislature. Filibustering tactics by the Nugent group were used to forestall the vote, which finally took place in the early hours of the morning on February 10. The affirmative vote of the twelve members of the Hudson delegation, led by Mayor Hague (who was now in the prosuffrage camp) helped swing the assembly to approval by a vote of thirty-four to twenty-four.[67] New Jersey had become the twenty-ninth state to ratify, with seven more states required to make the Nineteenth Amendment a part of the Constitution. Approximately six months later, on August 26, Tennessee became the thirty-sixth state.[68]

The national suffragist leaders had anticipated final approval of the Nineteenth Amendment. By early 1919 they began to look beyond passage and ratification and to prepare for the role women would play as voters. At the NAWSA annual convention held in St. Louis in March 1919, Carrie Chapman Catt proposed the formation of a new organization to replace the present one, a league of women voters.

The league was intended to be "non-partisan and non-sectarian in character" with "three chief aims":

> 1. . . . to secure the final enfranchisement of the women in every state in our Republic and to reach out across the seas in aid of the woman's struggle for her own in every land.
> 2. To remove the remaining legal discriminations against women in the codes and constitutions of the several states. . . .
> 3. To make our democracy so safe for the nation and so safe for the world that every citizen may feel secure and great men will acknowledge the worthiness of the American Republic to lead.[69]

The New Jersey League of Women Voters was to be organized the following year.

In the interim between ratification by the legislature and the organization of the state League of Women Voters in April 1920, the suffragists prepared for their new roles as voters. They felt almost certain that ratification would be completed in time for women to participate in the presidential election that fall and felt a responsibility to encourage a large turnout of women voters in this first important election. At a state conference held in Newark in mid-January, the NJWSA made initial plans to hold citizenship schools throughout the state that spring. The schools would seek the enrollment of leaders of the numerous women's organizations and clubs and offer classes on the science of government and politics. These leaders would, in turn, pass their newly learned knowledge on to their respective members. The purpose of the League of Women Voters was to be explained at these sessions.[70]

This final act of the suffragists was the first concrete indication of the direction many of them would take in the postsuffrage period. The suffragists rightfully believed that women needed to be politically educated. Women, after all, had been excluded from political life for generations. As a group, they were ill-informed about governmental structure, election laws, and practical politics. But many suffragists also believed that education was the key to correct voting. Men, they were convinced, had failed to be informed voters and voted merely out of party loyalty. Women would do better, they predicted. As educated voters they could rise above the harmful loyalism required by party politics.

The NJWSA held its final Victory Convention on April 23 and 24, 1920, at the Robert Treat Hotel in Newark. There it formally dissolved and reorganized as the New Jersey League of Women Voters. The convention delegates then elected nine league directors-at-large and eight regional directors. These directors were to elect the league officers at the organization's first regular meeting scheduled to take place later that month.[71]

At the Victory Banquet held on the final evening of the convention, political leaders from both parties offered toasts and delivered speeches to mark the euphoric event. Senator Edge was a featured speaker, and he had words of advice for the suffragists, urging them to join the political parties, "not to stand on the outside of the conference and throw bricks in, but to enter the conferences themselves."[72] Edge was addressing women who were united in the flush of victory. Indeed, all suffragists, both in the NJWSA and in the state branch of the WP, despite dissension over tactics, had shared one overriding goal over the years: to win the vote. But this unity of purpose would not survive in the years ahead. The senator had unwittingly identified one cause of a basic split that occurred in suffrage ranks after 1920 that was not entirely predictable: differences over whether to enter the political parties or maintain a strict, nonpartisan stance. The differences, however, went deeper. Within months of their victory, the suffragists went in two discernible directions. At the heart of the separation were two contrasting views the suffragists had of themselves and the role they felt women should properly play now that the vote was won. Indeed, these perceptions had provided the underlying rationale for the two types of suffrage argument: that based on justice and that based on expediency. The suffragists could hold both points of view at the same time, as they used both arguments in their campaign for the vote, but after 1920, as they entered public life as voters, they divided into two broad groups, each group giving emphasis to one viewpoint over the other. These positions, moreover, took on fresh meaning in these ensuing years.

The view underlying the justice argument was, as I have noted, that women were basically similar to men in their aptitudes and abilities. In the postsuffrage period, the suffragists who gave greater weight to this position—the Equal Righters—translated this to mean that women should be given equal opportunities in all areas of political and economic life. It is these women who joined the political parties, ran for and held office, and worked to improve the legal and economic status of women. By contrast, the basis for the expediency argument was that women had special capacities that made them different from men. Women were more compassionate, more concerned about family, more moral, and therefore less corruptible. In the postsuffrage era, those suffragists who emphasized this view— the Moral Prodders—translated this to mean that women should set themselves apart from the traditional operations of politics. Seeing themselves as different from and in many ways superior to men, they shrank from becoming an integral part of the male-dominated political system. They preferred the role of moral gadfly, hoping always to raise standards, right wrongs, and set goals. Thus, in the new era after winning the suffrage, they joined organizations that emphasized nonpartisanship and education for citizenship. Through these organizations they worked for specific goals they believed would create a better society. The newly organized League of Women Voters, to which I now turn, belonged to this category.

CHAPTER TWO

Moral Prodders I:
The League of Women Voters, 1920–1930

T HE New Jersey League of Women Voters, as successor to the New Jersey Woman Suffrage Association, was clear about its immediate purpose. As a nonpartisan organization it would work to educate the new women voters so that they would become informed citizens, and it would seek to pass specific legislation that would improve the welfare of the home and the larger community.[1] Within a short time after its founding, however, it became evident that the league was far less certain about the means by which these goals were to be achieved. As the league proceeded with its carefully articulated programs of work, it was confronted with two central dilemmas in the new decade. First, should it encourage women voters to join political parties and become fully integrated members of the party apparatus? Or should it advise women to give their first allegiance to the League of Women Voters (LWV) and to guard their nonpartisan stance above all? Second, should the passage of legislation be the league's first priority? Or was it more important to educate women so that they could vote intelligently for legislators, who would then pass the right laws? The league never found clear-cut answers, but by the end of the decade it demonstrated through its activities and stated philosophy that it had finally come to terms with these perplexing questions.

On April 30, 1920, eight of the nine directors-at-large elected at the final convention of the NJWSA met in Newark to choose, from among themselves, the officers of the newly formed NJLWV. They adopted a constitution which established a state board of directors, departments and standing committees, and a county organizational structure headed by chairmen to be elected by local leagues. Agnes Anne Schermerhorn, who had just completed a three-year term as president of the NJSFWC, was elected chairman. Mary Colvin was named vice chairman; Dr. Mary Hussey, secretary; Lillian Feickert,

treasurer; and May Hunter, auditor. With the exception of Schermerhorn, all had been members of the state board of the NJWSA.
Chairmen were also chosen to head seven departments: Ameri-
canization, Citizenship Schools, Child Welfare, Social Hygiene, Fair
Price (later called Production and Distribution of Commodities),
Unification of Laws concerning Women and Children, and Women
in Industry. An eighth department, Legislation, would be added at a
subsequent meeting.[2]

Meanwhile, some local suffrage groups were dissolving to become LWVs. The Newark WPU, for example, the largest local body,
declared on May 24, 1920, that it had fulfilled its purpose and that it
was turning over its property to the Newark LWV. Florence Eagleton,
president of the WPU, became the president of the new organization, which had a membership of four hundred.[3] The overwhelming
majority of the local suffrage groups, however, simply concluded
their operations. As early as 1916 the NJWSA had reported that there
were 215 suffrage societies in the state. Contrastingly, in October 1921
the state LWV chairman of organization reported the existence of
twenty-six local leagues and six affiliates. Early league membership
figures can only be surmised since state membership figures were not
reported until 1930. In that year the league noted that state membership had grown over the previous decade and had reached an approx-
imate state total of thirty-five hundred.[4]

It is obvious that the total LWV membership, at the time of its
founding, was far less than the 120,000 women claimed by the
NJWSA at the end of 1918. The stark contrast in the membership size
of the suffrage associations and the LWV must have been a disappointment to early league organizers. Clearly, the mass of organized
suffragists in New Jersey did not share the vision of Carrie Chapman
Catt, the victorious chieftain of the NAWSA, that "women having
attained their political independence should desire to give service in
token of their gratitude through a League of Women Voters." Winning the vote had been a grand cause that aroused the ardor of multi-
tudes of women. Many had undoubtedly joined suffrage groups simply to identify themselves with a movement in which they believed.
Many others had been willing to work for their objective. But with
suffrage won, it was not surprising that most organized suffragists
could not sustain the passion and commitment of earlier days.[5]

This was not true of the most active suffragists. In the 1920s the leaders of the NJLWV were drawn, in large measure, from the leadership ranks of the NJWSA. Moreover, suffragists held the two top leadership posts for most of the decade. In more than eight out of the first ten years of the league's existence, the positions of president and first vice president were held by suffragists.[6]

The founding of the NJLWV had its parallel in almost every state in the nation. By the end of 1920 the National League of Women Voters (NLWV), whose president was Maud Wood Park, reported that leagues had been organized in forty-six states. These leagues were embarking on programs similar to that of the New Jersey league, applying them to the conditions of their local environments. Furthermore, the experience of the NJLWV, in terms of membership, was repeated everywhere. Most women who had been members of suffrage organizations failed to join the new leagues. Total NAWSA membership in 1920 was two million, according to the national organization count, but in 1930 the NLWV had only about one hundred thousand members.[7]

The NJLWV constitution called for a broad program of study that would lead to support of specific legislation. The board was empowered to draw up a state program of study items, to be submitted for approval at the annual convention, which would then go to the local leagues. (This program included national study items that had been similarly approved by the national league.) After careful consideration by appropriate committees, positions were to be arrived at by consensus and a final program of recommended legislation would be adopted.[8] In actuality, the league concentrated on one activity after organizing: persuading women, through political education, to register and vote in the coming fall election. Under the chairmanship of Jennie Van Ness, who had been an active worker in NAWSA, the league continued to run the citizenship schools it had initiated while still a suffrage organization. These schools had relatively sophisticated programs on government and the political process. "The aim of the school," one flyer explained, "is to give women political education and to teach the new voter the best ways of using the ballot to advance the welfare of the home."[9]

Even at this early date in NJLWV history, the ambiguity of league purpose had become obvious. As members of the league, suffragists maintained that women should organize to make their presence felt as a nonpartisan force. But these same suffragists also declared that women should familiarize themselves with the political parties and become part of them as well. Carrie Chapman Catt encouraged women to "get into the parties and assume the responsibilities of office-holding and party formulation" while they worked simultaneously outside the party system in the league.[10]

A number of suffragists serving on the state board of the NJLWV, or in major league leadership positions, were doing just that. (A fuller discussion of the role of the suffragists in the political parties can be found in Chapter 4.) By May 1920 Lillian Feickert had been named vice chairman of the Republican State Committee and given the responsibility of organizing the Republican women of the state. Her first task was to name women to the new position of vice chairman of the twenty-one county committees. Of the ten of her appointees who became members-at-large of the Republican State Committee, two, Florence Randolph, and Mrs. John J. White, of Atlantic City, were on the NJLWV board.[11] Suffragists in the league were also assuming prominent positions in the Democratic party. Helena Simmons, former president of the Elizabeth Equal Franchise League and president of the Elizabeth LWV, was named to the vice chairmanship of the Women's Division of the State Committee. Marion McKim Garrison, of South Orange, a director of the league, was appointed to the State Committee, and made an elector-at-large. Caroline Wittpenn, of Jersey City, another director, was named delegate to the Democratic National Committee.[12] Van Ness became the most well-known league political activist. In the spring of 1920 she was named one of two women designated to run on the twelve-person Essex County Republican assembly slate. The other position was given to Margaret Laird, an officer of the WP. Van Ness and Laird won and became the first two women to sit in the state legislature.[13]

As Registration Day, September 14, and Primary Day, September 28, drew near, the league opened headquarters in Newark and Jersey City to offer women information about voting procedures and voter eligibility. League hopes for a large turnout of women appeared to be fulfilled, as their voters information booths were "swamped" with potential voters just prior to Registration Day.[14] Women registered in large numbers throughout the state, but the actual number of women voters failed to live up to league expectations. Registration figures for women and the percentages of women who subsequently voted in the election can only be pieced together from scattered evidence. The *Jersey Journal*, for example, reported that women registered in greater numbers than men in Hoboken and Jersey City, and "in Newark, Camden, Trenton, Paterson, New Brunswick, the interest of women was equally marked." The *Newark Evening News* noted that "reports and estimates indicate that more than fifty percent of the women of the state eligible to vote were registered." The percentage of women who finally chose to vote on November 2 is not known but was undoubtedly less. What is known is that women cast an estimated 30 percent of the total vote nationwide.[15]

The NJLWV was as disheartened by the results as the national league. "It was a great disappointment to find that comparatively few women cast their vote," the New Jersey chairman of the Get-Out-the-Vote Committee recalled in 1924, "and a great surprise to find how few MEN considered their citizenship a public trust." The NJLWV, like leagues elsewhere, seeing the need to increase voter participation, voted to continue its citizenship schools. Citizen education would be a league concern through 1923, and a major get-out-the-vote campaign was undertaken before the presidential election in 1924.[16]

The fact that the NJLWV was organized in 1920, a presidential election year, may have heightened the double pull political activity and nonpartisanship were exerting on suffragists on the league board. As a new organization the league was struggling to clarify its role and purpose. The minutes of the board shortly after Election Day reveal that dissension was already taking place. Feickert was pressing her view that women should join the political parties, and she was running into opposition. At a board meeting held in mid-December, differences came out into the open as some board members extolled the benefits of nonpartisanship and others, Feickert included, complained that they were being criticized for their political activities.[17]

In the next few weeks, Feickert apparently mulled over the dissatisfaction she felt with the direction in which the league was heading. On January 17, 1921, she sent a lengthy letter addressed "To the Directors of the New Jersey League of Women Voters—Friends and Fellow Citizens" that began: "I am very much disappointed for what is, apparently the plan for work by the League." Feickert noted that Mrs. Catt had envisioned the league "as a temporary organization to serve as a bridge between the passage of the Amendment by Congress and the completion of ratification by the States," to "last [not] more than three years." The primary task of women, she had advised, was to join the political parties. But Catt had evidently "changed her position" and now favored a permanent league. Feickert found the results disturbing. League activity in New York and Pennsylvania, she observed, was only drawing capable women away from political influence, thus making it possible for old antisuffrage politicians to be nominated and dooming important women's bills in the state legislatures to inattention and obscurity.[18]

"Whatever the experience of other States," she observed, "New Jersey women have been well treated by both the big political parties." Instead of avoiding political activity, the board should ascertain whether the parties were living up to their platform pledges, as well as encourage the political organization of women. But regrettably, that was not happening:

> Instead of that, we have gone back to kindergarten days, and spend hours talking about forming public opinion. We have been obliged to use the indirect method too long. Now that we have the vote we should become political workers. I, for my part, am through with creating sympathy in favor of industrial laws, child labor laws, etc. I want to see the women well organized in both parties, so that we can work for the measures we believe in by the direct method instead of the indirect method.

The "forming of public opinion," Feickert felt, should be left to organizations like the Consumers' League, the New Jersey Child Welfare Council, and the Congress of Mothers and Parent Teachers Association. The legislature was about to pass a law giving women equal representation with men on the municipal, county, and state party committees, she noted. But if women stayed out of the parties, she warned, "we will be worse off than we were in the past, when we stood on the sidelines and criticised the kind of men whom the men elected to these offices." Feickert said that she would be happy to resign if the board so wished. Her time "[would] be better spent organizing women for political work, in the Republican party." She hoped the board would understand that she was not suggesting that the league should disband but that its real function in preparing women for their new citizenship was to train them for political involvement.[19]

Feickert's letter was the first concrete evidence that the suffragists were breaking ranks. What is significant is that a division was taking place between suffragists who had previously had harmonious relations in the NJWSA. It was unanticipated. During the suffrage struggle, conflicts had flared up periodically between the NJWSA and the WP, particularly over tactics; but the suffragists in the NJWSA had always presented a united front. Now that the vote was won, that unity was coming apart.

Feickert (who severed her league connections when her term ended in April) and suffragists who joined her in the New Jersey Women's Republican Club (NJWRC), which she now organized and led, as well as those suffragists who became active in the Democratic party, were rejecting the league philosophy of nonpartisanship and education for citizenship and choosing instead to assert that women should have full equality with men in political life. They would not, in Feickert's words, stand "on the sidelines." They would "work for the measures [they believed] in by the direct instead of the indirect method."[20]

The dissension that marked the league's first year would not be re-peated. The new league board, elected in April 1921, and the new president, suffragist Florence Halsey, could now express, without op-position, what would become the accepted league point of view. A league pamphlet, published during Halsey's presidency, advised women to work in their parties but implied that the nonpartisan ap-proach of the LWV was preferable. Only through the league, it as-serted, could women work together as a body to improve conditions related to what they cared most about: home and family. Further-more, men did not share these concerns:

> Most women care more about babies and homes and happy
> human conditions than do most men. That is human nature. It
> does not matter whether a woman is a Republican or a Demo-
> crat, or a Socialist or a Prohibitionist or an Independent,
> where children and homes are concerned, she is willing to
> work with other women to help improve conditions. Her com-
> mon sense tells her that no one political party has a monopoly
> of principles or good intention, that it is only through mem-
> bers of the different parties who want the same thing working
> together that action will come.

Here was an expression of the classic Moral Prodder point of view, the heart of which was the belief that women were basically different from men. For suffragists and others in the league leadership, this meant that women, now that they had the vote, had to recognize that they had a separate political identity. That identity had to be guarded and not permitted to become submerged in partisan politics. Non-partisanship was particularly suited to women because of their "humanitarian point of view." The entrance of women into political life allowed the application of a new idea, heretofore untested: that individuals of all political beliefs could come together and work for the common good. The LWV was viewed as an ideal that could become a reality.[21]

Nonpartisanship, or rather "all-partisanship," was a movement that could be embraced, ultimately, by men as well as women, it was held. Many in the league leadership, it appeared, may have secretly hoped that political parties would eventually disappear altogether. In the late spring of 1922, for example, the NJLWV began a program to encourage local leagues to establish citizen leagues at the municipal level "composed of men and women of every political faith and religious creed, every class and colour." The objective was "to take municipal affairs out of partisan politics." Local matters certainly lent themselves to this "all-partisan movement," but the league saw the organization of citizens leagues as just a hopeful beginning. "Who will dare predict how far reaching its influence will be on the political life of our beloved Country?" it asked.[22]

Although a portion of the NJLWV leadership had these idealistic dreams, most league leaders accepted the fact that political parties were a reality and would remain so in the foreseeable future. By the early 1920s the NJLWV had resolved the question of how the league's nonpartisanship could be reconciled with political activity on the part of women. It was suggested that it was proper that women enter politics but that they should not merely replicate men's political activity. Women had a special role to play as public servants, the league believed, because of their experience and different point of view. As the author of an article in the *Civic Pilot*, the official publication of the NJLWV, explained, "not all offices are suitable for women," but women were especially qualified to head departments of public welfare, health, sanitation, maternity care, and the elderly, at city and state levels, and to serve in the state legislature and Congress, because of "their pride to keep their households 'spick and span'" and their "never ceasing motherly instincts." The happy results of women in government would be "clean, serviceable politics and many improvements in various public offices."[23]

The NJLWV struggle to clarify its role in these years was not unique to the state of New Jersey. It was being duplicated at the national league level and in other state leagues. As historian William Chafe observes, in his study of women's roles in society in the period between 1920 and 1970, from the moment of the league's founding, "The central issue confronting the new group was whether it wished to integrate women within the existing political system or segregate them as an independent political force." "In the end," Chafe observes, "the League resolved the conflict over its political role by compromise. Rather than create a new party, it determined to mobilize public opinion behind reform programs and to instruct women in the tasks of citizenship so that they could work more effectively within existing political organizations." Although individual women were advised to join the parties, as an organization the national league elected to remain independent. The vehicle through which the NLWV chose to work for the passage of legislation was the Women's Joint Congressional Committee (WJCC), which was organized in 1920 and was composed of ten women's organizations. By 1925 the league and the WJCC would justifiably assert that congressional passage of numerous bills, especially those that benefited women and children, were the results of their lobbying efforts.[24]

During the suffrage campaign, the suffragists had promised that, if granted the vote, they would "abolish child labor, sweat shops, the social evil, intemperance, dishonesty in office, cruelty and injustice." Now, suffragists in the league studied these topics and drew up legislative programs that would make good on these promises. Beginning in 1921 and over the next five years, they sought the passage of legislation, or support for existing legislation, with five broad objectives: the advancement of women's political and legal status; the improvement of labor conditions, especially as they related to women and children; governmental reform; social reform; and the preservation of world peace. Moreover, they worked for these objectives in cooperation with other women's groups. Through the Women's Cooperative Legislative Bureau, organized in 1920, which also represented the SFWC, the Consumers' League (CL), the State Council of Child Welfare, the Congress of Mothers and Parent Teachers Association, and the WCTU, suffragists in the league maintained an active lobbying presence in Trenton.[25]

One of the league's first legislative concerns was the advancement and clarification of women's political and legal status. A number of questions logically arose immediately following the ratification of the Nineteenth Amendment. What rights should women be granted in the political party structure? What rights should women have to hold office, both appointive and elective? Would women now be allowed to serve as jurors, a privilege previously withheld? Several bills dealing with these questions were being considered by the legislature in the fall of 1920 and winter of 1921 and had league support.

By May 1921, five bills had become law, to the considerable advantage of the new woman citizen. Women were granted "equal privileges in the holding of all office or employment"; women were to serve equally with men on municipal, county, and state party committees; a minimum of two positions on the newly enlarged state boards of health and education were designated for women; and women became eligible to serve as grand and petit jurors in civil and criminal matters.[26] The league also supported a federal measure, the Cable Act, which was passed in 1922, which granted women independent citizenship. Before passage of this act, American women who married aliens automatically lost their citizenship.[27]

The league believed that women had been wrongfully deprived of certain basic rights in the past and took it as a given that laws had to be passed to rectify this situation. In spite of this the league's basic perception of women as different—more moral and more humanitarian—remained dominant. Furthermore, there were limits to how far the league would go in support of equal rights legislation. When Assemblywoman Laird introduced a bill in the assembly in early 1922, ostensibly on behalf of the state branch of the NWP, providing that "women shall have the same rights, privileges, and immunities under the law as men," the LWV joined the Consumers' League and other women's organizations to oppose it vigorously. Similar bills were being introduced by the NWP in several states and also at the congressional level. The NLWV was advising state leagues to oppose them "on the ground that women needed special protection under the law and not equality."[28]

Blanket legislation on women's rights, as the WP bills were described, ran counter to league policy in a second area of league concern: working conditions. Through its Committee on Women in Industry and its Committee on Child Welfare, the NJLWV sought the passage of several bills that would give "protection" to women working in factories and in various other industries. Enactment of these bills would: shorten women's legal workday from ten hours to nine and shorten the legal workweek from sixty hours to fifty-four; establish a minimum wage commission; regulate sweat shop labor through effective licensing; prohibit women from working at night between the hours of 10 P.M. and 6 A.M. in manufacturing and mercantile establishments, and laundries and bakeries; and amend the 1911 Workmen's Compensation Act to include compensation for specified industrial diseases. The league also supported a bill that would "prohibit children from working in agriculture during the school session" and favored state ratification of the Child Labor Amendment, which had passed both houses of Congress in 1924. Only two measures became law in this period. In 1921 the fifty-four hour workweek for women was enacted in law, but the ten-hour workday, Monday through Friday, remained intact. In 1923 the legislature passed the Night Work Bill, which had been introduced under the auspices of the New Jersey Women's Republican Club. It lacked a punitive clause and never was effectively enforced.[29]

Throughout the 1920s and 1930s "protective legislation" was a major source of conflict between the NJLWV, the Consumers' League, and the WP. The WP declared that protection merely hampered women in their effort to gain access to jobs and to win equality with men. Laws improving working conditions should refer to men and women alike, it insisted. But the NJLWV saw protective legislation as an equalizer for women in the long run. Without state protection, it maintained, women were handicapped by "weaker bargaining power [and] difference in physical function." Protection would "give women true industrial equality . . . women should have equal rights and opportunities with men in industrial life but this does not mean identical rights."[30]

The third league objective, the reform of the state governmental structure and its institutions, was probably its most cherished. Many league leaders believed that the league should concentrate on making government more efficient, and thus more responsive to its citizens, to the exclusion of all other activities. Through its Committee on Efficient Government, established in 1922, the league worked for the passage of the City Manager Enabling Act, which became law in 1923, and studied the state taxation and budget systems. It recommended a survey of the state educational system and called for a biennial school census. It supported a bill that would establish a commission to revise and codify the state's election laws. The league's Committee on Production and Distribution of Commodities sought "to promote more efficient methods of retail distribution of food products in the cities of New Jersey" and successfully backed bills that established pure food standards.[31] In 1922 the league opposed a bill that would abolish the direct primary, which had been operating in New Jersey since 1903, and would, in effect, bring back the convention method of nominating candidates. The league fought this bill throughout the early 1920s, maintaining that it would set back the cause of democratic government and would make it more difficult for women to attain political office.[32]

The league's broad legislative program on behalf of social reform, its fourth objective, reflected league conviction that women, as the more moral and sensitive sex, had to lead the way to achieve a more ethical and humane society. Thus in the early 1920s, through its committees on social hygiene and child welfare, it supported the federal Sheppard-Towner Act, whose objective was "the reduction of the sickness and death-rates of mothers and babies," which was passed in 1921; a venereal disease control bill; a marriage licensing act that would "delay the marriage of persons infected with a venereal disease in a communicable stage"; and a child theater bill. The Sterilization Bill, first introduced in the legislature in 1924, and every year thereafter in the 1920s, had the league's special endorsement. The bill called for "the sterilization of chronic feeble-minded, chronic insane or habitual criminals who are mentally defective." The league fervently believed that feeble-mindedness and other mental defects resulted in crime and dependency, a net result of which was the overcrowding of state institutions as well as a high tax burden for the citizenry. Sterilization, the league maintained, was "a step forward in the protection of the health and raising of the standard of the race."[33]

Support of prohibition laws was also on the league social reform agenda. Although suffragists had not formally endorsed Prohibition, once the Eighteenth Amendment had been ratified and New Jersey had passed its state enforcement acts, suffragists in the NJLWV strongly favored "law enforcement." Before 1926 the league presented a united front with other women's groups, demanding more effective enforcement.[34] The league was convinced that the assurance given by the state's successive Democratic governors (Edward I. Edwards, George S. Silzer, and A. Harry Moore) that Prohibition would be upheld was mere rhetoric. Indeed, the state Democratic party did not hide its opposition to the federal Volstead Act and the state Hobart Act, declaring that these laws contravened the true meaning of the Eighteenth Amendment; it proposed, in their stead, laws that would permit the introduction of light beer and wines.[35]

League effort on behalf of world peace, its fifth objective, was but a larger extension of league belief that women must prod society into reforming itself in a more moral fashion. Nations had to be convinced that war, pursued as it now was on a worldwide scale, had to be outlawed. Further, nations had the imperative to come together to mediate their differences. In 1921 the NJLWV established its Committee on Limitation of Armaments, which remained a league department throughout the 1920s. Through the committee, the league in 1921 endorsed the convening of an international conference on the limitation of armaments and favored the entrance of the United States into the League of Nations World Court. The league joined the New Jersey branches of two national peace organizations, the Committee on the Cause and Cure of War and the Women's International League for Peace and Freedom. Several suffragists in the NJLWV—Mary Hussey, Florence Halsey, Miriam Early Lippincott, Florence Eagleton, Helena Simmons, Amelia Berndt Moorfield, and Lena Anthony Robbins—held leadership positions in these organizations.[36]

In early 1924 the league began to express frustration and disappointment with the results of its legislative program in Trenton. It had numerous bills it hoped to see passed, but its record of achievement was slim. The early enactment of bills granting women equal representation in the political parties, giving them access to political office and employment, and placing them on juries had promised future legislative success. But the ensuing years produced the passage of only a few measures.[37]

Steps were taken to improve matters. In October 1924, ten state women's organizations, including the NJLWV, met in Newark to form the New Jersey Council of State Organizations for Information and Legislation, with the object "to prevent overlapping of legislative effort by the various State Organizations" and "to enable organizations favoring the same legislation to unite their efforts to obtain its passage." Legislation was to be endorsed only after unanimous agreement by the membership.[38]

But despite this effort of women's groups to work together more effectively, the league judged that, as far as women were concerned, the 1925 legislative session was a failure. The bill favoring ratification of the Child Labor Amendment failed to get out of committee. The bill providing for a nonmandatory minimum wage commission had a similar fate. Although corporations were legally challenging the Night Work Law and flaunting it as well, the legislature continued to defeat bills that would assure effective enforcement. The school census bill was being considered at a snail's pace. The "one bright spot in our program was the passage of the sterilization bill in the Senate," it was noted.[39]

In the latter part of March 1926, twenty-one representatives of women's organizations received a letter from Mabelle S. Davis, president of the NJLWV, inviting them to a "small and confidential" meeting on April 7, to discuss the reasons for the failure of "measures [to] which the women's organizations have been especially committed." Representatives of approximately seven organizations attended that meeting and subsequent ones held in April and May. The most active participants were Juliet Cushing, of the CL; Lena Anthony Robbins, legislation chairman of the SFWC; Lillian Feickert, of the NJWRC; and Florence Halsey of the NJLWV. With the exception of Cushing, all had been active suffragists. Other organizations represented were the WCTU, the New Jersey Federation of Church Women, and the Anti-Saloon League.

Over these weeks the women poured out their frustration, anger, and bitterness about their experience with legislators in Trenton, and New Jersey politicians in general. "In what respect have we as women failed in Trenton?," they asked. The wrong men were elected, they agreed. Electing representatives from districts instead of from counties, the present method, it was suggested, might make a legislator more responsive to his constituency. As a start, women had to convince the political parties to nominate "the right men and women" to the county committees. But the blame lay elsewhere as well. "We need a united front," one participant observed. "Women never counted so little at Trenton as this year." "The men know the women are not united," added another, "even in their own organizations." [40]

The results of these unusual meetings were radical words and conservative measures. In early May a letter was circulated to approximately twelve women's organizations that read like a revolutionary manifesto. "The time has come for us to present an unbroken front to our common enemy . . . ," it began. Major headings were in full capitalization: THE PROBLEM; THE REAL ISSUE; THE CAMOUFLAGE ISSUE; THE REAL ENEMY; THE ACTUAL STRUGGLE; OUR POWER. The problem was how to get the voters to the polls; the real issue was whether government was representative or for the benefit of a few who made a living out of misrepresentation; the camouflage issue was "party loyalty," a mere screen to discourage independent voting; the real enemy was "groups of local politicians grasping for political power"; the actual struggle was between "selfish political machines and those who are seeking clean politics, civic decency, efficient government"; our power was the ability to prevent "vicious selfish groups" from delivering votes. [41]

Would women then storm the barricades and use their united voting power to convince legislators that they should be taken seriously at last? No. Orderly protest would be a more accurate description of their response. The creation of a "woman's bloc" was rejected. The plan of operation was a "joint questionnaire" to be sent to all legislators running in the spring primaries, asking them where they stood on specific legislation, thus putting them on record. [42] The final outcome·to the initial impassioned call for united action had an ironic, almost comic twist. In June the league board voted not to participate in the joint questionnaire "because there are several items in the questionnaire sent out that had not been included in the League's legislative program." Thus, the league's own method of study prevented it from taking the action it declared was so desperately needed. [43]

The meetings of 1926 would be the NJLWV's last gasp of organized protest that necessary legislation was not being passed. The meetings would, in fact, mark a turning point for the league, as they forced the organization once more to examine its purpose. The observed need to place responsible men and women on the party county committees called, by implication, for greater political involvement on the part of organized women and revived the old league dilemma of how to balance political activity with nonpartisanship. But the meetings also forced the league to come to grips with its second dilemma: What was its main function: to see that specific legislation was passed or to educate its members so that they would be knowledgeable voters?

In the June 1926 issue of the *Civic Pilot*, league member Margaret Porch Hamilton, reflecting on the legislature's failure to pass several bills favored by organized women, lay much of the blame at the feet of the women themselves. "Exactly what have we learned in the six years of our citizenship?" she queried. Hamilton acknowledged that the caliber of the legislators was poor. Women had to change that. But more important, she noted, women had failed to see that, having won the vote, they had an obligation to behave differently than they had in suffrage days. They were "no longer outside the government," but "inside," and should assume their "full duties of citizenship." Perhaps, she suggested, women had been too slow in taking up those duties through "the regularly established government channels."[44]

We in the league "have not clearly defined our own purpose," she went on. The league emphasized political education, yet it also endorsed legislation. It had not followed through on the second aspect of its program, which required more than endorsement and lobbying. It logically meant "the endorsement and election of men and women who could be trusted to go to Trenton and enact good laws," perhaps even a coalition of respected men and women. Perhaps, Hamilton conceded, political education was what the league was all about. In that case, she concluded, "this new trail" that the league had blazed had only led to a dead end. But there was still a way out. "Convinced that such a misfortune has overtaken us, we should be not only willing but glad to retrace our steps and make another try."[45]

But the NJLWV would not make another try. It had resolved the issue of political activity years before. With the failure of the 1926 meetings to achieve concrete results, there occurred a subtle, but perceptible, shift in emphasis. In the four years remaining in the decade, the league continued to work for specific legislation, but the special urgency of the past was gone. The passage of legislation was no longer a major objective. Citizenship education now became the prime goal.

Helena Simmons, who succeeded to the presidency in the fall of 1926, was a spokesman for the altered league philosophy. In her address to the league's state convention in 1927, she summed up "the fundamental policies of the League of Women Voters." There were three, she believed. First the league "specialized" in "basic facts":

> The League offers you study material and unbiased information not propaganda.

Second, the league was scientific:

> The League offers you a conference method based on carefully selected and scientifically worked out material whereby many persons of quite different views may sit down together, state their convictions and check up in the light of the first-hand evidence.

Third, the league would make the vote "effective":

> It can tell you where to put the emphasis, how to use the Primary, how to make a poll of your Representatives in Congress or the State Legislature and where and when, the best methods of lobbying for an important measure.[46]

The league now saw its task clearly. It would produce educated, unbiased women voters. As voters, women could demonstrate to the male-dominated political establishment that they could reform the political system and create a more moral and humane society. Facts would be the ammunition in their arsenal. Although they might meet with their representatives and lobby for legislation, their primary battleground would be the voting booth.

Through its various departments, the league continued to pursue its programs of study and legislative endorsement. It worked for much the same legislation it had supported previously and endorsed new legislation as well. Prohibition no longer had the league's undivided support. Division in the league, suffragists included, reflected the clear mid-decade shift in state sentiment for modification. In 1926 New Jersey delegates to the LWV national convention voted with the majority against a proposal "that it go on record against any modification of the Volstead Act or weakening of the Eighteenth Amendment" but did support law enforcement. The delegation also joined in voting down a resolution that would put the study of Prohibition on the national program. Prohibition, according to league leadership, was far too controversial an issue. "We are not a propaganda association," asserted a board member.[47]

One issue that was not controversial was governmental reform. Always a favored objective, governmental reform gradually became the gem of the league's program. The state and county governments indisputably needed to be made more efficient, and legislative procedures cried out for improvement. In the late 1920s the NJLWV developed programs to achieve these objectives, and it was in this area that it had its greatest success. Through its Efficiency in Government Department, the NJLWV encouraged its local leagues to study their town and county governments. Members were urged to become knowledgeable about the county and state taxation system and about voting procedures. Is our government truly representative? was the fundamental question members were to ask.[48]

By 1930 several bills that had received league support had become law. These bills established a commission "to study, codify, and revise the election laws"; created the Legislative Reference and Bill Drafting Bureau; and in 1929 created within the Department of Labor the Bureau for Women and Children, to be headed by a woman. The league Committee on Women in Industry rejoiced that New Jersey, in establishing the Women's Bureau, had joined with other industrial states, such as New York and Pennsylvania, in its recognition of the needs of working women and children. The bureau's task was to supervise the licensing of industrial homework, to oversee enforcement of laws relating to women, and to make periodic inspections of mercantile establishments where women were employed. Factory inspections remained the province of the Department of Labor.[49] The passage of other bills having league endorsement looked promising: an enabling act to allow the introduction of voting machines and a bill to put a mechanical voting device in the assembly to tally the votes of its members.[50]

In their activities on behalf of governmental reform, suffragists and their fellow members of the league had found their true calling. If there was a dark cloud developing on the league horizon, it did not seem to dampen the new league optimism. Sometime in mid-decade, patriotic societies, such as the Daughters of the American Revolution, began to accuse the NJLWV and other leagues in the nation of joining in a "spider-web campaign" to undermine national strength. Ties to Communist Russia were alleged. By 1927 these allegations were stepped up. Addressing the state convention that year, President Simmons dismissed the accusers. They were engaged in "ridiculous lying and self-interested stuff." "Their patriotic efforts [were] along the safe and sane lines of 'flag ceremonial' and of getting up card parties to pay for bronze tablets in memories of dead heroes."[51] The NJLWV printed a special publication to deal with the "spider-web" indictment. "Who Are the Patriots?" it asked. "The men and women who are living on the reputation of their ancestors services to their country,—or those who are trying to become honored ancestors to their posterity by unselfish devotion to high ideals of citizenship?"[52]

By the end of the decade, the NJLWV was secure in the knowledge that it had become a respected nonpartisan presence. The dissension of earlier days that had threatened to tear it apart was over, and the dilemmas of the past had been resolved. Its members did not doubt that it was they who were the true patriots who trained women to become better citizens; lobbied for efficient and effective government; and sought, among their many objectives, ratification of the Child Labor Amendment, protective legislation for women and children, protection for new mothers and their babies, and the creation of international machinery to assure lasting peace.

CHAPTER THREE

Moral Prodders II:
Other Reform Organizations, 1920–1930

I T WAS logical that a large number of the suffragist leaders
joined the League of Women Voters and served on its state
boards in the ensuing decade, as it was the direct successor to
the New Jersey Woman's Suffrage Association. Many suffragists also
sought to maximize the effectiveness of their newly won right to vote
through activities in other organizations that worked for political
and social reform. Four main groups in this category were the New
Jersey State Federation of Women's Clubs (SFWC), the Consumers'
League of New Jersey, peace organizations, and the New Jersey
Woman's Committee for Law Enforcement.

Many of the women were continuing memberships they had
held for several years before 1920 in the Women's Clubs and the Consumers' League. Affiliations with peace organizations and the New
Jersey Committee for Law Enforcement were more recent. The agen-
das of the SFWC and the CL had much in common, while the peace
organizations focused on their one area, and the Law Enforcement
Committee had as its sole raison d'être the enforcement and non-
modification of the Prohibition laws. Together, though, these organizations shared with one another, and with the League of Women
Voters as well, a certain point of view: Women had different concerns
than men. As wives and mothers they would see to it that the home
would be safeguarded, civic and political life would be cleansed,
working women and children would be protected, the law would be
respected and upheld, and the causes of war would be studied and
understood so that the now global pestilence could eventually be
eradicated.

Although suffragists and their fellow members in these organizations saw the winning of the vote as a great victory for women,
they eyed entry into the political system with caution. The concern
for the good of the community would not be subordinated to party
needs that put loyalty and the winning of public office first, they held.

Rather, women's prime role would be to serve as a moral force, essentially outside the political structure, though not disassociated from it. Women would act as prodders to remind those within the system what course they must properly pursue.

Suffragists had played an active role in the SFWC since its organization in 1894. Antoinette Brown Blackwell was the federation's first vice president, serving from 1894 to 1896. Mary Hussey, Florence Howe Hall, and Mary Philbrook were officers in subsequent years. The stated purpose of the SFWC was "to bring the women's clubs of the State into communication, for acquaintance and mutual helpfulness." Like its parent body, the General Federation of Women's Clubs, founded in 1890, the federation brought existing women's clubs under a single umbrella. Some of these groups were literary, others cultural, and still others political. At the time of its formation the federation included fifteen clubs with a total membership of eleven hundred women.[1]

The founding of the SFWC was a part of the establishment of a number of women's organizations that began, in the state and in the nation, shortly after the end of the Civil War. The phenomenon reflected the need of leisured, middle class women to come together for social purposes and to provide an outlet for their intellectual energies. Many had benefited from the recent opportunities to receive a college education. The drudgery of household care had been lightened by the numerous advances of the industrial revolution, such as indoor plumbing, improved cooking stoves, and the sewing machine. In addition, the swell of immigrants to the United States after 1880 provided an available labor pool for housework.[2] But the emergence of many of these organizations in the latter part of the nineteenth century was also an aspect of the rising middle class demand for social, political, and economic reform, termed *progressivism*. In the Progressive Era, which spanned the years from approximately the late 1890s to the end of the First World War, reformers sought to reverse the disorder and injustices of society created by the forces of industrialization, urbanization, and immigration. Through governmental efficiency and expertise, they held, the needs of society could be met.

State Federation of Women's Clubs leaders viewed the role of clubwomen as "purifier" of social and civic life. They also believed, as did other social reformers in the Progressive Era, that the problems of modern industrial life were not inevitable but could be solved by methodical, rational planning and implementation. Thus, in addition to federation cultural committees on art, literature, and music, there were those on civics and town improvement, public health, conservation, household economics and pure food, and industrial and child labor. A legislative department worked for the passage of several bills, including one to build a reformatory for women and another to prohibit children under fifteen from working at night in factories.[3]

Suffragists in the SFWC urged federation endorsement of the suffrage cause at a number of state conventions held in the early twentieth century, but they encountered strong opposition. A majority in the SFWC leadership warned that clubwomen would lose their special moral position if they became voters. "To have one great section of the community out of the turmoil of political machinery, out of personal contact with the forces that most arouse passion and prejudices," one official observed, "is to give that section immense weight and influence in spreading public enlightenment. That is woman's supreme opportunity today." When the SFWC finally did enlist in the suffrage campaign in 1917, the idea that women had a special moral role to play in public life did not die but was incorporated into the rationale for the importance of granting women the vote.[4]

By 1920 the SFWC had grown to a membership of twenty-six thousand and was, by far, the largest of the women's organizations in New Jersey. (Similarly, the General Federation of Women's Clubs was the largest national organization of women, with an estimated membership of 2.5 million.) Twenty-six years after its founding it was proudest of two of its past accomplishments: in 1897 "saving the Palisades from commercial development" and subsequent creation of Palisades Interstate Park in the early twentieth century and in 1918 the establishment of the New Jersey College for Women "after fifteen years of persistent effort."[5]

Several suffragists who had served on the SFWC committees prior to 1920 continued to do so after passage of the Nineteenth Amendment: Beatrice Stern, Lena Anthony Robbins, Caroline Wittpenn, Geraldine Livington Thompson, Helena Simmons, Melinda Scott, Agnes Cromwell, and Florence Halsey. Agnes Schermerhorn, president from 1917 to 1920, was the SFWC's most prominent suffragist. It was Schermerhorn who spearheaded the drive to win federation support of the Nineteenth Amendment, and it was she who became the first president of the NJLWV.[6]

In 1917, during Schermerhorn's administration, the SFWC established its Women's Legislative Bureau in Trenton, which lobbied for bills supported by the federation and kept the local clubs informed of current legislative activity. Under Beatrice Stern's direction, the bureau gained status and recognition. In 1920 it was renamed the Women's Cooperative Legislative Bureau and became the lobbying agent of six women's organizations, representing forty thousand women.[7]

In her retiring address, in May 1920, Schermerhorn set out the federation goals for the new decade. It was a rousing speech and a call to action. Clubwomen must prepare themselves for their new citizenship, which now seemed a certainty. They must know the issues, so as to make proper judgments; "therefore read, read, read; study, study, study," she declared. Schermerhorn advised members to join the new LWV. As voting citizens, women would have a great opportunity, she observed. They would create a larger society, like their own homes, in which fine schools, good health, recreation, and friendly relations would prevail. "This means participation in the politics of one's community. Right and proper! All these years of preparation have been for this—to understand and obtain the needs of our homes, our families and our friends, who are the world at large."[8]

With the ratification of the Nineteenth Amendment, then, suffragists and their fellow members of the SFWC entered the decade of the 1920s with a special sense of purpose and the feeling that they could shape a new order. Through their committees, they worked for many of the same objectives as the NJLWV (and the CL): advancing women's legal and political status, improving the working conditions of women and children, improving the quality of state institutional life, upgrading the efficiency of the state government, and securing world peace.

In the early and mid-1920s suffragists were prominent in all these committees, often working in the very same areas in which they were involved in the NJLWV and the CL. In addition, suffragists who held prominent public posts worked in SFWC departments. Thompson and Wittpenn, for example, both members of the State Board of Institutions and Agencies, served on the advisory committee of the Department of Institutional Cooperation. Cromwell, a member of the State Board of Education, was a director of the Legislative Bureau. Halsey, state chairman of the Women's International League for Peace and Freedom, was a member of the Committee on International Relations.[9]

Suffragist influence was clearly evident in this period. The legislation and various social welfare departments were alive with activity. Clubwomen expressed an eagerness to become good citizens, to learn about governmental operations, and to take their voting responsibilities seriously. The Department of American Citizenship gave courses in citizenship training. Although as an organization the SFWC prized its nonpartisanship, individual clubwomen were urged to run for positions on the county committees and local school boards. In 1924 and 1928 the SFWC conducted its own get-out-the-vote campaigns, offering a prize to the club that achieved the highest percentage of women who registered and voted.[10] Moreover, suffragists, because of their multiple memberships in other women's groups, were influential in advancing the federation's joint organizational activities. The SFWC participated in numerous conferences on women in industry, on education, and on state institutions. It joined the Council of State Organizations for Information and Legislation and attended the NJLWV-sponsored meetings in 1926.

In spite of the fact that it had much in common with the CL and the NJLWV, the SFWC had its own perspective that set it apart. The CL was committed to one area of interest: the betterment of women's and children's working conditions. The LWV had been created specifically to prepare women for their new role as voters. In contrast, the SFWC had a broad cultural program as well as a program of legislative activism that was more than twenty years old. Moreover, its purpose had not changed since its founding. As President Schermerhorn declared in her final address:

The finest thing in all this club movement is that it is SOCIAL, in the best sense, but not society! The club should be and the Federation is open to all types of women—rich and poor, urban and rural, educated and uneducated, trained and untrained, broad and narrow, conservative and radical—for under and back of it all is the sisterhood of women and fellowship of ideals.[11]

The federation thus focused on women themselves, recognizing their special interests and viewpoints as mothers and homemakers. Home life was what clubwomen were all about. It was what bound them to one another and created a "sisterhood of women." It was what made them different from men, whose world revolved around business and commerce. Women, then, came together in their clubs primarily for sociability but also to work for a better society, modeled on the homes that were their province. Just as they guarded the morality of their homes, they would work to improve the moral quality of public life.

Clubwomen believed that, as voting citizens, they had gained new power to "purify" civic life. In the 1920s they worked with special fervor for legislation that would bring "moral reform." These bills provided for uniformity of the marriage codes, particularly as they related to venereal disease, sterilization of the criminally insane and mentally unfit, birth control, regulation of highway billboards, and censorship of motion pictures and theatrical productions. The SFWC also supported strict enforcement of the prohibition laws throughout the decade. (Not until the 1930 convention did the federation's unyielding position collapse, when it voted overwhelmingly to table a resolution that would put it on record against any modification of the Eighteenth Amendment.) [12]

The final piece of moral reform legislation supported by the SFWC in the 1920s was a motion picture bill, first introduced in 1927 by suffragist Assemblywoman Florence Haines, Republican from Essex County. The bill made the showing of "obscene, lewd, indecent, immoral drama, play, exhibition, motion picture show or entertainment" a misdemeanor subject to appropriate police action. The SFWC asserted that the public required "this much needed protection." It agreed with Haines, who declared, "We protect the public and our own children from physical ills. We insist by law upon pure food, uncontaminated water supply, supervised milk. Why should we not legislate against moral harm in like manner?" After its initial defeat, Haines reintroduced the bill in 1928, 1929, and 1930, but each time it was unsuccessful. [13]

By 1930, when the federation had grown to include more than forty thousand women and approximately three hundred clubs, its place as a respected reform organization was secure. In 1927 as testimony to its place in the public eye, Governor A. Harry Moore appointed Lena Anthony Robbins, who was chairman of the federation's important Department of Legislation from 1925 to 1928, as the only woman member of the commission to study the relationship between Rutgers University and the state of New Jersey.[14]

Ten years after winning the vote, the traditional SFWC perspective that woman's primary sphere was that of her home and family had not fundamentally changed. It was merely altered. As the SFWC saw it, clubwomen's new political activism still came back to the home. It was ultimately to benefit the home that clubwomen had sought the vote, and for the same reason that they now used it. When women did become involved in politics, they would contribute their much needed special qualities, "intuition and ideals." They would shun extreme partisanship and the spoils of office that men pursued.[15]

Looking back, the 1920s stand out as a period in which political involvement became an important priority for the federation. This emphasis would not be seen in subsequent years. It is the suffragists in the SFWC who must be credited with the considerable amount of political activity that did occur in this period—the focus on citizenship education, the encouragement to join the parties, the drive to get out the vote, and the joint lobbying in Trenton with other women's organizations. All of these efforts brought clubwomen into public life more than ever before and won increased recognition for the federation. To that degree, the suffragists played an important role in the federation's growing prestige.

Only a handful of suffragists served on the state board of the CL of New Jersey before 1920. Perhaps this was because the CL never chose to enlist in the suffrage movement, confining itself to its special and only interest: improving the working conditions of women and children. But after 1920 and throughout the 1920s, several suffragists joined the CL board—Helena Simmons, as second and third vice president, and Bertha Shippen Irving, Mary Colvin, Florence Eagleton, Florence Halsey, Caroline Wittpenn, and Melinda Scott as members. Scott was the only known representative of organized working women in the CL. President of the New Jersey Women's Trade Union League (NJWTUL) (which she had founded in 1917), a small organization run by a cadre of middle class and working women dedicated primarily "to improving female laborers working conditions and their status in the labor movement," she was probably best known as an organizer of the United Textile Workers of America.[16]

Most of these suffragists were also members of the NJLWV and were undoubtedly drawn to the CL by the similarity of many of the objectives of the two groups. Binding the CL and the NJLWV was the latter's Committee on Women in Industry, whose chairman was Juliet Cushing, the CL's president and founder. It was Cushing who made the NJLWV aware of CL activities, who called joint conferences on women in industry, and who pressed for mutual support of legislative measures. Moreover, in matters relating to industrial legislation, it was the CL that led the way.

The CL had been founded in 1900, one year after the establishment of its parent body, the National Consumers' League (NCL). Other leagues had sprung up in major cities earlier in the decade. The formation of these organizations reflected the conviction of educated middle class women, living in major industrial states, that working women, because of their weaker physical makeup than men and their family obligations, were sorely in need of protective legislation. Long hours, night work, lack of seats, unhealthful and unsafe working environments were major complaints. Shortly after its establishment the New Jersey league embarked on an ambitious program to "educate consumers to recognize their responsibility for the conditions under which the goods they purchase are manufactured and distributed." It launched a publicity campaign to advertise the impact of the Christmas shopping season on female department store clerks and succeeded in gaining the agreement of store owners to promote early shopping and to shorten the work day. It encouraged the voluntary cooperation of factory employers to maintain healthful working conditions for their employees and to comply with the existing ten-hour day and sixty-hour week factory law. It awarded the NCL label to factories that met those standards and began a series of investigations of industrial homework (work done primarily by women and children in their own homes for a contractor) and, finding the licensing standards rarely enforced, began lobbying for a strong licensing law.[17]

By 1920 the CL had a number of legislative accomplishments: in 1904 the establishment, owing in part to CL efforts, of the State Department of Labor, whose main tasks included the collection of labor statistics, the periodic inspection of factories, and subsequently, the licensing of industrial homework; in 1909 the requirement of seats for women engaged in commercial employment; in 1912 the limitation of the working hours of women employed "in any manufactory, mercantile establishment, in any bakery, laundry or restaurant" to ten in any one day and to sixty in any one week; and in 1914 the regulation of child labor, through the passage of compulsory education and child labor laws.[18]

Throughout the 1920s the CL remained a small organization of middle class women who lived in the major cities and towns in the northern part of the state. It reached its highest membership figure, 675, in 1922. (The NCL remained relatively small as well, despite its initial spurt in growth. Although the NCL had "64 branches in 11 states" in 1904, by 1930 it had but eleven branches with a total membership of forty-one thousand.)[19]

The CL never suffered the ambiguity of purpose of the NJLWV in the postsuffrage era. It did not agonize over the question of nonpartisanship versus political action. Its mode of operation had been, and continued to be, that of the nonpartisan lobbyist. Its work went through three clearly defined stages: investigation, consumer education, and lobbying for the passage of legislation. The league was the fact collector, the exposer, the enlightener. As it lobbied for bills in Trenton, it relied on arousing public sentiment in its favor. It did not press for the election of women legislators who would introduce favored bills and fight for their enactment, nor did it encourage its members to run for office or join the political parties. It felt confident that its legislative efforts would be handled by sympathetic male legislators and the few women who were elected to office.

The CL believed it had a special responsibility to industrial working women, who, lacking "time, money, [and] influence," needed outside, concerned allies to improve their oppressed condition. The need for this support was heightened because working women, unlike men, were rarely organized. "The industrial woman worker is handicapped," it maintained, "by youth, inexperience, lack of training, poorer pay and lack of organization." The CL held that women entered the work force out of economic necessity but that their prime obligation—to their children, their husbands, and their homes—had not changed. Their burdens had merely increased. "People," Scott declared, "talk of the sacredness of motherhood and the sacredness of home like magpies. What sacredness can there be in a home when a mother works nine or ten hours in a mill and then goes home to work still?"[20]

Night work was particularly injurious to women workers, the CL declared, and should be banned. Not only did it affect women's health but it made it impossible for a mother to look after her children and care for her home properly. The results could, in fact, be deadly. Citing evidence gathered by the Children's Bureau in the U.S. Department of Labor, the CL maintained that "the overwork of mothers is one recognized cause of high infant mortality and the rising deathrate of women in childbirth."[21] The number and percentage of industrial women workers in New Jersey who actually worked at night were relatively small. In 1923 the state Department of Labor reported that, out of a total of approximately 116,000 women engaged in manufacturing and mechanical pursuits, 1,567 women worked at night in factories—a little more than 1 percent. Nevertheless, by that time, passage of a Night Work Bill had become a major cause of the CL and other women's organizations.[22]

The CL first introduced the Night Work Bill in 1918 and backed similar legislation in the next three years with no result. The bill's ultimate passage, in 1923, was in large part due to the fact that, in 1921, the New Jersey Women's Republican Club agreed to be its sponsor. Moreover, both political parties now supported limitation of night work for women. In spite of the active opposition of several Passaic textile manufacturers, the passage of the bill had become politically expedient.[23] Several factors, however, made the bill's passage nothing more than a hollow victory for the CL. First, the law did not go into effect for two years, at the request of several manufacturers, who maintained that they needed time to make the necessary machinery changes. Many of these same manufacturers, in 1925, instituted a legal suit against the law. Finally, the law was ruled by the state attorney general to be unenforceable, as it lacked a penalty clause. Later efforts to add that clause were unsuccessful.[24]

The failure to achieve an effective night work law was a major setback for the CL's drive for protective legislation. It demonstrated, the league declared, that New Jersey was backward compared with other industrial states and most industrial nations. Thirty European countries as well as Japan had already banned night work, it noted, and New Jersey remained the only eastern industrial state that still permitted this hazard to women's health.[25] But an even greater threat to that drive arose in the early 1920s with the introduction of an NWP's equal rights amendment (ERA) to the federal Constitution. Although several women's organizations, such as the NJLWV, the NJWTUL, and the SFWC, opposed the ERA, the CL was perhaps its most vigorous opponent. The CL, and leagues throughout the nation, warned that congressional passage of the ERA could negate all existing legislation it had sponsored on behalf of women over the past twenty years. The most important issue for industrial working women, its leadership asserted, was not sexual equality, as the NWP insisted, but finding realistic solutions to the actual problems working women encountered in their day-to-day work.

The dispute between the CL and the NWP soon took on the characteristics of a major battle, with each side declaring the other's pronouncements to be misleading. The CL was particularly angered by NWP statements in *Equal Rights*, the NWP publication, that New Jersey working women were opposed to the Night Work Law and that, once enacted, the law had forced all women who worked at night to lose their jobs. Most working women favored the Night Work Bill, the CL retorted, and those few who came before the legislature to declare their opposition had been brought there by the mill-owners. Moreover, it pointed out, no women had lost their jobs because the law's operation had been postponed for two years.[26]

By the mid-1920s the angry words had subsided considerably, as it became evident that the ERA had little immediate chance of passage. In 1928, when the Women's Bureau of the federal Department of Labor completed a study of the effects of protective legislation on women's employment opportunities and found that such legislation had little influence on women's job chances, when compared with other factors, the CL rejoiced. The bureau also found that women's hours legislation set a general standard that tended to improve conditions for men as well as women, a further coup for the CL.[27] These were only moral victories, however. By the decade's end, the CL's lobbying activities had yielded few concrete legislative results. With the exception of the night work law, only two major laws had been enacted: in 1926 "radium necrosis" was added to the list of compensable diseases under the Workmen's Compensation Act, and in 1929 the Bureau for Women and Children was created. Suffragists and their fellow members on the CL board shared the frustration of other organized women with the failure of the legislature to pass many of the bills it supported. In the spring of 1924 the CL called the initial meetings of nine women's organizations that resulted in the formation of the Council of State Organizations for Information and Legislation to permit joint lobbying for social legislation. The CL was also an active participant in the impassioned 1926 meetings of women's groups called by the NJLWV.

But the CL, unlike the NJLWV, did not alter its methods and objectives after 1926. It had known failure before, and the indifference of legislators. The experience of two and a half decades had shown that dogged determination, careful collection of facts, and persistent education of the public resulted in a steady accretion of laws that made the working lives of women and children continually better. Despite the legislative record, the league believed that in its role as exposer and enlightener it had performed its greatest public service. In 1922, for example, it began an educational campaign for a minimum wage law for women. In that same year the CL asked the federal Women's Bureau to undertake a study of New Jersey women's wages and cost of living. The bureau agreed. Its published findings, in late 1923, revealed that 50 percent of all women working in factories and mercantile establishments received less than a living wage, which it calculated at fifteen dollars per week, and 25 percent received less than twelve dollars per week. The CL used these facts to back its demands for a minimum wage commission which would set standards for a minimum wage for women.[28]

The CL also urged stronger industrial homework laws and helped publicize pitiful sweatshop conditions. The CL had been a leading advocate of a homework bill that was passed in 1917. Subsequent investigations after 1920, however, conducted by the State Department of Labor, revealed that a slipshod method of licensing still permitted women and young children to work long hours in homes where disease and unsanitary conditions prevailed. The CL circulated the department's findings and, in 1924, supported a bill to provide for more rigorous inspection and regulation of industrial home work.[29]

The league's most spectacular investigation and publicity campaign began in 1924, when the Orange Board of Health requested that it study the causes of serious illness or death of several female employees of the United States Radium Corporation of Orange, whose job it was to paint illuminated dials on watch and clock faces.

One of the most important results of the league's inquiry was a heightened public awareness of a relatively new hazard of modern life: industrial disease. Although all of these employees suffered the same symptoms—trouble with their teeth, followed by sore and deteriorated jaws, and for four women, ultimate death—neither the corporation or the state Department of Labor could find any connection between the employees working conditions and their illness. In its investigation, which involved consultation with medical and scientific experts, the CL found that the employees were dipping their brushes in an illuminant containing a radioactive substance and then putting these brushes in their mouths to create a fine point. Physicians who examined the sick women "found that the girls' mouths were all radio-active." State newspapers gave considerable coverage to the CL findings. Public horror over the suffering of the victims made passage of a bill to add this new occupational disease—"radium necrosis"—to the list of compensable diseases, a foregone conclusion. The law, not being retroactive, could not compensate any of the families of the dead women, but it was conjectured that the CL publicity may have been responsible for the United States Radium Corporation's out-of-court settlement with three of the claimants.[30]

Finally, the CL made the public aware of the problem of migratory labor in the state, espcially as it affected children. In 1925 it undertook an investigation of migratory children, from both New Jersey and Pennsylvania, who worked on the truck farms and cranberry bogs in southern New Jersey, leaving school in early spring and returning in late fall. Children involved in this work numbered in the thousands, the CL reported. The league found that absence from school often resulted in marked retardation in learning. Children were engaged in excessively heavy labor, it declared, and living conditions in the migrant camps were well below an acceptable sanitary standard. This was an old CL project. Earlier investigations had been made in 1905, 1914, and 1921, in cooperation with Pennsylvania authorities and the federal Children's Bureau. In 1927 the league sponsored a migratory children's bill that would prohibit children from working in agriculture while school was in session. The bill was introduced in 1928 and 1929 but never succeeded in passing both houses.[31]

Perhaps because of its narrow purpose and the fact that it shared similar objectives with other women's organizations, the CL began gradually to lose members by the mid-1920s. By 1930 its rolls had shrunk to five hundred.[32] But the CL's size and small budget were in no way related to its accomplishments, Katherine Wiley, its executive secretary declared. It was not and had never been a "popular" organization like so many other social welfare clubs and societies. Yet, she noted, the record proved that the CL had "influenced public opinion and so legislation probably more than any other organization."[33]

The league's prestige and public recognition remained high. In April 1930 the CL celebrated its thirtieth anniversary with a dinner at the Robert Treat Hotel in Newark, honoring Juliet Cushing, who was retiring as president after thirty years of service. One hundred and twenty women were patrons of the dinner, and twelve hundred invitations were mailed. The occasion also marked the installation of a new president, Helena Simmons, a suffragist who had led the NJLWV through most of the past decade.[34] As evidence of the prestige of the CL, in November 1930 President Herbert Hoover invited Simmons and Wiley to participate in the White House Conference on Child Health and Protection.[35]

In her report on April 9, 1930, Wiley observed that the work of the league was still incomplete. "Shall we ask ourselves today why in 1930 we are organized as consumers to promote the welfare of women and children in industry?" she asked. "Has social organization in the last thirty years wrought changes which may absolve us from further responsibility concerning those workers whose services are devoted to making what we consume?"[36] The challenges of 1900 remained in 1930. Changing industrial conditions required new study, new consumer education, and new lobbying efforts directed toward the passage of legislation.

Very little is known about suffragist involvement in the peace movement before 1920. All the record reveals is that in 1905 an organization called the New Jersey Peace Society was established under the auspices of the SFWC; subsequent activities of the society remain unknown.[37] The period after 1920 is better documented. As I noted earlier, suffragists in the postsuffrage period supported peace efforts through the NJLWV and the SFWC and through memberships in the state branches of two peace organizations: the New Jersey Women's International League for Peace and Freedom and the New Jersey Committee on the Cause and Cure of War. In addition, a num-

ber of suffragists were members of an ad hoc group, the World Court
Committee of New Jersey. The two most prominent suffragists in the
New Jersey peace movement in the 1920s were Amelia Berndt Moor-
field, who was president of the Women's International League
(WIL), and Florence Halsey, president of the organization's north-
ern branch.[38]

The parent WIL was founded in 1915 by a congress of women
from several nations that convened at The Hague. "The immediate
object of the founding congress, "according to the organization's historian," was to try to stop the [World] war, the outbreak of which
had been a profound shock to all progressive and liberal-minded
people. In a longer perspective, the aim was to abolish the war system and to replace it by ordered cooperation among the nations." To
achieve its long-range objective, the WIL sought to establish a permanent mediation arm, manned by neutral nations, which would
be available to diffuse periodic flare-ups of national differences that
threatened to lead to war.[39]

The parent Committee on the Cause and Cure of War (CCCW)
was a purely national body and was founded in 1925, at a conference
of nine women's organizations held in Washington, D.C. The CCCW,
which named Carrie Chapman Catt as chairman, declared in its first
report:

> The women's organizations of this country, which have
> been working, through their respective programs, for an or-
> dered human society, feel deeply their responsibility in this
> realm of war and peace.
>
> They believe it is time for their organizations to unite in
> taking steps to study the causes and cures of war.[40]

The first annual New Jersey Conference on the Cause and Cure
of War was held the following year in Montclair, with nine women's
organizations participating: the SFWC, the Council of Women for
Home Missions, the New Jersey State Council of Jewish Women, the
NJWCTU, the national board of the Young Women's Christian Association (YWCA), the American Association of University Women,
the Federation of Women's Board of Foreign Missions of North
America, the NJLWV, and the NJSFCWC. The conference was a
spectacular demonstration that the major women's organizations of
the state supported the peace movement.[41]

In the 1920s suffragists and their fellow members in the peace organizations supported a number of positions: convening of an armaments limitation conference in 1921; U.S. adherence to the World Court; cooperation with individual League of Nations Departments, particularly the Economic Section and the International Labor Organization; the creation of a division in the Department of State to be headed by an under secretary of peace; and Senate ratification of the Kellogg-Briand Pact, the first international treaty to outlaw war.[42] They held that women could act as an influential moral force to convince nations that war was an illogical way to resolve differences. War was a matter of choice, they maintained, and was not inevitable. Nations could choose to go to war, or they could not. It was as simple as that. The claim of self-defense, the historic justification for war, was no longer acceptable, they declared. The process of law, that is, mediation and arbitration, had to replace the national rush to attack or avenge. After centuries of slaughter and destruction, war could finally be outlawed. Should an outcast nation refuse to abide by the rule of law, the united nations of the world could use force to punish the offender, but only as a last resort.[43]

More fundamentally, women in the peace groups believed that their sex was tempermentally better equipped than men to lead the way to end war. Thousands of years of human history had shown that men resorted to impulse, not reason—vengeance, not facts, when it came to settling international disputes. Moreover, profit, not morality, was often the real motive behind war. The World War had proven that. "Shall we forever bow to the will of the few big financial interests that profit by war?" Mary Hussey of the NJWIL asked. "Shall we always be fooled by false slogans? Did the last and greatest war *end war*?"[44]

Women, on the other hand, were more temperate and objective, evidenced by the fact that they were working for "an ordered human society" "through their respective programs."[45] Through the careful collection of facts about the causes of war, they could influence public opinion to work for peace. As bearers of children and mothers of the race, they could no longer countenance the holocaust of war. The place to begin was in the home. Peace began by living it, day by day. "While our ideals are set for peace, we are still leading imperialistic lives," Halsey contended. "We must first learn what ideas will prevent war and strive to change the thought of another generation." It was up to women, who were charged with the moral guidance of their children, to teach the next generation. War could be prevented, read a CCCW resolution, "by such teaching of the children in the home, substituting stories of the achievements of peace for those of war, . . . By influencing the Schools, the Press, the Pulpit, and the Public Platform of all kinds that these shall strengthen and further such home teaching."[46]

The suffragists in the peace movement were distinguished from their counterparts in other reform organizations in that they were working solely for national and international objectives. It was national, not state, politicians who had to be convinced of the imperative to create the international machinery for peace. It was not unexpected, therefore, that they used indirect political action to achieve their goals. Senators and congressmen were to be bombarded with letters. Telegrams were to be sent to the president. Resolutions were to be drawn up and announced to the public. Nevertheless, it is the similarity, not the difference, that stands out, when comparing these suffragists with other suffragist reformers. What bound all of them to one another was a point of view that women had a special obligation to educate the public and to prod the political establishment to work for moral ends.

By 1930 the peace advocates could validly assert that the decade had produced some concrete achievements. The Washington conference in 1921 had resulted in the Four Power Treaty in which the signatories agreed to limit their naval tonnage and "to respect each others rights in the Pacific." The Kellogg-Briand Pact had been ratified by the United States, and "most of the nations of the world had followed suit." But there was disappointment as well. United States membership in the World Court, a cherished goal, remained an unaccomplished objective. Collective security was not yet a reality.[47] By decade's end, the peace organizations were still an impressive lobbying presence, representing thousands of organized women. Membership figures of the WIL, which was undoubtedly the smaller of the two peace groups, are not known, but the CCCW had not only retained its broad constituency but grown. Its roster of participating organizations now totaled eleven and included the New Jersey Federation of Business and Professional Women's Clubs.[48]

No organization better expressed the Moral Prodder's view that women had a responsibility to preserve the integrity of home and family and to reform society through the passage of appropriate legislation than did the Woman's Committee for Law Enforcement. The committee was established in April 1924 at a national convention held in Washington, D.C. Described as a "'Second Crusade' of the womanhood of the nation," it drew women from thirty-nine states who collectively represented ten women's national organizations. It pledged to uphold the Constitution, especially the Eighteenth Amendment, and proposed a series of measures to make federal enforcement of Prohibition more effective. Within a month a New Jersey Woman's Committee for Law Enforcement was formed, as were other state committees throughout the country. The New Jersey committee had a nucleus of one thousand women. Its chairman was suffragist Miriam Lee Early Lippincott, of Camden. Lippincott had been a member of the Republican State Committee since 1921 and was a delegate-at-large to the Republican national convention. She was a member of the state boards of the NJLWV and the New Jersey Women's Republican Club, and New Jersey representative on the national board of the YWCA. Officers and executive committee members included suffragists Helena Simmons, Geraldine Livingston Thompson, the Reverend Florence Randolph, Lillian Feickert, Florence Halsey, and Jennie Kerlin. In 1927 Lena Anthony Robbins joined the executive board, when she was elected organization secretary. Other noted members of the board included nonsuffragists Mrs. Thomas Alva Edison and Juliet Cushing.[49]

It is important to examine the circumstances that led to the founding of this organization, particularly as they relate to developments in New Jersey. The stated need to establish the national and state committees was "the drift toward lawlessness," a phrase that succinctly described the growing smuggling, bootlegging, and less than effective enforcement of the prohibition laws only a few years after the federal Volstead Act had gone into operation. Certain states were clearly less enthusiastic than others about the dry situation. In New Jersey opposition developed immediately. Only months after ratification of the Eighteenth Amendment in early 1919, the state Democratic party announced its opposition and reserved the right to wait for Supreme Court judgment on the amendment's constitutionality before accepting it as law. The party's platform, adopted in September, pledged its opposition to the Eighteenth Amendment and its intention to work for its repeal. The Republican party, on the other hand, pledged "to uphold and defend the Constitution of the United

States."[50] Prohibition was thus established as a major political issue in New Jersey, with the sides closely drawn. In the fall election campaign of 1919, the Democratic gubernatorial candidate, Edward I. Edwards, promised to make New Jersey "as wet as the Atlantic Ocean." With the support of Mayor Frank Hague of Jersey City and the votes of a majority of urban "New Americans," as one historian termed them, Edwards won the election.[51]

By the fall of 1921, party differences remained striking. The Republican party, which continued to control both houses of the legislature, reaffirmed its unqualified support of law observance and the Eighteenth Amendment. The Democrats finally accepted Prohibition as a reality but sought the defeat of the first state enforcement law, the Van Ness Act, on constitutional grounds. (The law allowed search and seizure without a warrant and failed to provide for jury trials.) They also called for modification of the Volstead Act to permit beer and light wines.[52] Nevertheless, a crack in the Republican armor could be observed that year. Stung by the unpopularity of the Republican-sponsored Van Ness Act, as evidenced by the returns of the recent election, state Republican Chairman Edward C. Stokes warned in mid-November that the severity of the law was losing votes for the party. Democratic Hudson County had increased its plurality of Democratic votes; and Van Ness, author of the enforcement act, was the only member of the twelve-person Essex County Republican slate to be defeated. The Republicans experienced a major setback only a few months later. Within a year of its operation, the Van Ness Act was overturned by the state courts, and in 1922 a new law, the Hobart Act, was passed in its stead.[53] By 1923 the Republican party, which still controlled the state legislature, had publicly divided over the issue of Prohibition into three distinct groups: wets, drys, and modificationists. In their party platform that year, Republicans indicated, for the first time, that they were prepared to support changes in the dry law "to harmonize with any modification that may be made in the National Act."[54]

The New Jersey Woman's Committee for Law Enforcement (CFLE) was founded, then, at a time when sentiment in the state was growing in favor of some form of modification of the prohibition laws. Moreover, New Jersey's most prominent political leaders— Democratic Governor George S. Silzer and U.S. Senators Edward I. Edwards, Democrat, and Walter E. Edge, Republican—were now in the modificationist camp.[55] The CFLE was not alone in its fight against modification. Its most ardent ally was the state Anti-Saloon League, which claimed to represent "1,357 churches with a membership of 464,223." The fact that Committee President Lippincott served on the board of the league helped to strengthen the ties of the two organizations.[56]

Throughout the mid and late 1920s Lippincott was the most visible and vocal spokesman for the suffragists and their fellow members in the CFLE. She enunciated their beliefs that women had a moral obligation, indeed, a "divine" calling, to keep the nation dry. Women, the committee believed, were law abiding, and it was up to them to demonstrate that laws, once passed, were meant to be obeyed and enforced. But, of course, CFLE members fervently believed in these particular laws. They felt that the situation before Prohibition had been intolerable and cried out for remedy. Prohibition laws served to protect what women cared about most: the family, especially children.

> The most valuable product in this nation is CHILDREN. This is primarily woman's industry. Women demand PROTEC-TION of the essential product as the first duty of city, state, and Nation. They pledge themselves to renewed effort through education as loyal citizens to support the Constitution and the law, especially the great PROTECTIVE LAW, the Eighteenth Amendment.[57]

"Protection" was a word that conjured up visions of its alternative: the drunken husband and father who either failed to show up at work or stumbled home late from work, oblivious to his children and abusive to his hard-working wife. There were no gradations of alcohol content, as far as committee members were concerned. Alcohol in any form—beer, wine, or liquor—meant the saloon, the way station between home and work. Even the young were not immune to its temptations. University students could be lured from their studies into its dusky interior. "THE SALOON MUST NOT COME BACK!" the committee declared.[58] To the counterargument that Prohibition had failed to achieve its original purpose, that drinking was, in fact, on the rise, the CFLE answered that the manufacture and sale of liquor had declined; saloons had been closed; and drinking and drunkenness on the job, a problem which had plagued industry, had been drastically reduced.[59]

The CFLE not only fought modification of the state prohibition law but modification of the federal law as well. By 1926, a congressional election year, it joined the national body to make the public aware of the need to return dry congressmen to office. "Our country is facing a crisis," Lippincott wrote the membership in February. "Our present Congress is dry, but it is in the NEXT Congress that the brewers and saloon keepers who are supporting the wet bills in Congress count on making the big drive." [60]

Lippincott soon found a perfect national forum for her views. In April she appeared before the Senate Judiciary Committee in Washington. The Senate committee was holding hearings on the Volstead Act and was giving both the pro and anti forces an opportunity to be heard. "When it was announced that Mrs. Lippincott would take the stand," reported the *Jersey Journal*, "many knew that fireworks were in order." "Mrs. Lippincott bore in her arms a rolled-up paper, fully two feet in diameter, which she later described as being a protest against the Edge beer and light wines bill." The petition bore the names of sixteen thousand persons. At the hearing, Lippincott asserted that the overwhelming majority of New Jerseyans were law abiding and were opposed to any changes in the dry law. How was it, then, asked a Judiciary Committee member, that New Jersey had elected a wet governor as well as two U.S. senators now on record for modification? Unfortunately, Lippincott answered, most New Jerseyans did not take the trouble to vote their convictions. The result was the election of politicians who did not truly represent the people. [61]

At its June convention in 1927, attended by representatives of the SFWC, the Daughters of the American Revolution, the WCTU, and the State Federation of Church Women, the CFLE drew up plans to pressure both state political parties to declare, in their platforms, their support of the "enforcement of the Constitution" well before the 1928 presidential election. Candidates for the legislature, and for Congress, who failed to take an unequivocal dry position would be singled out for defeat. Of course the committee could only realistically hope to influence the Republicans. The Democrats, traditionally opposed to Prohibition, were beyond redemption, but the Republicans had only recently strayed from the dry camp. Senator Edge, whose term expired in 1931, was a prime target. [62]

But the committee was fighting a losing battle. The mood for modification, and even for outright repeal, was growing. The Republicans, in their platform adopted in July 1927, suggested for the first time that a referendum on modification of the Volstead Act be submitted to the people of the nation. By January 1928 a total of six bills, authored by Republicans and Democrats, had been introduced in the state senate and assembly calling for referenda on modification, on Prohibition in general, and for repeal of the Volstead and Hobart acts.[63] Most New Jerseyans who now opposed Prohibition favored modification rather than repeal. The formation, in May 1929, of the New Jersey branch of the Women's Association for Prohibition Reform reflected this growing demand for modification, or "temperance," as it was called. Suffragist Marion McKim Garrison, a former Democratic state committeewoman and one-time staunch supporter of strict enforcement, became an active board member of the new organization and was a vigorous exponent of this point of view. "I believe in temperance," Garrison declared. But, she noted, ten years of Prohibition had only retarded the cause of temperance and blown up the liquor issue so far out of proportion that other more pressing issues were not being addressed. The prohibition law as it now stood was ineffective and had to be amended.[64]

These developments did not persuade the CFLE that public opinion had changed, however. Over the next two years it continued to assert that powerful lobbying interests were masterminding the campaign to undermine Prohibition. "Are you going to allow the bootleggers, the liquor interests, and the politicians who protect vice to dominate New Jersey?" Lippincott asked in a letter she distributed statewide in November 1929.[65] Lippincott urged committee members to "know your courts"; by that she meant that members should make it their business to be on-the-scene observers of the courts in their localities when those courts dealt with cases of nonobservance of the prohibition laws. Court watchers were to take note whether true "enforcement" was taking place and were to report their findings to the state committee.[66]

By the spring of 1930 the CFLE had become increasingly isolated. The NJLWV had disassociated itself from the committee four years earlier. The SFWC had just tabled a motion that it declare its support of the Eighteenth Amendment. The recently published findings of the *Literary Digest* indicated that, out of a total of 227,727 New Jerseyans it had polled, 180,513 favored modification or repeal and 42,214 favored enforcement, a ratio of 4.3 to 1 in favor of the wet position, figures that appeared to repudiate the CFLE's assertion that most state residents were dry.[67] But most devastating to the CFLE, the Republican party had completely crossed over to the wet camp and now called for repeal of the Eighteenth Amendment. Prohibition enforcement should be left to the states, it now maintained.[68] Moreover, one of the three Republican candidates for the senatorial nomination, Dwight Morrow, former ambassador to Mexico and the most favored to win, had just declared that he supported repeal of the amendment. Morrow's stands posed a dilemma for the CFLE and proved to be internally divisive. When the committee decided to endorse Representative Franklin Fort, the only dry candidate, it lost the support of one of its most eminent board members: Republican National Committeewoman Geraldine Livingston Thompson. In a public statement Thompson declared that she had decided to support Morrow in spite of her "sincere disappointment and distress" over his Prohibition stand. Ambassador Morrow was the most outstanding candidate, she noted. He had "the best chance of winning in November," and the Republican party needed more senators in Washington. "Therefore," she said, "I am prepared to subordinate in this one primary election the issue of the repeal of the 18th Amendment to a position of secondary importance."[69]

The clash over the Morrow nomination was symbolic of what had happened to the CFLE by the end of the decade. What had begun in 1924 as a "'Second Crusade' of the womanhood of the nation" had become, in six years, a matter of "secondary importance" to those committee members who put party interest first. By 1930 the CFLE could see that "law enforcement" was doomed, although it dared not acknowledge it to others or to itself. It continued to assert that the majority of New Jerseyans wanted a law-abiding, decent, and safe society. It continued to hope that morality would ultimately triumph.

Of the four groups of Moral Prodders—the CL, the SFWC, the peace organizations, and the CFLE—only the last experienced a loss of influence as the 1920s came to an end. The suffragists who joined the other three organizations (along with their counterparts in the LWV), stating that voting women had an obligation to serve as nonpartisan workers, were rewarded with public recognition and approval. These suffragists had fulfilled their campaign promises that women would behave differently from men once granted the vote.

They had proven that women did not seek to challenge male dominance in the sphere of politics, which was, at bottom, self-serving, but to extend their own sphere beyond that of their homes. Their moral perspective, they declared, was at long last bringing an urgently needed dimension into public life.

CHAPTER FOUR

Equal Righters I:
The Political Parties, 1920–1930

My home is the center, but not the circumference of my life,
just as it is the center, but not the circumference of the life of
every right-living husband and father. The responsibility of
home-management rests upon the woman, it is true, but why
should that fact keep her out of politics any more than the fact
that most men in public office or in party organizations are
business and professional men first and politicians afterward?
The men have their responsibilities in most instances apart
from politics and the women can follow their example.
—Jennie Van Ness, Essex Republican Assembly Candidate,
    September 10, 1920.[1]

Don't allow anyone to tell you that a separate woman's party
would be a good thing. I never believed in such an arrange-
ment. I have had enough of ladies auxiliaries. Do you know what
they always do? They earn all the money and the men spend
it. We want to be in politics on an equal share with the men.
—Lillian F. Feickert, president, New Jersey Women's Republi-
    can Club, April 12, 1924.[2]

BOTH of the above women were suffragists. In contrast to the
view held by the Moral Prodders, their statement reflected
the belief held by another group of suffragists that women,
having won the vote, should become equal participants in political
parties because it was their right and because it was the best way to
work for the passage of legislation they favored.

In 1920 and in the few years that followed, the future looked
bright for those suffragists who sought equal rights for women in the
political party structure. Politicians were eager to court the woman's
vote and sought to include many suffragist leaders in their inner councils. But by mid-decade matters had already gone awry. Suffragist influence in politics was beginning to wane noticeably. Politicians were

expressing their dissatisfaction, even disgust, with the policies of many of the suffragists. By the end of the decade suffragists could no longer be counted an important factor in party matters. A new group of party women, with a different point of view, had taken their place. While a substantial portion of the blame for the suffragists' ultimate failure to achieve true political equality can be laid at the feet of the male political establishment, the fault also lay with the suffragists themselves.

It is important to describe, briefly, the political world into which New Jersey women entered in 1920. The New Jersey state government was headed by a governor, who served a three-year term, and a bicameral legislature consisting of a sixty-member assembly and a twenty-one-member senate. Assemblymen served one-year terms, and senators, three-year terms. The office of governor, in the judgment of one political scientist, was "a weak one." The governor "could not succeed himself," and his veto could be overridden by a simple majority. Many state agencies were independent of gubernatorial direction; some department heads were chosen by the legislature; and the appointments of many officials were beyond gubernatorial control.[3]

Power lay elsewhere. The fact that the county was a unit for the election of state senators, assemblymen, and freeholders and had been so since 1893 gave power to county party officials exceeding that found in other states. County party committeemen were elected by the voters in a primary election. Real control, however, resided with the county executive committee and especially the county chairman. The executive committee picked the party slate, raised funds, and co-ordinated the political campaigns. A prime example of the strong county chairman was Mayor Frank Hague, of Jersey City, in Hudson County. Hague could count on regular Democratic majorities of such magnitude in Hudson County that he became the most important power broker in the state.

By 1920 true party competition was not the rule. Certain counties were known to be safely or strongly Republican or Democratic. Republican strength lay in the northern and northwestern counties of Bergen, Morris, and Essex and in the rural southern counties. Democrats had strong organizations in Warren, Hunterdon, Salem, Hudson, and Middlesex. By virtue of the number of counties in which the Republicans were able to command a majority, the Republicans controlled the state legislature throughout the 1920s. The Democrats, on the other hand, won statewide majorities in this period and elected governors in 1919, 1922, and 1925. In 1928 the Republicans shared in the Hoover landslide and succeeded in electing their candidate, Morgan F. Larson, to the governorship.[4]

New Jersey suffragists had fought long and hard for the vote. Immediately after their triumph, the political parties moved with alacrity to respond to the new reality. Well before the passage of legislation in 1921 that granted women the right to hold office and to serve equally on municipal, county, and state committees, and even before full ratification of the Nineteenth Amendment, the state Republican and Democratic parties took measures to incorporate women into their party apparatus. Suffragists figured prominently in their leadership choices.

The Republicans acted first and most decisively. In May 1920 (as noted in Chapter 2) the party named Lillian Feickert, the state's most well-known suffragist, vice chairman of the state committee. It created the Women's Division of the state committee with its own vice chairman (Feickert) and ten members-at-large. Of these ten, seven were suffragists: Florence Dillon Whitney, Geraldine Livingston Thompson, Florence Randolph, Edith Hyde Colby, Mrs. John J. White, Agnes Cromwell, and Mrs. Robert Huse. (Women became full-fledged members of the committee in 1921.) The party also turned to a suffragist to organize black women voters. Randolph, president of the SFCWC, was appointed to head this effort. The Republicans had good reason to hope that large numbers of the new women voters would flock to the party banner. A straw vote taken at the final convention of the NJWSA in April indicated that the association's membership favored the Republicans over the Democrats, four to one. The suffragists' heavy tilt toward the Republican party could best be explained by the fact that most suffragists were native-born Protestants from the middle and upper middle class, a population group that traditionally voted Republican, and also that Republican legislators, both state and federal, had a better record in support of suffrage than the Democrats.[5]

In later years Feickert asserted that her acceptance of the vice chairmanship was part of a bargain she had struck with Republican Chairman, and former governor, Edward C. Stokes, which ultimately brought about the passage, by the Republican-dominated legislature, of the various bills that advanced women's political and legal status.

I was not willing to accept the vice-chairmanship without making a bargain. I laid my terms before the men who offered it to me. These were that all political committees should be composed of an equal number of men and women; that there should be women on all juries, and that at least two members of the State Board of Education and the Department of Health should be women.

Feickert's assertion, which was made more than once, appears to be accurate, as it was never refuted by Republican party officials. Her appointment to such a strong post undoubtedly reflected the party's respect for the strength of the organized suffragists and its admiration for Feickert's leadership ability.[6]

Once installed, Feickert worked quickly and efficiently. By September she announced that she had appointed vice chairmen to fifteen of the twenty-one county committees, and they, in turn, were organizing the women political workers in the counties. That same month she opened a two-day school for Republican party women in Asbury Park in which specific campaign techniques were taught for the upcoming election. State Chairman Stokes had high praise for Feickert. "Under her leadership," he said, "there will be an addition of 2,000 women workers to the 2,000 men who now handle the party's machinery."[7]

Around mid-1920 Feickert, with party blessing, organized the New Jersey Women's Republican Club. Modeled after the NJWSA, the NJWRC was set up as a grass-roots organization with local groups located in towns and cities and affiliated with county councils. The state club operated independently but received some funding from the party. Republican women were clearly eager to join the new organization. By the spring of 1922 the NJWRC reported that it had a membership of sixty thousand and was planning a drive to enroll one hundred thousand members by the fall. Feickert later claimed that three-quarters of the suffragists joined the NJWRC. Although the accuracy of her statement cannot be ascertained, a high proportion of the club's early state boards was made up of suffragists.[8] Once Feickert had publicly opposed the nonpartisan direction of the

NJLWV in January 1921, then completely severed her ties to it when her term as league treasurer expired in April, her commitment was totally to politics, and obviously she commanded the allegiance of large numbers of suffragists, who joined her in active participation in the NJWRC.

The Democratic party's efforts to organize women were less structured. Because it appeared that the overwhelming number of suffragists favored the Republicans, the party probably did not try to place as many suffragists in prominent positions. By mid-1920 the Democrats had established a six-person women's executive committee as an adjunct to the state committee. Three members of the committee were suffragists: Caroline Wittpenn, Helena Simmons, and Marion McKim Garrison. Simmons was appointed state chairman of the Executive Committee, but her position, unlike Feickert's, lacked authority, for the party undertook no statewide effort to organize women. The inclusion of women in the party apparatus was, apparently, left to the county organizations. Nor did the Democrats encourage women to set up an autonomous organization; there was no Democratic women's group comparable to the NJWRC. In contrast, party officials continually advised women about the importance of joining the regular Democratic party clubs. The basic approach used by the party was the mass rally, held in various cities and organized specifically for women.[9]

The swiftness with which New Jersey women were accepted on an equal basis on the local, county, and state levels of the political parties was by no means duplicated everywhere in the nation. As late as 1950 only eleven other states had enacted similar fifty-fifty legislation, "either by statute or party rule of both parties": Colorado, Florida, Indiana, Kansas, Missouri, Montana, Oregon, South Dakota, Utah, and West Virginia. In most states, the parties granted women equal representation on their state committees only, but parties in eight southern and western states declined to do even this.[10]

Women fared better at the national party level. In this instance the Democrats were the pioneers. Women had been "associates" on the Democratic National Committee since 1919. In 1920, two months before ratification of the Nineteenth Amendment, the party made women full partners with men. A suffragist, Emily Newell Blair, was named vice chairman of the national committee. The Republicans were slower to share power. In 1919 the party set up a "woman's division" of the national committee and appointed a suffragist to head it, but it was not until 1924 that equal representation became the rule.[11]

The political parties in New Jersey clearly had a healthy regard for the anticipated power of the new women voters. By early September 1920, as Registration Day and Primary Day approached, major questions about the women's vote were being raised. Would women vote in large numbers? Would they vote as a bloc on certain issues? Would women prefer one party over another? And would they tend to vote for the party that ran women for elective office and supported bills that women favored?

Not only were women planning to go to the polls for the first time, but several were running for office as well. Although women were undoubtedly seeking numerous local offices, their number is not known. But in that first year a total of eleven women were nominated for the office of assemblyman. (In the 1920s an increasing number of women ran for all the major county and state offices, reaching a high of twenty-nine in 1926. The majority of these women ran for the assembly.)[12] The major parties, and the third parties, too, had placed women on their assembly tickets. The Democrats had nominated four, the Republicans three, and the Socialist and State Tax parties had each nominated two. Three of these new aspirants to office were suffragists: Bertha Shippen Irving, a Democrat from Camden County, and Jennie Van Ness and Margaret Laird, Republicans from Essex County. The Essex Republicans had chosen to place two women who were suffragists on a slate whose election was assured. Thus, the Republican party had the honor of sending the first two women to the state legislature. Mayor Hague and the Hudson Democrats could have made a similar decision but chose not to. The Hudson slate remained all male until 1921, when one woman, Katherine Whelan Brown, a nonsuffragist, was nominated and, of course, won. Perhaps rethinking the wisdom of his decision, Hague announced in mid-September that five of the fourteen Democratic presidential electors from New Jersey would be women. Four of the five who were ultimately named were suffragists: Garrison, Wittpenn, Simmons, and Elizabeth Pope. In 1921 Hague named a second suffragist, Rose Anne Billington, of Jersey City, to serve on the Democratic National Committee.[13]

The outcome of the election on November 2 gave tentative answers to some of the questions raised about the effect of the woman's vote. The total, as I have already noted, did not live up to expectations. But those women who did vote, clearly favored the Republican party over the Democrats. Had the attention paid by the Republican party to women, and to suffragists in particular, made a difference? What is clear is that other factors were influential. While the electorate in general preferred Harding, the Republican presidential nominee, to Cox, the Democrat, newspaper accounts indicate that old-stock Protestant Republican women were more inclined to register and vote than new-stock Catholic women, whose affiliations were likely to be Democratic. As one historian of New Jersey politics in the 1920s observes, "Newer American" women were not encouraged to vote by their husbands, and they did not see the relevance of politics to their daily lives.[14]

Thus far, it looked as though the suffragists' successful drive for the vote had yielded a bonanza for the Republican party. Suffragists were active in both political parties, but they predominated in Republican circles, and it was through the NJWRC that the suffragist leadership was most prominent and had its greatest impact on political affairs. When the NJWRC held its first annual convention in Atlantic City in April 1921, the mood of the gathering was ebullient. Speaker after speaker declared that the party had fulfilled its pledges to Republican women. The club drew up a legislative program and decided to focus its energies on encouraging more women to run for the municipal and county committees. In subsequent months the NJWRC began to write both planks in the party platforms advocating action to be taken and specific laws it wished to see passed. There were five that first year, including one on pure food, two related to education, and another calling for passage of the CL-backed Night Work Bill.[15]

The Night Work Bill proved to be the cause of early sharp conflict between the NJWRC and the Republican leadership. Early in 1922 the NJWRC-sponsored bill was introduced in the legislature. It passed the assembly easily but ran into trouble in the senate. The Senate Committee on Labor and Industries, chaired by Horace M. Fooder, Republican from Gloucester County, which was considering the bill, was being pressed on all sides by different interest groups: the women's organizations, which favored the bill; the textile manufacturers, who opposed it; and several hundred night workers, who demonstrated at a public hearing in the senate chambers and maintained that night work was essential to their livelihoods. The committee, loathe to take action, considered postponement or, as an alternative, adding amendments. The NJWRC leadership responded with anger. There were to be no changes in the bill. The proposed delay, it charged, was merely a stalling tactic.[16]

The Night Work Bill eventually died in committee that spring, but a bad taste lingered on. Senator Charles White, Republican from Atlantic County, a supporter of the bill, subsequently observed that the Republican women had been inflexible and had unnecessarily insulted several senators, including Mr. Fooder, whom he considered "[men] of integrity." Their methods, he said, "made it very difficult to bring about any sensible compromise at the end of the session." The leadership of the NJWRC also continued to smart over the recent events. That May, Feickert observed that the Republican clubwomen were growing impatient with the legislature for its failure to consider any of the legislation that the women favored. The matter would be raised with party leaders, she advised.[17]

The fall 1922 campaign provided time for a welcome truce. Owing to NJWRC efforts, the platform plank calling for a night work law was reinserted, and two new planks, one supporting the existing Direct Primary law and another calling for the appointment of the commissioner of education by the State Board of Education instead of the governor, were added. The Republican women worked diligently in behalf of the party's gubernatorial, senatorial, and legislative candidates. But the reintroduction of the Night Work Bill in the legislature in February 1923 reignited the antagonism of the past and deepened the feelings of ill will on both sides. The senate passed the bill, but this time a caucus of Republican assemblymen was urging an amendment that would postpone operation of the law until December 31, 1924, a delay of almost two years strongly opposed by the NJWRC. When the bill came to the floor for a vote, Feickert, who had been in regular attendance with other NJWRC representatives, was ejected from the chamber by Speaker Walter W. Evans, on the grounds that "lobbyists" could not be present. The votes for the amendment had been garnered, and on March 16 the Night Work Bill passed almost unanimously. Feickert's ejection from the assembly aroused an immediate furor. Not only were the Republican women highly incensed, but numerous state newspapers deplored Speaker

Evans's action and came to Feickert's defense. Several of these papers criticized the Republican leadership for weakening the impact of the Night Work Bill.

When Governor George S. Silzer signed the bill into law on March 21, Juliet Cushing of the CL, NJWRC leaders, and representatives of other women's organizations were there. The victory was primarily the CL's, as the organization had sought the Night Work Law for many years. To the NJWRC went the credit for forcing the legislature to act. But as far as the Republican women were concerned, there was no cause for celebration. The conditions under which the Night Work Bill had been passed only unleashed their fury. In the April issue of the *New Jersey Republican*, a new monthly publication of the NJWRC, the leadership declared that the Republican legislators had broken their promises to the party women. Those assemblymen who voted to amend the Night Work Bill had not kept the faith, they asserted. Moreover, the legislators had failed to carry out their other platform pledges, particularly those related to education. In the 1922 election Republican women had put party first despite the poor legislative record of its members. But now, in the coming primary elections, with no candidates running for major office, things would be different. Those legislators who did not work to keep the Night Work Bill intact would be singled out for defeat. "Swat the promise-breaker!" was the new slogan of the NJWRC.[18]

At its annual convention, held in May in Atlantic City, at which Jennie Van Ness, Geraldine Livingston Thompson, and Mrs. Robert Huse were featured speakers, the NJWRC repeated these charges and drafted its new legislative program: support for United States entry into the World Court; strong law enforcement and opposition to Republican Senator Walter E. Edge's bill to allow beer and light wines; and "the selection of honest men and women to represent them in the primaries of the Republican party." "We won't be fooled again," Feickert warned.[19]

This dissension between the NJWRC and the male republican party leaders was grist for the Democratic mill. For example, at the first convention of Democratic women, held in Asbury Park in September 1923, the assemblage drew up a resolution criticizing the Republicans for their treatment of their party women. On repeated occasions, moreover, Democratic political leaders, without direct reference to the NJWRC, relished telling Democratic women that it was inadvisable to form an independent organization. The right path for women was working within the existing party structure, they cautioned.[20]

Mary Norton, a nonsuffragist from Hudson County, who in 1921 had become vice chairman of the Democratic State Committee, particularly enjoyed pointing out the contrast between women's experience in the Democratic party and in the Republican organization. Women were well treated by the party, she declared. They needed no expensive state club. "We have a great many district and ward clubs throughout the State, each working out its own problems and all working in harmony with the men of our party and for the greater good."[21]

Despite the conflicts over legislative objectives, the NJWRC, as of late 1923, remained committed to the party organization. Granted many of its goals had not been achieved, it also conceded that Republican party leaders had made valid efforts to recognize women's interests. Feickert remained optimistic about the role organized women could play in the Republican party. She still had a vision of women actively involved in the party organization who would be supported by a loyal female following. But while she could repeatedly state that women should "be in politics on an equal share with the men," her definition of political equality had apparently evolved with the passage of time and was not what it seemed. She hoped to see women on the municipal, county, and state committees in order to influence party policy, to choose candidates for office, and especially to work for the passage of specific legislation. But she did not necessarily see women running for office; at least that was not her major priority. "Women are not looking for gain in politics," she told a group of Republican women in 1924, "in that they differ from the men. Few women, if any, want any political jobs. Women are in politics for what they can put in it, not what they can get out of it."[22]

Feickert appeared to be having difficulty reconciling her stated belief in political equality with her view that women were bringing a new perspective to political affairs. On the one hand, Feickert's noted disdain for women's auxiliaries and her desire for an equal share in politics was a classic expression of the Equal Righters' point of view. On the other hand, her assertion that women were above the spoils of office negated her demand for equality. What she was actually saying was that since women were more moral than men, it was their task to keep the political parties on the right course. Although still adhering to the belief that activism in party affairs was primary, Feickert and the NJWRC leadership had moved closer to the view of the Moral Prodders that stated that women were different from men and had to behave differently.

Earlier Feickert had counseled Republican women against permitting the issue of Prohibition to become divisive, but she was unable to follow her own advice. The modificationist stand of the Republican party, added to other alleged failures, proved too much for Feickert and the NJWRC membership. In December 1923, at a convention of approximately three hundred women, held in Newark, the NJWRC passed a resolution, introduced by Feickert, demanding the ouster of State Chairman Stokes as well as the reorganization of the entire state committee. The club voted to "personally obey all laws to enforce Prohibition, whether approving them or not." In a subsequent letter to the Republican clubwomen, Feickert denounced the legislature for its overall poor performance. She promised a "ceremony of putting on the map the legislative promise keepers and promise breakers" at forthcoming regional conferences.[23]

The resolution passed at the Newark convention and Feickert's letter together constituted an open revolt against the party leadership. In the past the NJWRC had criticized individual Republican legislators and had chastised Senator Edge, but now it stood in defiant opposition to the entire political establishment. Feickert's call for the defeat of Republican legislators who did not pass women's bills and party leaders whose views the NJWRC opposed brought back the excitement of suffrage days. Indeed, Feickert was, in effect, refighting the campaigns of 1918 and 1919, when she worked to mobilize a large body of suffragist women in an attempt to defeat antisuffragist candidates. She felt confident now, as she had then, that women would band together to fight for what they believed. Women, she was certain, would put issues first, party second.

It initially seems difficult to understand the depth of the animosity the NJWRC felt toward Republican politicians in view of the club's recognition of the party's accomplishments for women. Upon reexamination, two factors appear to have influenced its actions. First, it is likely that the Republican women could not forget that many of these same men had not been their allies in suffrage days.

The legislators' failure to pass women's bills only bore out the women's basic belief that most male politicians gave them grudging acceptance at best. Second, the Republican women felt isolated from the party organization. As much as the women spoke in favor of entering politics, it remained, in 1923, a terra incognita. The inner chambers of the political parties had not really opened up to them. The male political establishment was obviously reluctant to share power. The county chairmen were all male, and female county vice chairmen were little more than figureheads. At the state level, the state chairman still retained ultimate authority.[24] Furthermore, the independent route taken by the Republican women contributed to their isolation. Independence had its drawbacks as well as its advantages. A major advantage was that the Republican women retained their identity and were not swallowed up by the party apparatus. Their voices were heard and recorded. They spoke out on issues; they wrote platform planks; and they lobbied in behalf of legislation. But in so doing they had also isolated themselves from the male politicians and were not being exposed to the arguments and concerns of the real power structure.

The Republican women were largely responsible for their sense of isolation in another important regard. They wanted to enter the political parties but shuddered at the thought of playing the political game. First, compromise, the stuff of which politics is made, was anathema to them. They sought the truth, knew the truth, and would not budge from their chosen path. Those who opposed them were to be exposed in public and defeated. This position led to indifference about a second cardinal political rule: the primacy of party loyalty. "We women are for the Republican party right, but not right or wrong," Feickert often remarked. Third, the Republican women set themselves above the rewards of office, another fundamental accepted by traditional politicians. In 1926 Van Ness, NJWRC legislative chairman, grudgingly announced that women would accept political jobs. But, she added, "It's not that we want the jobs themselves . . . but they seem to be the only language the men understand. We don't really want these $200 a year jobs. But the average man doesn't understand working for a cause."[25]

The NJWRC resolution and Feickert's letter proved to be watershed events, as they were instrumental in bringing about the ultimate decline in the fortunes of the NJWRC. In addition, Feickert's advice to clubwomen, in the fall of 1924, not to vote for the party nominee, Senator Edge, in the primaries for U.S. Senate only exacerbated the situation. Together, they brought about swift criticism from Republican politicians, dissension and defection in club ranks, and ultimately, the unseating of Feickert from the state committee.

There had been "rumors" of unseating Feickert from her position of state vice chairman as early as 1923. What was required was her defeat as state committeewoman from Somerset County. By 1925, when Feickert was up for reelection, the party leadership was ready to take that step. The Republican voters, including many women voters, had recently demonstrated, in their support of Senator Edge (who won both the nomination and the election), that they no longer agreed with Feickert's views, particularly on Prohibition.[26]

The four-year terms of all the members of the State Committee were expiring. Seven suffragists were up for reelection in the June primary: Feickert, Thompson, Miriam Lippincott, Edith Colby, Dr. Mary Cummins, Huse, and Mrs. Charles Woodruff. With the exception of Colby and Huse, all were opposed by Edge. Lippincott, president of the New Jersey CFLE, was a major target. Feickert later charged "that the Edge machine spent fifty thousand dollars in Camden County, in its efforts to defeat her." As for her own campaign, Feickert said, "about ten thousand dollars was spent" by Edge.[27]

Woodruff and Feickert were defeated, and Lippincott won by only a slim margin. "The defeat of Mrs. Woodruff," Feickert declared, "was the most disgusting of all because she has always been so fair and kind in her treatment of even her open enemies in the county, and she was opposed merely because she stood firmly for the things in which our Club believes—honesty in office, law enforcement and the keeping of promises." As for herself, "My own defeat . . . was neither a surprise nor a disappointment." She had learned through a friend, she said, that the county politicians felt that "she was constantly interfering with their plans." She was actually "relieved not to have the responsibility of organizing the women for the coming campaign."[28]

The Democrats once again exploited the clash between the NJWRC and the Republican leadership. Over the next few years Norton repeatedly pointed out that the Democratic party, unlike the Republican party, kept its promises to women and backed women for office.[29] Norton herself was the supreme example of what the

Democratic party had done for women. In 1920 Mayor Hague had appointed Norton, who had been chairman of the Queens Daughters Day Nurseries, to organize the Democratic women of Hudson County. In 1921 the Mayor had replaced Simmons and had named Norton to the vice chairmanship of the state committee, a position she continued to hold. In 1923 she was designated to run for the Hudson County Board of Freeholders and was elected with the rest of the slate. And in 1924 Norton was picked by Mayor Hague as candidate for the nomination to the House of Representatives from the Twelfth District. Her election gave her the distinction of being the first Democratic woman to serve in Congress and the first woman from any party to serve from the East.[30]

Norton had definite views about women's role in the political parties, and they stood in bold contrast to those of the suffragists and their fellow members in the NJWRC. Norton emphasized the importance of women gaining their political education through involvement in day-to-day political work, however menial. This work was to be done in existing political clubs or in women's auxiliaries closely allied with the regular party organization. Women were Democrats first, Democratic women second. Initially, men were to be the teachers, women the pupils. Women need not initiate legislation. Party programs and policies were to be accepted. Norton was confident that, as women's political experience grew, the party leadership would give them increased responsibilities—political jobs and political office.[31]

The women in the NJWRC, on the other hand, were proud of their independence, their insistence on the passage of specific legislation, especially those bills that benefited women, and the fact that they did not take party loyalty for granted. The most important place for women, they believed, was on the party committees, where they could guide party policy and select the right candidates. Moreover, they felt that their suffrage experience had prepared them for rapid entry into political life. They had given public speeches, written pamphlets, organized rallies, and run major campaigns. Most important, they had proven their ability. They had won the vote.

Despite the sharp differences between the independent Republican women and Norton, who spoke for the organized Democratic women, both groups believed that women's activities in political affairs should be channeled through the political parties. Norton's assessment of women's proper political role would prove to be more realistic than that of the NJWRC, as it coincided with what most male politicians believed. Indeed, the suffragists' strident self-assurance, drawing on their earlier campaign experience, had proven to be a political liability. But in one important respect, Norton was mistaken. The political future of women in New Jersey would not improve with time, for the Republicans or for the Democrats. The political parties' respect for the anticipated power of enfranchised women was beginning to wane.

Although Feickert had lost her important post on the Republican State Committee, the NJWRC had by no means been read out of the party. Her claims, as late as 1926, that the NJWRC membership was one hundred thousand may have been exaggerated, but the club was still a force with which to be reckoned. Feickert continued to be re-elected to the presidency, and she retained the allegiance of many of the original suffragist board members. Moreover, Feickert had the continued support of the organized black Republican women.[32] It gradually became apparent, however, that the NJWRC could no longer claim to be the sole representative of the organized Republican women. By 1926 there were references to two types of party women: the "independent" Republican women, and the "official" or "regular" Republican women. The titular head of the "official" women was Margaret E. Baker, of Morristown, Feickert's successor to the state vice chairmanship. There was, as yet, no statewide organization to rival the NJWRC, but "official" Republican women's clubs were springing up in several counties.[33]

The emergence of a new group of party women brought about a significant change in Republican party affairs. After 1925 planks backing specific legislation or action favored by women, which had been a familiar hallmark of the NJWRC, were no longer to be found in the party platforms. Thus, pledges were no longer demanded of the party leadership, which would then have to be kept. Baker did not see the extraction of party pledges, especially those related to social welfare legislation, as her responsibility. "My job is a partizan (sic) job," she observed, "concerned with the welfare of the Republican party . . . as a party leader my task is for better election laws, and for the furthering of party interest and for the advancement of party success." What she was ready to fight for, she said, was the direct primary, which had been threatened by the newly introduced Stevens bill, calling for the nomination of governor and U.S. senators by the convention system. Her defense of the direct primary, in her role as party leader, was appropriate, she held, because its continued use was essential to the democratic process and to "the influence of women in public affairs." Senator William A. Stevens, of Gloucester County, was the author of the convention bill, but Vice Chairman Baker did not choose to attack him personally or call for his defeat, as the NJWRC would have done in the past. To the contrary, Baker supported Stevens, as she did all the Republican candidates in the 1926 election. That was her job, and she had carried it out.[34] Baker, and the "official" women, were typical of a new breed of political woman, not seen earlier in Republican party life: the loyal party woman. Republican women were beginning to resemble their counterparts in the Democratic party.

"Beginning in mid-decade . . . women's standing in the eyes of politicians dropped precipitously." These words, which William Chafe uses to describe the experience of women on the national scene, could have been applied to New Jersey with equal accuracy. Chafe observes that in 1920 the major political parties had viewed women as a "potent political force," resulting in congressional passage of numerous measures urged by the newly formed Women's Joint Congressional Committee. But by 1924, he notes, several measures endorsed by the WJCC were getting nowhere, and recent laws and newly created agencies were threatened with budget cuts. The Child Labor Amendment, the Sheppard-Towner Act, the Women's Bureau, and the Children's Bureau were major examples.[35]

There were other indicators that national politicians were less in awe of women as a political group. As Emily Newell Blair, vice chairman of the Democratic State Committee until 1927, later observed, by the mid-1920s suffragist leaders were gradually being replaced in the party apparatus by party women "of a different type . . . who [were] without achievement or previous leadership of women."[36] What had happened? The national parties had relaxed and were no longer uncertain about the impact of woman suffrage. Women were not voting as a bloc, and women were not voting in the numbers that had been predicted. Although more women appeared to have voted in the 1924 presidential election than in 1920, they were not a swing force. Women, in fact, were not voting any differently than their husbands. On only two issues, Prohibition and peace, did there appear to be something resembling a woman's vote.[37]

In New Jersey a similar scenario was unfolding. Women were definitely increasing their voting participation, but it was clear that they were not united. Women who voted Democratic chose to do so for the identical reasons as men. The same was true of women drawn to the Republican party. The Republican sweep of the new woman's vote in 1920 reflected, as I have noted, the tendency of native-born Protestant women to vote while immigrant or new-stock women, who would have voted Democratic, stayed at home. But gradually the "Newer American" women acquired the voting habit, and it was reflected at the polls. The Democratic party was building up its female constituency, and it had demonstrated that it was not necessary to set up a separate woman's organization to attract the female vote. The party did make a major effort to appoint and elect women to office, but even this was starting to change. In 1923 and 1924, for instance, Mayor Hague had placed two women on the eleven-member Hudson assembly slate; and in 1925, 1926, and 1927 he increased that number to three. But after 1927 only one woman was designated to run from Hudson County. Women who were active in the Democratic party immediately protested that women had been treated unjustly, but to no avail. Further, the much vaunted participation of women in the party apparatus had become a mere sham, a former vice chairman of the Union County Democratic Committee declared. "It is absolutely senseless to send an independent with real constructive ideas and ideals of government for the good of the cause to the state committee. . . . She would be snowed under and ruled out."[38]

The change in the Republican party's attitude toward women was more dramatic. At the outset, the party had given women, particularly suffragist women, complete freedom to chart their own course. The women's independent organization, the NJWRC, was supported with party funds. The independent women won election to the state committee and authored several party platform planks. But male Republican leaders soon discovered that the methods and objectives of the NJWRC were not supported by a substantial number of female Republican voters, and they learned too that many Republican women put party loyalty before issues. The abrasive approach of the NJWRC had rankled Republican politicians for years, and the NJWRC's legislative goals were often at odds with those of the party. By mid-decade the replacement of the "independent" women with "official" women had become an important party objective.

The decline of the NJWRC and the ascendancy of the "official" Republican women proceeded rapidly after 1925. The number of suffragists on the state committee, who were also members of the NJWRC, continued to dwindle. In 1925 there were seven suffragists on the committee, and in 1926, five. By 1927 and 1928 there were only three suffragists remaining on the committee: Lippincott, Thompson, and Huse. These years were the last that suffragists served on the state committee in the 1920s.[39]

The NJWRC had lost its power to write planks in the party platform, but it still lobbied actively in Trenton. Early in 1926 the club sponsored two bills that were introduced in the legislature—one that added a penalty to the Night Work Law and another that equalized the dower and curtesy inheritance rights of husbands and wives. It also fought to retain the direct primary. By the fall of the year, however, the club was clearly suffering from inactivity and poor attendance. The *New Jersey Republican* had not been published for several months. Feickert was not active in New Jersey throughout the summer and early fall, having gone to upstate New York to work for the defeat of U.S. Senator James Wadsworth, a former antisuffragist.[40]

The fall elections had come and gone without any campaign activity on the part of the NJWRC. Official party women were pressing for the formation of a new statewide women's club. It was suggested that the leader of the new organization be a "harmonizer" who could appeal to all factions of the Republican women.[41] Moreover, loyalists in the NJWRC were becoming concerned about the club's future. The Prohibition issue was putting the club, with its official rigidly dry position, increasingly outside the mainstream of Republican politics. Feickert, too, had become a matter of concern and dismay. Her articles in the *New Jersey Republican* had become angrier than ever. What particularly distressed club members was the fact that Feickert appeared to have become antiparty. Her statements, in effect, rejected party affiliation. "*The New Jersey Republican*," she wrote in April 1926,

believes that all women's organizations should stress bipartisanship rather than non-partisanship, and the perfor-
mances of our own (alas that we should have to express any
ownership in them!) legislators in the session just closed at
Trenton, will very likely bring about a coalition of Republican
and Democratic women in New Jersey . . . most of the legislation the women want, they want irrespective of party lines.[42]

Feickert's call for bipartisanship on the part of women was a far
cry from her earlier hopes for women in the political parties, which
she had expressed in 1921. She had believed then that women cared
more about certain social problems than men but that the best way
for women to solve these problems was by becoming equal partners
with men in every area of politics. But now, five years later, she had
become disillusioned. The political parties had ignored women, she
maintained, or had treated them as second-rate partners at best.
Women's participation in these first five years of their enfranchisement had killed their independent spirit and the unity they had
known in suffrage days. The best means of reviving that unity, she
concluded, was to organize a bipartisan coalition that could reestab-
lish women's influence.

There were no immediate changes, however. The formation of a
new state women's Republican club would not be realized until 1929,
and Feickert's visions of the establishment of a bipartisan coalition of
women remained a dream. In April 1927 the NJWRC held its seventh
annual convention in Asbury Park and reelected Feickert to the presidency once more. The club still retained the allegiance of a large
number of Republican women, particularly those who fought the
modificationist and wet views of the party leadership. Further, club
members believed that there was still evidence that NJWRC political
influence had not completely ended. The passage of the long sought
dower and curtesy bills and their signing into law by Governor A.
Harry Moore on March 15, in the presence of the representatives of
several women's organizations, including Feickert, was, to loyalists,
an important achievement.[43]

In the beginning of 1928 Feickert announced that she would be a
candidate for the Republican nomination for U.S. senator. She had
assembled, she said, a campaign staff of 150 and an active working

staff of 50. "Of course, I will run on a strictly dry platform, provided the other three candidates are wet," she noted. Running against Feickert were Edward C. Stokes, Hamilton F. Kean, and former State Senator Joseph F. Frelinghuysen, who were declared modificationists.[44] The campaign was marked by angry words and sensational headlines. Stokes accused Feickert of being "obsessed" with Prohibition and of being a one-issue candidate. Feickert retorted that she had positions on many issues: world peace, the civil service, national defense, and the direct primary. As for Prohibition, she declared, it was only a political issue for the wets; it was they who wanted to change the law. The drys merely wanted to enforce it.[45]

Just before the primaries on May 15, the unthinkable occurred. Feickert was accused of being "politically dry but personally wet." A companion who had traveled with Feickert in Europe the previous summer declared that Feickert had drunk wine in copious amounts while abroad. Feickert labeled the accusations "a fantastic lie" circulated by the Frelinghuysen camp. But the *New York Times* and *Newark Evening News* headlines that read "Woman Dry Candidate Accused of Drinking," and "Friend Says Mrs. Feickert Emptied Bottle at Sitting," made Feickert the object of public ridicule. This was not the first time Feickert's personal life had been exposed to public scrutiny. One year earlier, the public learned that Feickert's twenty-three-year-old marriage to Edward Feickert had ended in divorce in 1925. A headline in the *Newark Evening News* read: "Husband Preferred Blond, Mrs. Feickert Testifies." Her husband said that his wife's nonstop political activities had caused him too much "suffering." These personal matters were, of course, extraneous to the political disfavor in which the NJWRC found itself. But the unsympathetic reporting of these stories by the newspapers reflected the degree to which the independent Republican women had fallen in the eyes of the public.[46]

Kean won the Republican nomination, and in the November election the Republicans made a clean sweep of the major state political offices. Morgan F. Larson became the first Republican to win the governorship in the 1920s. The time was ripe for the formatiion of a new women's state organization. In April 1929 a state federation of Republican women's clubs was proposed. The federation idea permitted the inclusion of all the Republican women's clubs under one overall administration, including the NJWRC. The NJWRC leadership rejected the proposal, however, seeing it as an effort to end the club's independent voice, and voted to continue as a fully autonomous body.[47]

But the existence of the NJWRC was obviously coming to an end. In November Feickert tendered her resignation effective the following February, offering hopes that the NJWRC would reorganize with a stronger central administration. "The women who are so terribly worried about pleasing 'the boys' had better resign and work with them," she added caustically.[48] That same month the Women's State Republican Club of New Jersey, the official Republican women's club, was formally launched. Its president was Helen Berry, who had succeeded Baker to the state vice chairmanship in 1927. There were now "regular" county Republican clubs in at least nine counties in addition to numerous municipal clubs throughout the state.[49]

Meanwhile, the fortunes of the NJWRC were continuing their rapid downward spiral. That spring, when it found that it could not support the highly respected and party-backed candidate for the Republican senatorial nomination, Dwight W. Morrow, because of his wet position and supported instead Franklin W. Fort, the dry candidate, the NJWRC moved permanently outside the regular Republican orbit. In December 1930 the NJWRC disbanded and reorganized as the State Council of New Jersey Republican Women, with Feickert as president. But the new group was a shadow of its former self. It was held together primarily by its dry position, a position that commanded the support of fewer and fewer voters with the passage of time. A once dynamic body of eager new voters and party workers numbering in the tens of thousands had become, in ten years, a small maverick club out of touch with the political climate in the state.[50]

In retrospect, the decline of the NJWRC was an overall loss for the democratic process and for the cause of equal rights. In the days when the NJWRC was respected and its counsel taken on the state committee and in the legislative halls, new ideas and proposals were added to the Republican party's legislative program. There was pressure to pass bills that might not otherwise be considered—bills that attempted to improve the working conditions of women and children, to benefit the educational system, and to advance the legal status of women. In its heyday, the NJWRC symbolized strong, independent women in politics who felt free to speak their minds and to influence the direction of party affairs. Both parties, Republican and Democratic, now had what they wanted: women whose loyalty they could depend upon. But the parties had lost the active and informed participation of a group of women who had demonstrated their willingness to give of their time, energies, and talents toward goals they deemed important for the welfare of society.

By 1930 suffragist presence in political life had not entirely ended. There were still a few suffragists in important appointive and elective political posts. Thompson, a Republican, and Wittpenn, a Democrat, were members of the Board of Control of Institutions and Agencies. Irving, a Democrat, and Cromwell, a Republican, were members of the State Board of Education. Billington was serving on the Democratic National Committee. And Florence Haines, a Republican, was reelected to the state legislature as assemblywoman from Essex county for the fourth time.[51]

These suffragists had survived, but with the possible exception of Thompson, the party loyalist,[52] they lacked real influence in the party organizations. The suffragists' drive for equal rights in the political arena had suffered from major defeats from which it would not recover. One other group of Equal Righters—the Woman's Party— had retained its organization and membership by the end of the decade.

CHAPTER FIVE

Equal Righters II:
The State Branch of the Woman's Party,
1920−1930

T
HE suffragists who joined the New Jersey state branch of the
Woman's Party in the 1920s were Equal Righters in the purist
sense. They believed that women should receive equal treatment with men in every area of human endeavor, both public and
private. In their ideology and activities they went well beyond their
fellow Equal Righters who concentrated on winning equal participation in the political sphere. Because women and men were equally
human, they declared, women should no longer be treated as men's
inferior in any sphere. The winning of the vote was merely a first step
toward achieving true equality in education, work, the professions,
government, church, citizenship, legal status, and marriage.[1]

The NJWP's unwavering devotion to the principle of equal rights
had two important results. First, it brought the organization into direct public conflict with the other large body of suffragists in the major reform, nonpartisan organizations, as well as with the NJWRC,
over the issue of protective legislation. The conflict made it painfully
apparent that organized women were not united and, further, that
extreme hostility existed between these factions. Second, it led to the
NJWP's sponsorship of numerous bills which were passed by the
state legislature, bills that immeasurably improved women's legal status. In this less publicized endeavor, the NJWP received the approval
of several women's organizations. This body of laws constituted a
permanent equal rights legacy to the women of New Jersey. The unexpected success of the legislative campaign for legal equality encouraged the Equal Righters in the NJWP to believe that the future
looked bright for equal rights in general, but their failure to gain the
broad-based support of organized women was an indicator that their
achievements would be limited.

As of 1920 the NWP had made no apparent plans for its program in the postsuffrage era. Its single goal between 1914 and 1920 as the CU and then as the WP had been passage of the federal suffrage amendment. Indeed, once the amendment had been ratified, the NWP went into temporary limbo until it formally reorganized in February 1921.[2] During the first year of its new existence, the NWP gradually formulated three long-range objectives. First, it announced that it would work for passage of a federal equal rights amendment to the Constitution to wipe out all discrimination—political, economic, and legal—against women. Second, it planned to lobby for the passage of similar equal rights amendments to every state constitution. Finally, it sought passage of state laws to eliminate specific discriminations found in the individual states and in the nation as a whole. (At the federal level, for example, the NWP worked for equalization of the nationality laws, which resulted in 1922 in the passage of the Cable Act, which granted women independent citizenship rights and stated that "the right of any woman to become a naturalized citizen shall not be denied or abridged because of her sex or because she is a married woman." Further liberalizing revisions of that act in 1930 and 1931 were due, in part, to NWP efforts.)[3]

The New Jersey state branch of the WP had ceased operation as well once ratification was achieved. Never a grass-roots organization, but rather a centrally run group with close ties to the national body, it followed the lead of the NWP. The NJWP was revived informally in early 1921 with a small nucleus of members. Two suffragists, both attorneys, held the main leadership positions. Mary Philbrook became temporary state chairman, and Paula Laddey, legislative chairman.[4]

Between 1921 and 1923, with NWP encouragement, other state branches were reorganized throughout the country. The NWP set plans in motion to put its three-pronged program into full operation. In addition to revitalizing the state committees, it had established a legal research department to undertake the massive task of researching the laws of the states as they applied to women and of drafting bills for introduction into the individual state legislatures. Also, in consultation with the state committees, it carefully prepared its draft of the ERA, which it hoped to introduce in Congress shortly.[5]

The transitional organization in New Jersey lasted for approximately two years. By early 1923 the NWP was pressing the state committee to organize formally and to build up its membership. Burnita

Shelton Mathews, an attorney who headed the National Legal Research Department, and her team of assistants had already drafted several bills for New Jersey, and she was particularly anxious to have them introduced during the current legislative session.[6]

At a meeting held in Newark on February 23, the New Jersey state branch of the WP was officially organized. Elizabeth Vroomam, of Ridgefield Park, was elected state chairman. Minnie S. Karr, Lucy Karr Milburn, and former Assemblywoman Margaret Laird, all from Newark, were elected treasurer, secretary, and legislative chairman, respectively. Both Karr and Laird had been active suffragists, Laird having served as NJWP state treasurer from 1916 to 1920.[7] During the succeeding decade the NJWP gradually grew, but it never came close to the membership goals envisioned by its early leaders. By 1930 its list of members totaled two hundred women, predominantly from the middle and upper middle classes. Much like its suffrage predecessor, the NJWP remained a central organization with congressional district chairmen but without local offshoots.[8]

A number of other suffragists subsequently became active members in the NJWP in the 1920s: Rose Anne Billington, Mary Dubrow, Bertha Shippen Irving, Agnes Campbell, Grace Osgood, Helen P. Finley, Gussie L. Vickers, Clara Laddey, and Helen Paul, younger sister of Alice Paul. Four of these women, as already noted, were active in the political parties. Laird, in addition to having served in the assembly, was president of the Newark Women's Republican Club. Vickers was a member of the Jersey City branch of the NJWRC. Irving, a Democrat, had been an assembly candidate from Camden County in 1920, and Billington was serving on the Democratic National Committee. For all of these suffragists, the new direction of the NJWP appeared the logical outcome of years of effort on behalf of the federal suffrage amendment. Women were entitled to self-government, they had emphasized in the suffrage campaign, a right men in a free society took for granted. Now that the vote was won, the new demand that equal rights be guaranteed in the federal and state constitutions, and that women's inferior legal status be finally ended, seemed a reasonable extension of their earlier demand for political equality.[9]

In embarking on this new course, the suffragists in the NJWP identified most closely with the founders of the woman's rights movement in the nineteenth century, particularly the three women whom they called the "Pioneers": Lucretia Mott, Susan B. Anthony, and Elizabeth Cady Stanton. Along with their fellow members in the NWP, they regularly paid homage to these three, observing the anniversaries of their births, laying wreaths at their statues at the Capitol in Washington, D.C., and recalling the objectives that they sought. It was no mere coincidence that the NWP Declaration of Principles, adopted on November 11, 1922, was modeled after the Declaration of Sentiments adopted at Seneca Falls, and copies of the documents were prominently displayed side by side in a 1923 issue of *Equal Rights*. Similarities in wording and format are clearly seen. "The history of mankind," began the 1848 document,

> is a history of repeated injuries and usurpations on the part of man toward woman, having in direct object the establishment of absolute tyranny over her. . . .
> Resolved [it concluded] that the speedy success of our cause depends on the zealous and untiring efforts of both men and women for the overthrow of the monopoly of the pulpit, and for the securing to woman an equal participation with men in the various trades, professions, and commerce.

"Whereas, Women today," the 1922 Declaration of Principles began,

> although enfranchised, are still in every way subordinate to men before the law, in government, in educational opportunities, in the professions, in the church, in industry, and in the home. Be it Resolved. . . .

The resolutions that followed paralleled many made by the earlier feminists that all discriminations against women and barriers to equal rights be removed. "In short," it concluded,

> THAT WOMAN SHALL NO LONGER BE IN ANY FORM OF SUBJECTION TO MAN IN LAW OR IN CUSTOM, BUT SHALL IN EVERY WAY BE ON AN EQUAL PLANE IN RIGHTS, AS SHE HAS ALWAYS BEEN AND WILL CONTINUE TO BE, IN RESPONSIBILITIES AND OBLIGATIONS.[10]

In their eagerness to state their case, the NWP had, of course, chosen to overlook the fact that women had vastly improved their economic and legal position since the time of the adoption of the first declaration. But, albeit at the cost of accuracy, it had correctly dramatized the fact that, despite having won the vote, women were still far from the goal of true equality.

Given the strained, even hostile, relations between members of the NJWP and the majority of the suffragists in the NJWSA at various times during the suffrage campaign, it was only natural that the reorganization of the NWP in 1921 and the establishment of the interim New Jersey branch should elicit a wait-and-see attitude among suffragists who had joined the various reform organizations in the state. Within a year, however, it had become clear to the Moral Prodders that the new drive of the NWP for federal and state equal rights amendments threatened the protective legislation they so strongly favored.

Early in 1922 both the NJLWV and the NJCL warned that it was imperative to defeat Assemblywoman Laird's resolution calling for the creation of a commission to investigate discriminations against women, to be followed by a recommendation for a state ERA. Laird's resolution was ultimately defeated by four votes, but the closeness of the vote must have alarmed Moral Prodders that their programs in behalf of protective legislation might be in jeopardy.[11] Indeed, an open, bitter clash occurred just one year later over this very issue. The NJWP was strongly opposed to the Night Work Bill being considered by the legislature in early 1923, but it had reorganized too late to do any effective lobbying. The bill was passed and became law in March. The first major NJWP criticism of the bill's passage appeared in an article in a May issue of *Equal Rights*. The article, based on a report from the NJWP, not only vastly exaggerated the number of working women who opposed the Night Work Bill, but in its assertion that "approximately ten thousand women will be thrown out of employment," ignored an important section of the bill that called for the delaying of the law's operation for almost two years.[12] This careless reporting was guaranteed to bring an immediate counterattack from the bill's proponents. More important, the article, and a subsequent article's acid criticism and derision aimed specifically at the state's women's reform organizations, elevated the dispute to that of major battle with no room for compromise. "Among the most dangerous of human kind," a NWP editor asserted, are philanthropists. They are forever rushing in where angels fear to tread, and as they do not have to endure the results of their own beneficence they learn nothing from experience. Especially in labor circles are they a menace, for they conspire, for their own comfort, a variety of utopian schemes which bear no relation to the hard pan business of earning a living.[13]

Another confrontation occurred between the NJWP and several women's reform organizations in late 1925. On December 8 a special committee of the legislature appointed to investigate the conditions of working women in the state held its initial meeting in Newark, to which various interested organizations were invited. Attending the meeting were representatives of the CLNJ, the YWCA, the NJWCTU, and the NJWP. The legislative committee was particularly interested in the status of women's wages. Juliet Cushing of the CLNJ urged prompt investigation, which she believed, based on her organization's own preliminary studies, would reveal that a large proportion of working women in New Jersey earned less than a living wage. It was imperative, she held, that the legislature act to relieve the desperate plight of these women. Leila Enders, speaking for the NJWP, protested against the idea of the committee even embarking on the investigation. The results of such a study were well known, she said, from past experience. "As night follows day, they are always followed by an attempt to place restrictive laws, such as forty-eight hour week or minimum wage law, for women upon the statute books." Working women in New York had opposed a forty-eight hour week, she contended, because they knew that such a law would force them to accept lower wages than men and even to lose their jobs altogether.[14]

The NJWP, like the NWP, had a logical and persuasive argument for opposing all forms of protective legislation, whether it be seats for women, minimum wage legislation, maximum hours laws, or night work laws. It believed that valid as these provisions might be, women should not be singled out to receive their so-called "benefits." If such measures were indeed beneficial, it maintained, then every effort should be made to have them apply equally to men and women alike. Should there be a basic living wage? Then see to it that society guarantees it regardless of sex. Does working at night endanger the safety of women? Then make the streets safe at night, so that all may walk them with assurance. Is it also dangerous to women's health? Then outlaw it for all workers. The NJWP was convinced, moreover, that protective legislation was more accurately termed *restrictive* legislation because it limited women in their bargaining position vis-à-vis getting and keeping their jobs. Because the employer was legally bound to pay women a certain scale, could only hire them in the daylight hours, and had to limit their work week, he would naturally turn to men when he made his hiring choices, the NJWP held. The result was bound to be fewer jobs for women and, more likely, unemployment.[15]

What was the point of view of the women's organizations adamantly opposed to the equal rights position? It helps to recall that the position of women in the work force in the early twentieth century was quite different from that of today. While contemporary working women are most likely to be married and middle aged, the average working woman in the 1920s was young, single, divorced, or widowed. Moreover, she was far less likely to be a union member than a man. The CLNJ, the NJLWV, the NJWTUL, and the SFWC continually pointed out that women's youth, inexperience, and lack of unionization put them at a disadvantage when bargaining for a job. The facts were, they declared, that women worked for lower wages than men and their working conditions were often worse, particularly those engaged in sweated labor. Protective legislation merely made an unequal situation more equal. Of course underlying the Moral Prodders' demand for protection was their perception of women as physically weaker than men and having the double obligation of running a home. The unequal position of women in the work force served to support this basic perception.[16]

There was logic on both sides of the argument, and it seems possible, from a present vantage point, that the suffragists and their fellow members in both camps could have found ways to bridge their differences. But the methods of the NJWP precluded that option. Moreover, a further impediment to compromise was the Moral Prodder's strong suspicion that the NJWP was not basically interested in improving women's working conditions. They noted the failure of the NJWP and the NWP to commit themselves on this issue, as evidenced by statements such as these in *Equal Rights*: "The Woman's Party is not a labor organization and does not presume to say what is the best method of improving labor conditions—whether by organi-

zation, by legislation, or by reconstructing the form of our society";
"The WP is neither for nor against the minimum wage in itself but it
is against a sex basis for a minimum wage law." The NWP made such
comments over and over. For a group such as the CLNJ that had devoted its entire organizational life to improving the working conditions of women and children, these words only served to escalate the
dispute over a central and sensitive issue.[17]

The NJWP attack on the Night Work Bill, as well as on other forms
of protective legislation, threw a harsh spotlight on the divisions
within the ranks of the suffragists. These disputes were tailor made to
receive publicity. Yet beyond the glare of public attention, the NJWP
was engaged in another long-range effort of considerable importance. From the time of its reorganization the NJWP began a dia-
logue with the national body to plan for the enactment of its legislative program to eliminate state legal discriminations against women.
Throughout the 1920s correspondence flowed between the NJWP
leadership and two major NWP figures—Emma Wold, legislative
secretary, and Burnita Shelton Mathews, legal research secretary—
regarding the details of the legislative campaign. (By late 1924 the
NJWP presidency had passed from Elizabeth Vrooman to fellow
nonsuffragist Leila Enders, a young schoolteacher also from Ridgefield Park. Enders retained the presidency through the 1920s and
1930s.) The national office was in large measure the initiator of the
effort to introduce bills into the legislature, with the state leadership
indicating those bills it thought had the best chance of being passed.
"We would like five or six bills for our legislative program," Enders
wrote Mathews in September 1925, for example. "That gives us a
chance to pick favorites as well as Senators and Assemblymen." The
national office also provided a careful analysis of the meaning of the
laws it had drafted, or of the changes it was making in the existing
laws. Enders found this extremely useful: "Thank you very much for
answering all my questions in regard to Senate #10 so promptly," she
wrote Mathews in March 1925. "You have enabled me to talk to the
legislators convincingly."[18]

Interchange took place in other ways. The national office continually checked whether its bills were being introduced. It also advised the NJWP, as it did all the other state branches, that it not only
push the introduction of its own bills but back any bills sponsored

by other groups or individuals that met its equal rights criterion. Whereas the stance of the NJWP regarding protective legislation was in opposition to that of most other women's organizations, the NJWP still sought to develop a spirit of cooperation where possible. As Alice Paul, now vice president of the NWP, regularly observed, "It seems to me that it is immaterial whether the bills which are passed are those which we have drawn up, or those which some other organization has drawn up. I think we should consider any Equal Rights legislation which is introduced as our legislation and support it."[19]

By early 1923 NWP research on the laws of New Jersey as they affected women was nearing completion. As early as December 1922 Paula Laddey, state legislative chairman, had received three drafted bills from the NWP relating to "equal alimony . . . equal criminal liability for non-support, and . . . establishing a settlement for poor relief, so that a married woman may have a settlement of her own account not dependent on her husband's domicile." These drafts were the first in a stream of bills sent to the state branch during the decade. By the end of 1924 the Legal Research Department had drafted a total of fifteen bills for New Jersey, and more were to come.[20]

Although the NWP had declared in its Declaration of Principles that women had moved not one jot beyond the legal status of the early women's rights leaders with the one exception of winning the vote, this was, of course, were dramaturgy. The astute Legal Research Department clearly knew that numerous laws had been passed in the states in the intervening years to improve the legal status of women, particularly married women; and this was true for New Jersey as well. Until 1852 the legal status of married women in the state had been defined by English common law. While single women had many of the same rights and privileges as men, they lost those rights upon marriage. Husband and wife become one person in the eyes of the law, but it was the husband who assumed the rights as well as the obligations of both. The property, possessions, and even debts of the wife became the husband's. Upon passage of the Married Woman Act in 1852, married women regained many of the rights they had as single women—to retain their real and personal property, of which the husband could not dispose, to acquire new property, and to have contracts made before marriage considered legally valid. Because their debts were no longer assumed by their husbands, married women could now sue and be sued. A subsequent law in 1864 permitted married women to draw up a will, in which they could dispose of their personal, but not their real, property.[21]

Although women's educational and professional opportunities had considerably improved during the latter part of the nineteenth century, their legal status had not basically changed. What had yet to be done in the 1920s to equalize the legal rights of New Jersey women with men? Although the winning of the vote had made it possible for women to serve on juries; participate equally on municipal, county, and state party committees; and enjoy equal privileges with men in holding office and employment, the research of the NWP revealed that many discriminations still existed: in married women's property rights; in guardianship rights; in contractual capacity; and in rights to sue fully, to be executors and trustees, to make deeds, to receive fully equal jury status, to receive equal pay as school teachers, to retain earnings earned in their homes for third persons, and to have a separate domicile from their husbands, among others. In addition, a single woman did not have the legal power to compel the father of her illegitimate child to pay support. These and other discriminations were described and illustrated with cases in the NJWP twenty-four page leaflet "How New Jersey Laws Discriminate against Women" published in 1926. The leaflet was written by Mary Philbrook and printed jointly by the state branch and the NWP.[22]

The introduction of NJWP equal rights bills into the legislature began in early 1924 and continued in succeeding sessions throughout the rest of the decade. The NJWP had no problem finding sponsors for its bills. Senator William B. Mackay, Jr., Republican from Bergen County, introduced all NJWP bills in the senate until his term expired in 1929. Enders described Mackay as "a strong and faithful leader in the movement to advance the position of women in New Jersey." Subsequent bills were introduced in the senate by Ralph Chandless, Republican from Bergen, and Morgan F. Larson, Republican from Middlesex. Between 1924 and 1928 most NJWP bills were introduced in the lower house by then Assemblyman Chandless; Assemblywoman Isabelle Summers, Republican from Passaic County; and Emma Peters, Republican from Bergen.[23]

In 1925 the first NJWP bill was passed: "An act prohibiting discrimination on account of sex in the employment of teachers," albeit over Governor George Silzer's veto. Discrimination against women teachers in New Jersey, like that in many other states, though not codified in law, was practiced by many local school boards. A law was deemed necessary, the NWP asserted, to wipe out all such practices. The teacher's law was invoked successfully in 1929 and 1930. In the first instance ten married school teachers in the city of Gloucester brought against the local school board charges of salary discrimination, and in the second, sixteen women teachers in Perth Amboy brought a similar suit. State Commissioner of Education Dr. Charles D. Elliott ruled that these boards must set the same salary scales for men and women and, further, that the appealing teachers must be compensated retroactive to the beginning of the school year. *Equal Rights* had high praise for this action: "Commissioner Elliott deserves the highest commendation for enforcing the law he is sworn to enforce." [24]

Over the next five years another nine NJWP bills were passed by the legislature, all dealing with the various discriminations against women that the Legal Research Department had cited (for a detailed listing of these laws, see Notes). The NWP considered drafting of a bill to rescind the Night Work Law but rejected the idea because it determined that many night workers were exempted from the law's restrictions and especially because, lacking a penalty clause, the law was totally ineffective. Not all NJWP bills that were introduced received legislative approval, but those that were passed after 1925 were signed by Governor Silzer's successor, A. Harry Moore. Moreover, these ten laws were not the sum total of the equal rights laws passed in New Jersey during this period. Others were sponsored by other organizations or individuals, most notably, the Dower and Curtesy Bill, passed in 1927, introduced on behalf of the NJWRC. Following Alice Paul's dictum, the NJWP was pleased to support all equal rights bills from whatever source. Similarly, organizations which opposed the ERA but still favored the advancement of the legal status of women—such as the NJLWV, the SFWC, and the NJWRC—gave the state branch campaign their open approval. [25]

The NJWP, apparently, had little difficulty in moving its successful bills through the legislature. For example, the act granting married women the same power to bind themselves by contract as if single passed in 1927 with the formal backing of leading bankers in the state. Another, requiring the fathers and mothers of illegitimate children to provide "support and education" as if married, was passed unanimously in 1929. Indeed, by 1927 the NJWP had received such ready cooperation from the legislature that Mathews suggested to Enders that less popular measures be introduced simply to educate the legislators about the inequities of the existing law. In effect, Mathews was saying that the senators and assemblymen could benefit from a consciousness-raising session about equal rights. "Your campaigns on the legislature in New Jersey have been wonderful," she wrote in 1928. "I congratulate you on your success. I only wish more women would join the New Jersey branch and thus become part of the woman movement." [26]

In its campaign to improve the legal status of woman, not only had the NJWP been dramatically successful, but by the end of 1929 it had brought New Jersey to a leading position among states in the number of legal discriminations removed. In a report to the NWP convention that convened on December 8, 1929, Mathews reported on the work of the Legal Research Department and reviewed its achievements, state by state. Five hundred pieces of legislation had been drafted since 1921, she noted; eighty-nine equal rights bills, either drafted or supported by the NWP, had been passed in twenty-three states, Puerto Rico, an the District of Columbia. Louisiana took first place with eleven bills passed; New York, second place with ten; and Maryland and New Jersey tied for third place with nine. [27]

It is particularly significant that so many equal rights bills in New Jersey were introduced after 1920. Winning the vote gave impetus to the suffragists and encouraged them to demand dramatic improvements in their legal status. Although the Moral Prodders supported this aspect of the drive for equal rights (the NJLWV, for example, established its Committee on the Legal Status of Women in 1927), it was the Equal Righters who were the most militant and effective in this regard. The suffragists who sought to enter the political parties, particularly the organized Republican women, were largely responsible for the legal advancements of women in terms of their public rights. But it was the suffragists and their associates in the NJWP who demanded that women be made equal with men both in their public and private lives. Moreover, the unusual success of the NJWP in removing legal discriminations against women was the result of action taken at the right time. Once the suffrage was won, New Jersey male legislators gradually became more sympathetic to the demands for legal equality that the WP dramatized so well. These legislators were no longer prepared to accept the legal assumption that women, once married, surrendered their rights to their husbands. In the hands of supportive sponsors in the senate and assembly, NJWP bills were thus enacted into law with relative ease.

Notably, the effective NJWP campaign was the undertaking of a few able leaders, particularly Enders and Laird, who were knowledgeable about legislative procedure. It was not the culmination of a groundswell of activity on the part of the membership. It is interesting to observe the differences between the NJWP methods of operation and those of the NJLWV. The league saw the education of its membership as a basic objective. Issues were studied by local chapters, and as the result of a consensus, positions were established. Lobbying for the passage of appropriate legislation then followed. In contrast, the leadership of the NJWP took upon itself the right and the obligation, together with the national office, to set policies and to pursue its legislative program. Although enjoying the support of its membership, the leadership made no effort to encourage broad-based participation.

An occurrence in 1929 revealed the elitist nature of the organization. Minnie Karr, now NJWP vice president, wrote a long letter to Mable Vernon, NWP secretary, seeking NWP help in unseating Enders. The NJWP, she declared, had never been properly organized, as Enders had not been elected to the presidency, but appointed to her post by the old board. There were no annual business meetings. The current executive board was thus a mere fiction. Membership, moreover, had suffered. "Each year," she observed, "the numbers of those that renew their membership grows smaller." That same month Gussie Vickers sent a similar letter to Vernon, noting that it appeared there had never been a proper election of officers. "Shouldn't 'Washington' correct this?" she asked. But the call for a change in leadership went unheeded. The national office was apparently satisfied that Enders was doing a fine job. Enders, meanwhile, was publicizing NJWP achievements through press releases and radio broadcasts. "Equal rights progress so fast in New Jersey," she declared in a statement to the *Newark Evening News* at the end of 1928, "that it is almost bewildering."[28] In addition, press coverage was laudatory. In 1929 a *Newark Evening News* article reporting passage of the ninth equal rights bill had this headline: "As Usual the National Woman's Party Scores Again."[29]

By 1930, with passage of yet another of its bills, the NJWP looked back on the decade with satisfaction, assured that the cause of equal rights had indeed been advanced. There is no doubt that the legislative campaign had brought tangible benefits to the women of New Jersey in that women, and married women in particular, had gained greater rights as individuals. The achievements of the suffragists in this regard, both in New Jersey and throughout the nation, have not been well recognized.

But, having said this, it must also be said that these Equal Righters had overestimated the degree to which women had achieved greater equality with men over the previous ten years. In particular, the advancement of women in the political process, a major resolve of the NWP as stated in its Declaration of Principles—"That women shall no longer be discriminated against in civil and government service, but shall have the same right as men to authority, appointment, advancement and pay in the executive, the legislative, and the judicial branches of the government service"—was still to be accomplished. Moreover, the suffragists in the NJWP had done nothing directly to help bring this about.[30]

These suffragists, by their single-minded fight for the federal suffrage amendment, had implied that they attached great significance to women's right to participate as equals in the political system. But in the postsuffrage period, although a few individual members of the NJWP were active politically, the organization itself ignored politics altogether. It did not encourage women to vote, to enter the political parties, or to run for office. (This was not as true of the NWP, which launched its Women in Congress campaign in 1924 and again in 1926.) At the end of the decade, as their fellow Equal Righters in the political parties were disillusioned and losing influence, they seemed oblivious to the fact that women's earlier high hopes for political equality were being dashed.[31]

There was one exception to the NJWP's lack of interest in politics. In the fall of 1928, the state branch directed the NWP campaign in New Jersey to support Herbert Hoover and Charles Curtis, Republican candidates for president and vice president respectively. The NWP decision to actively oppose the election of Alfred E. Smith, the

Democratic presidential candidate, was precipitated by Smith's declared support of a night work law in New York State and apparently influenced by the fact that as a U.S. senator, Curtis had introduced the ERA in Congress in 1923. The NWP focused its campaign in New York and New Jersey, where Smith's chances were judged the greatest, placing Enders in charge of the New Jersey effort. "We still look upon Mr. Hoover as our greatest hope for achieving equality before the law for women with men throughout the United States and all her territorial possessions," Enders declared shortly before Election Day. The NJWP's sole foray into politics was thus on behalf of the WP equal rights position, nothing more. It did not reflect a decision to encourage political activity for its own sake.[32]

Judged solely in terms of its specific objective to win legal equality for women, the NJWP had succeeded resoundingly. But it had also failed in several ways that were less obvious. Not only had it failed to encourage women's participation in politics, a logical path to have taken as a consequence of having won the vote, but it had failed to gain the support of the vast majority of suffragists, and women in general, in its campaigns to pass federal and state equal rights amendments. These objectives were certainly visionary and advanced for their time, but the NJWP must be faulted for its inability to compromise on the issue of protective legislation, thus increasing divisions among organized women in a period when unity was crucial. There was evidence, after all, that both sides could cooperate. The Moral Prodders readily declared in the 1920s that they shared the NJWP's view that many legal discriminations against women had yet to be eliminated, and they credited the NJWP with its legislative achievements. But the basic split between the two camps over the ERAs continued to overshadow this area of agreement.[33] Finally, within its own ranks of not more than a few hundred women, the NJWP had failed to develop a body of participating, committed members. Ignoring democratic procedure, its leadership perpetuated itself in power and governed in an elitist manner.

In retrospect, the legislative accomplishments of the NJWP on behalf of women's legal equality remain a lasting achievement of the Equal Righters in the 1920s. The party's failures would take on an added significance in the decade ahead.

CHAPTER SIX

After Ten Years

O N March 26, 1930, the branches of the New Jersey League
of Women Voters joined in a nationwide celebration marking the tenth anniversary of woman suffrage. Westfield,
Plainfield, and Elizabeth celebrated together. In Newark an "Uncle
Sam Luncheon" was held at the home of Amelia Berndt Moorfield,
organization president, to which all members were invited. Members
of the Monmouth County League marked the birthday gala with a
box luncheon held at the Municipal Building. At exactly 2 P.M., the
women, along with league members in forty-five states, turned their
radio dials to the local NBC station to hear addresses by Belle Sher-
win, NLWV president, and other national officers from the St. Regis
Hotel in New York City.[1] It was a time to rejoice, a time to reminisce
about suffrage days, and a time to evaluate the record of a significant
decade.

In fact, the suffragists had been busy. From the moment of ratification of the Nineteenth Amendment, they dove with zest into a number of activities, not content with the knowledge that the ballot was
at long last in their hands. They joined existing organizations and
formed new ones. They discussed the implications of their new political weapon and formulated strategies to make it more effective.
They plunged into strange political waters and urged women to learn
about the male world of government and political parties. They lobbied in the state legislature with a new sense of vigor. Despite the
philosophical differences which separated the Moral Prodders and
the Equal Righters, the suffragists as a body worked for six clearly
discernible objectives throughout the 1920s. Four of these fell under
the category of the public welfare; that is, they were objectives that
affected the larger society. Two were related to the broad rights of
women.

First, mitigating the harmful effects of the industrial system on women and children through the passage of appropri-

ate legislation. Although a small, influential group of suffragists asserted that women should not be singled out for
special legislation, the great majority held that government
must intervene to protect the health and welfare of working
women.

Second, improving the efficiency and effectiveness of state
and local government. Underlying this suffragist effort was the
conviction that good government, benefiting all citizens,
would be its inevitable result.

Third, elevating the esthetic and moral quality of life. Although some legislation which the suffragists sought to pass or
retain appears conservative, or even repressive, to contemporary eyes, the suffragists were motivated by a genuine desire to
minimize crime and dependency, eliminate pornography, reduce the deleterious effects of alcoholism in the marketplace
and in the home, and encourage respect for the law.

Fourth, supporting the creation of international machinery to prevent war and studying the causes of war. Recoil-
ing from the horror of the First World War, the suffragists
asserted that mankind must not subject itself to mass destruction ever again, that modern nations could, through legal
means, prevent such barbarism from reoccurring.

Fifth, increasing the participation of women in politics
and expanding the number of appointive and elective positions
for women in the political system. Suffragists were the prime
movers in the drive to get out the vote and in the effort to
induce women to join the political parties and to run for office.

Sixth, eliminating the remaining legal discriminations
against women so that the legal status of women would be
equal to that of men. Suffragist demands for equality in the
jury box, in job access, and in the marital relationship heightened the awareness of legislators, as well as the entire citizenry,
of the degree to which women had yet to be made fully equal.

The record of the activities of the New Jersey suffragists indicates that, for one state at least, and contrary to the conclusions of
several historians, feminism was far from dead after 1920. For in New
Jersey the woman's movement did not fall apart after the vote was
won. It was alive and active well into the 1920s. Galvanized by their

newly won right to vote, the suffragists and other women without strong suffragist ties joined with one another to bring about social, political, and legal reform, much of which benefited women as a group.

But by 1930, something else could be observed of equal importance. A postsuffrage portrait of the suffragists was gradually emerging. The Moral Prodders had remained strong and had, in some cases, increased in numbers, while the Equal Righters had lost ground. The NJLWV reported a "satisfactory increase in membership"; the SFWC had jumped from twenty-six thousand members in 1920 to forty thousand in 1930; and the peace groups represented many thousands of women. While the CL had lost members, it remained a viable organization with loyal supporters, attested to by the outpouring of patrons and donors at its thirtieth anniversary dinner. Only the CFLE was fighting for its life, bucking the relentless tide of public opinion against the obvious failures of Prohibition. In contrast, the ranks of the Equal Righters had been decimated. Once numbering thousands of women, mostly in the NJWRC, they consisted in 1930 of the two hundred–member WP and the small State Council of New Jersey Republican Women, newly built on the ruins of its former self, the NJWRC.

The emergence of the Moral Prodders as the dominant group of suffragists was the gradual result of developments that occurred over the entire previous decade. In retrospect the division that arose in the NJLWV between suffragists who wished to become active political party members and those who preferred the nonpartisan course was a formative event in the early postsuffrage era. The split that occurred reflected the sharply different views the suffragists held about their political roles, marking them clearly as Moral Prodders and Equal Righters. The significance of this event was the revelation that although women, in their campaign for the vote, had appeared to be demanding equal partnership with men in the political arena, many had expected the voting privilege to mean something quite different. For this segment, it meant retaining a separate political identity as women, without formal entry into the party system. In the postsuffrage period, nonpartisanship took on a new meaning for women. It did not mean fence-straddling or disinterest in politics, for the nonpartisan women in the NJLWV, the SFWC, the CLNJ, the peace groups, and the CFLE were intensely interested in politics. They wanted to know about the issues and about the candidates. They studied carefully. They also voted. But, in the main, they refused to become directly involved in political party life. Women, they maintained, as the more moral and humane sex, must not be swallowed up in the day-to-day business of politics in which party loyalty, winning of office, and patronage played such a vital part. Women were different, they said. Having won the vote, woman as wives and mothers, would exert a beneficent influence on party life in ways they could never have done before.

The survival and success of the Moral Prodders was not predictable but it is not surprising. The Moral Prodders' belief that women had a different viewpoint from men and that women's concerns were primarily related to their homes and families complemented the prevailing reality and mood of the decade, both in New Jersey and in the nation. The experience of women in terms of their work status is illustrative. Many suffragists had hoped that winning the vote would lead to greater economic equality for women. Indeed, as Alice Kessler-Harris observes in her history of wage-earning women in the United States, there were perceptible changes in the female labor force in the 1920s that boded well for the improved economic position of women. First, the proportion of married women in the female labor force rose dramatically between 1920 and 1930, from 22.8 percent to 28.8 percent. The earlier proscription against married women working, most rigid for middle class women, lost its persuasiveness in a new era in which women could vote, have greater sexual freedom, and shed the more cumbersome dress. Second, an array of new jobs in the white collar sector opened up for women as the United States assumed its position in the world as a creditor nation. The First World War had provided new occupations for women but briefly. The small percentage who entered the work force for the first time during the war had returned to their homes when hostilities ended (not all willingly, but in many cases because their jobs were resumed by men), and most women workers who had shifted to war-related occupations had resumed their old peacetime jobs. But there were other opportunities. There were expanding new industries in the 1920s such as banking, finance, advertising, and insurance, and these recruited women to work on their office staffs and at the lower levels of management. For the first time, the number of women in white collar positions exceeded those in industrial occupations, as well as in domestic service and agriculture.

Despite these significant shifts within the female work force, statistics at the end of the decade revealed that women's economic status had not substantially changed. By 1930 a large majority of women were still full-time homemakers. Although the actual number of working women rose by two million during the decade, the proportion of women in the work force had increased only one percentage point, from 23.3 percent in 1920 to 24.3 percent in 1930. The numerical increase of women who worked reflected essentially the growth in population and the expansion of the economy rather than any significant change in the proportion of wage-earning women. Moreover, the initial promise of substantial economic opportunity for women in the 1920s had not materialized. As the decade wore on, Kessler-Harris points out, "the portion of the marketplace allocated to women became increasingly credentialized, segmented and hierarchical. That was the paradox of the twenties. . . . Women were invited into the work force and again invited not to expect too much of it." Women who did work, professional, clerical, and industrial workers alike, consistently received lower wages than men and were engaged essentially in occupations commonly described as "woman's work"—as teachers and nurses, as typists and stenographers, and as textile and apparel workers.[2]

Perhaps as a backlash against women's brief fling with wartime jobs and their entry into the expanding business world, or out of concern that winning the vote might truly alter women's traditional position as full-time wife and mother, educators, journalists, writers, and psychologists began in the 1920s to stress that women's natural role was determined by their biological makeup. This image of women was not new, of course. It echoed an earlier nineteenth century view of women as frail, delicate, prone to illness, and dominated by their biological functions, but it was couched in more modern terms.[3] A woman might attend college, if she chose, and have a job before marriage, but these activities were mere preliminaries before assuming her main role in society. A woman was meant to bear children, to nurture them, to create a happy home, and to serve as helpmeet to her husband. By nature she was loving, intuitive, emotional, idealistic, and moral. Unlike men, she was not aggressive and competitive. Women were advised how important and how satisfying homemaking, housework, and child rearing could be.[4]

But what about the so-called "New Woman" of the 1920s, said to be working and living on her own? How did she feel about the current "glorification of domesticity," as William Chafe terms it? Was she not pursuing a career, thereby rejecting the ideology that woman's sphere was still circumscribed by activities associated with the home? Although she was engaged in all areas of business and the professions, the New Woman had apparently been made to appear more radical than she actually was. In an article appearing in *Harper's* in 1931, Anne Rogers Hyde observed that although more women in the nation were working more than ever before and a high proportion of female college graduates were going to work, the chances that these women could become financially successful were "extremely thin." Women, Hyde said, were basically not interested in becoming successful. They viewed work as a temporary situation to be followed by marriage. After marriage they might work, but it would be secondary to their family obligations. Women, Hyde maintained, were more interested in a congenial working atmosphere than a job with a potential for financial advancement. They gravitated to jobs considered "ladylike"—such as teachers, librarians, and editors—jobs with the lowest pay scales. They did not take money seriously. Money was viewed as a medium of change rather than as a tool for investment. Finally, she noted, women did not take themselves seriously. They never sought the better position nor expected higher pay than they received.[5]

If the young, educated working woman of the 1920s still basically thought of herself as a potential wife and mother, what about the even younger college coed who apparently had rejected Victorian morality with a passion? Certainly the women on the college campuses who discussed sex openly, who smoked in public, and drank and danced late into the night were asserting their complete equality with men. Was not the Moral Prodder point of view of women as essentially different from men anathema to them? Paula Fass, in her study of college youth in the 1920s, found that despite the change in personal behavior of college students, both male and female, students contemplated no radical overhaul of the structure of society. Both men and women expected to marry, Fass notes, but "while men looked toward marriage as a vital part of their lives, women looked toward it as their primary and almost exclusive goal; all other aspirations became secondary." What had changed was that both men and women had greater expectations about the marriage relationship. Marriage was to be a true partnership in which the views of each partner would have equal weight. But in this schema, both men and women agreed: after marriage, woman's place remained in the home. "By the 1920s," Fass concludes, "the young seemed to believe in complete equality in the home but not outside it."[6]

Why had the Equal Righters failed to persuade the majority of educated young women that their position favoring women's equality in all areas was worthy of support? Why had not the WP's successful campaign to improve the legal status of women drawn young women to its banner? And why did young women rarely share the eagerness of many suffragists to enter the political parties?

Again, the national experience is instructive. In an article appearing in *Harper's* in 1927, Dorothy Dunbar Bromley contended that an unbridgeable gap had developed between modern, young career women and the older generation of feminists who had fought for the vote and who continued to fight for equal rights. Granting their courage and their suffrage victory, she declared that the philosophy, the methods, even the appearance of the older feminists were extremely distasteful to the young:

> "Feminism" has become a term of approbrium to the modern young woman. For the word suggests either the old school of fighting feminists who wore flat heels, or the current species who antagonize men with their constant clamor about maiden names, equal rights, woman's place in the world, and many another cause . . . *ad infinitum*.

The main difference between contemporary young women in their twenties and thirties and the older feminists, Bromley said, was that the former were out in the world, forging ahead with their careers, marrying, and having children—determined to combine the two successfully—while the militant feminists were still talking, talking, talking. "Is it not high time that we laid the ghost of the so-called feminist?" she asked. Modern woman should properly be labeled "Feminist—New Style." For the new feminist, unlike the old, Bromley observed, was happy to dress prettily; liked men; was ready to flirt—but in a clever way; wanted her marriage to be an equal part-nership, sexually and otherwise; was ready to end it if it failed; and refused to get hung up over small matters like keeping one's maiden name or who should darn the socks.[7]

Possibly because Bromley wrote her article four years before Hyde, she felt confident that "Feminist—New Style" was going to continue working after marriage and children. Hyde was not con-vinced that most women would follow this pattern. But most impor-tant, Bromley had sketched a portrait of the suffragists (undoubtedly members of the WP) as seen through the eyes of young women: an-tagonistic to men, unyielding in their beliefs, given to slogans not action, petty, and unfeminine.

Bromley did not mention politics, but the reader could extrapo-late her remarks to mean that younger women were more concerned about their personal lives than about political involvement. This was true, as well, of female (and male) college youth. According to Fass, "the young were politically apathetic . . . [They] were not terribly concerned with the details of political life." What mattered to them, Fass observes, was being able to behave as they wished without inter-ference. Only two issues aroused college students to some degree: Prohibition and peace. Student opposition to Prohibition was par-ticularly marked in eastern schools, but it was found everywhere. By mid-decade students were calling for modification or repeal of the prohibition laws by more than 75 percent. At Princeton University a poll taken in 1926 revealed that 87 percent of the student body favored an end to Prohibition. Students also registered their approval of in-ternational disarmament and of U.S. entry into the World Court. But, Fass notes, few student conferences were called over either the Prohibition or peace issue, and student action that did occur often came after a call from college administrators for student involvement.[8]

The apparent lack of interest of young women, both in the working world and on the college campuses, in politics and in equal rights causes did not mean that they had rejected organizational life altogether. Many had merely postponed such activity for a later pe-riod. As they married, had children, and established homes, a num-ber of them would join groups like the LWV, the women's clubs, and the peace groups, whose outlook so closely conformed to their own.

On the tenth anniversary of woman suffrage, journalists and writers assessed the impact of winning the vote in the nation at large. Their comments, in several cases, were remarkably similar. The following statement in the *Newark Evening News* was typical:

[the] participation of women in politics . . . has not disrupted the home, destroyed the church nor undermined the pillars of the state anymore than it has purified politics, made human welfare the main concern of government or brought universal peace.[9]

Commentators also noted that women were holding public office from the town hall to the state house to the Congress. Women, they said, were influential in the convening of international peace conferences and in the passage of major legislation, such as the Sheppard-Towner Act to improve maternal and infancy care and the Cable Equal Citizenship Act.[10] In spite of a careful tally of achievements, the general portrait was, in balance, a rather bland one. Nothing truly momentous had taken place. The prophets of doom as well as the prognosticators of utopia had been refuted. Woman had made a good beginning. They were educating themselves in their new role as voting citizens. They were gradually making themselves felt in the political system. They would, it was judged, surely do more in the years to come.

Despite this common assessment, a few nationally known women were much more critical of what their sex had accomplished during the decade. Emily Newell Blair, for example, who had served as vice chairman of the Democratic National Committee for seven years, observed in 1931 that women had not achieved equality with men in politics because of their own shortcomings. Women in office and in party posts, she declared, were followers of men, not leaders of women. They were not committed to the feminist goal of bringing more women into politics, nor did they work for women's measures; and equally important, women voters were not prepared to back female candidates for office.[11]

There were comments by Rheta Childe Dorr, speaker for the Republican National Committee, and Nellie Tayloe Ross, current vice chairman of the Democratic National Committee, on the suffragists predeliction for an excessive moral stance on picayune matters and for their preference for nonpartisanship. Both attitudes, they noted, hindered women in their effort to attain equal rights in political affairs. Women focused their energies on such matters as an anticigarette campaign in Nebraska, for example, and the beat

Wadsworth-for-Senator campaign in New York (Wadsworth being a former antisuffragist). "The suffrage battle is over," Dorr observed. "It doesn't take a brilliant mind to see," Ross asserted, "that so long as women workers in politics exhaust their efforts as free lances on the outside, not knowing what plans and strategies are being developed on the inside, there is going to be a sad waste of time and effort and money and considerable duplication of work that men are doing independently." [12]

The record of the suffragists in New Jersey indicates that, for one state at least, the basically colorless evaluation of women's progress since winning the vote was inadequate and incomplete. Much more had occurred than the obvious fact that women were gradually becoming politically educated and part of the political process. More could be said, as well, than the criticism Blair had leveled that women who did enter politics had failed to assert their right to equal partnership with men.

What stands out about the New Jersey experience is that the suffragists who had led the fight for the vote had, in the main, chosen to remain outside of the political arena once the vote was won. Most suffragists believed that the proper role for enfranchised women was as informed and concerned citizens who lobbied through their organizations for legislation and voted but who essentially remained aloof from the formal operations of the political parties. Moreover, they held that, as organization members, women ought not work for the election or defeat of individual candidates. In this role, which did not threaten the male political establishment, these suffragists had thrived. Indeed, much as the nineteenth century sisters had been placed on a moral pedestal for all men to admire, men in public life in the 1920s held up the suffragists and their associates in the reform, nonpartisan organizations as moral exemplars who carefully studied the issues, whether matters of government, social welfare, or peace, and were unsullied by tainted partisan considerations.

Those suffragists who chose to assert that enfranchised women should be given equal access to the political parties, to government service, and to economic life had not fared as well. Although they had significant legislative success, they had run into opposition from men and had alienated other women, suffragists included. Most of the suffragists who bravely attempted to become active participants in the political parties were hampered by their lack of political acumen and by the conflicts they had over whether to become loyal party workers or keep their independence. This group was far more threatening to male politicians, who still preferred to deal with women as their moral superiors and political inferiors. But most important, the lack of sophistication and ambivalence of these women regarding their proper political role helped bring about their loss of influence.

The New Jersey experience had been one of accomplishments, to be sure. The Moral Prodders had helped women assume their new voting responsibilities by establishing citizenship schools, providing voting information, and initially offering encouragement to participate more fully in politics. They had also helped to pass a number of laws that advanced the cause of social reform. The Equal Righters were instrumental in the passage of several laws that improved the legal and political status of women. But it was also one of suffragist failures: failures to exert power that the voting right had granted and failures to grasp opportunities that had been offered in good faith by male party leaders. The period that lay ahead would demonstrate whether the pattern set in the first ten years had been temporary or permanent.

CHAPTER SEVEN

Six New Jersey Suffragists

T HE record of the activities of the New Jersey suffragists is about the organizations they joined and the specific goals for which they worked, but it is also about the suffragists themselves—their ideas, their attitudes and their motivations. The following Moral Prodders and Equal Righters are a small sample of the many women who were leaders in the state suffrage movement and who continued to play a vital role in public life after the vote was won. Their stories, of course, necessarily involve jumping ahead in the sequence of events.

Moral Prodders

Helena Simmons

Like many of her fellow suffragists, Helena Neilson Simmons discovered, through activity in the suffrage movement, the satisfaction of working for the public welfare. From 1914, the year of her initial involvement as a suffragist at the age of thirty-eight, until her death in 1942, Simmons was involved as a leader in a variety of church, social reform, and political activities that easily could have kept two or three persons busy. Something seemed to push her to live her life to the fullest in the pursuit of some noble ideal. She believed in the importance of having a worthwhile goal and working toward it. Her hopes for the NJLWV expressed this personal philosophy. "All that is needed is faith, a vision and work," she observed in 1927, when she was its president. "We all work at something. It is whether we are productively employed which is our real question." [1]

All that is known about Simmons's early family life is that she was born in New Brunswick in 1876 and was educated by private tutors. In 1898 she married Harriman N. Simmons and moved to Elizabeth, where she resided for the next forty-four years. She raised two daughters and a son. In 1915 she became president of the Elizabeth

Equal Suffrage League, retaining that position until 1920. When the league reorganized as the Elizabeth LWV, she was elected its first president. During these same years she was beginning to expand her horizons. In the late teens, in addition to her suffrage activities, she assumed the chairmanship of the Elizabethtown Red Cross and became president of the Elizabeth CL.[2]

Unlike most Moral Prodders, who devoted themselves exclusively to nonpartisan social reform, Simmons believed that women should make their voting privilege effective by becoming active political workers. In addition to serving as president of the NJLWV through most of the 1920s and serving on the state board of the CLNJ, she entered the world of politics. In 1920 Simmons was appointed chairman of the Democratic Woman's Executive Committee, a temporary body set up until women became fully incorporated into the party structure. (She was replaced the following year by Mary Norton, who became vice chairman of the Democratic State Committee.) Between 1921 and 1925 she served on the state committee representing Union County. Simmons saw no conflict between nonpartisan affiliation in the NJLWV and political involvement. Indeed, in 1928, at a time when the league was starting to soft-pedal its calls for party activity, Simmons exhorted the membership to join the parties. "The usefulness of the league," she noted, "would be greatly hampered if the women trained in its methods and point of view failed to practice what they preach and abstained in practical work for great issues."[3]

For all her political activism (she became chairman of the Democratic Women's Luncheon Club in 1932), she was distrustful of the parties and politicians. Politicians were more interested in furthering their own interests and those of their party, she held, than in dealing honestly with the issues. The average citizen, she believed, suffered in the long run. That was where the LWV served its essential purpose. "If the League of Women Voters, can help in any way to clear the air of political propaganda and partisan 'bunk,'" she observed in 1928,

and train a generation of voters to demand of their parties and candidates clear and honest platforms and speeches; to insist that there shall be no equivocation and no promises which cannot be carried out; and then to watch campaign workers so that as few misstatements as possible creep into party speeches, interviews, and publications, it will have justified its existence.[4]

Whatever Simmons did, she believed in deeply—which included working for world peace (as a member of the World Court Committee) and enforcement of the prohibition laws (as a member of the CFLE)—but she seemed to experience greatest fulfillment during her tenure, from 1930 on, as president and executive secretary of the CL. In these Depression years she became dedicated to the elimination of poverty, not through philanthropy, which she considered merely a temporary antidote, but through governmental programs. As Simmons saw it, New Deal administration goals and the CL's meshed perfectly. Both groups were working for "health protection, a living wage and social security," which she described as the foundations of a democratic society. Every citizen, she believed, was entitled to these basic rights. CL efforts on behalf of working women and children were vital, she maintained, as they helped to improve the lot of the most underprivileged and unrepresented segment of the labor force. Moreover, industrial homework, which the CL had consistently sought to license and control, was an abomination that must ultimately be prohibited.[5]

Simmons never retired from her double-time work regimen. At the time of her death she was still CL executive secretary and she had just entered a new field, consumer protection. As chairman of the Consumer Interests Committee of the Council of National Defense (to which she was appointed in 1940), a body which included representatives of women's groups, labor and farm groups, and retail merchants, she fought hoarding and artificially pegged prices and monitored labor standards in the state. Wartime conditions were raising new challenges for New Jersey citizens, and Simmons was preparing to tackle them.[6]

Lena Anthony Robbins

Lena Anthony Robbins shared with Helena Simmons the need to work constructively. What motivated her to assume leadership positions in numerous women's organizations was her conviction that women, as wives and mothers, had an obligation to be informed about the important issues of the day and to contribute to the formation of public opinion. "Women are beginning to want to know," she declared in 1939 when she was president of the NJLWV. "It is not so fashionable nowadays as it used to be for women to boast ignorance of public matters that vitally affect them and their homes and children."[7]

But Robbins had always wanted to know. Her origins were in the American West. Born in a covered wagon in the late 1870s in Colorado, she grew up in Lincoln, Nebraska. Her father was a builder. In an era when few women went to college, she attended the University of Nebraska and graduated in 1901. She was married that year to Leonard Robbins, a fellow Nebraskan, a writer and newspaperman. The couple moved shortly thereafter to Newark, where Leonard went to work for a local city newspaper. (He later became a feature writer for the *New York Times*.) As far as is known, they had one child, a daughter.

Within a short time Robbins became active in the women's club movement and in the suffrage movement. By the late teens she had become president of two women's clubs, the Irving Club of Irvington and the Contemporary of Newark. As a member of the executive board of the Newark WPU, she lobbied on behalf of suffrage in the state legislature, and in the spring of 1920 she helped organize its citizenship schools.[8]

Robbins believed that the vote had given women tremendous political power but that its potential was barely realized. New Jersey's needs were not being met, she held, because politicians paid more attention to national issues, which made vote-getting headlines, than to state matters. The citizenry, moreover, was often better informed about the problems of its larger urban neighbors—New York and Philadelphia—than its own. Women had the opportunity to address these neglected concerns, she contended, and she believed they could do it most effectively unencumbered by political ties.[9] Robbins chose to devote most of her time and talent in the 1920s to the SFWC, becoming state chairman of legislation in 1925. During her three-year tenure she made the department one of the federation's most important. She alerted clubwomen about every bill of interest being considered by the legislature. She wrote columns in the *New Jersey Club Woman* and the *Civic Pilot*, giving legislative news and explaining the basis for federation support of or opposition to state and national bills. Her leadership was clearly an important factor in the SFWC's strong lobbying stance during this period.

In her talks before various women's groups Robbins regularly advised that women had to do more than study the issues and propose legislative solutions. They also had to make certain that their solutions worked, and that meant looking at finances. "The time has come when women must think of legislation as men do—in terms of money, " she counseled members of the College Club of the Oranges at a tea held in the spring of 1928.[10] Indeed, Robbins's own familiarity with tax matters as well as her close connection as an active clubwoman with the founding of the New Jersey College for Women had made her Governor A. Harry Moore's logical choice that year as the sole woman to serve on the commission to study the future role of Rutgers, which was not yet the State University. Among the commission's recommendations were the establishment of the Board of Regents and the tightening of ties, financial and otherwise, between the university and the state.[11]

There were other causes in the 1920s—particularly temperance and peace—that claimed her efforts. By the 1930s, however, her greatest commitment was to the LWV, having served on its state board since its inception, becoming its vice president in 1930 and its president in 1935. In these years she steered the league in its drive against patronage, its lobbying for voting machines, and its leadership in the movement to revise the state constitution.

All through her busy life Robbins had focused her energies on what women, as nonpartisan workers, could do to improve society on behalf of their homes and families. After her retirement from the LWV presidency in 1942 she began to shift her attention to the position of women themselves. In a new role as chairman of the Committee on the Economic and Legal Status of Women for the state branch of the American Association of University Women, Robbins opposed the ERA but championed women's right to equal opportunity in employment regardless of marital status. She also looked ahead to the role women would play in the postwar world, a time she did not live to see, for death came in September 1945. "Men and women must continue to work side by side in the post-war world, as in war," she wrote in late 1943, "sharing responsibilities and in maintaining a better world order."[12]

Caroline Wittpenn

Caroline Bayard Stevens Wittpenn was probably one of the best known suffragists in the state of New Jersey.[13] At the time of her death in 1932 at the age of seventy-three, she was serving on the State Board of Institutions and Agencies; had been recently appointed, in 1929, to the International Prison Commission by President Hoover; and was president of the state branch of the League of Nations Association, director of the Hoboken Unemployment Relief Commission, and a member of the board of trustees of Stevens Institute of Technology. In many ways Wittpenn's life and career paralleled that of another prominent suffragist, her good friend Geraldine Livingston Thompson. Both lived on large estates (Thompson in Lincroft, Wittpenn in Hoboken); both were friends of presidents (Thompson of Franklin Delano Roosevelt, Wittpenn of Woodrow Wilson); both served on national party committees (Thompson for many years on the Republican National Committee, Wittpenn briefly on the Democratic National Committee during Wilson's administration); both gave unstintingly of their time to charitable and prison reform activities; and both were instrumental in organizing the State Board of Charities and Corrections (later called Institutions and Agencies), to which they were appointed by Governor Walter Edge in 1918, the first two women to serve on a state board.

It was quite appropriate that Wittpenn, a woman of privilege all her life, was born in a "castle." The date was November 21, 1859, and the "castle" was Castle Stevens, the family home at Castle Point, Hoboken. The Stevens family had made an important imprint on the state's recent past. Caroline's grandfather, Colonel John Stevens, had served as "treasurer of the revolutionary government of New Jersey." Her father, Edwin Augustus Stevens, and his brother Robert, both engineers, had organized the Camden and Amboy line, "one of the first railroads in the United States." The founding of the Stevens Institute of Technology in 1847 on the site of the family estate was the result of Edwin Stevens's beneficence and foresight.[14]

Caroline grew up in a world of beautiful furniture, beautiful clothes, private tutors, abundant domestic help, trips to Europe, and membership in the elite social clubs of New York City and northern New Jersey. Like many other well-to-do women of her day, she was trained to devote a substantial portion of her time to philanthropic work. Her mother, Martha Bayard Stevens, was a strong influence in this direction, and it was through her that Caroline saw the harder side of life. At the age of twenty, for example, Caroline was encouraged by her mother to become involved in the Industrial Society for Manual Training, an organization of working girls from Hoboken and New York City. The society remained her lifelong interest.

In 1879 Caroline was married to Archibald Alexander of Princeton, a Columbia University professor. They had one son. When the marriage ended in separation sixteen years later, she threw herself into public service. The list of her activities from that date forward on several state boards—among them the State Institution for Feeble Minded Girls and Women, the State Board of Children's Guardians, the New Jersey Reformatory for Women—and as Hudson County probation officer (serving for thirty years from the year of her appointment in 1902) reflected her conviction that the wayward, the needy, and the sick had been dealt an unfair card and should be helped by those in happier circumstances. Women, she believed, were especially suited to this task. Their unique natures helped them relate as human beings to those who were less fortunate. This was what counted in social service work, she held, far more than the efficiency and expertise of the professional social worker.

A devout woman, Mrs. Alexander never divorced. She remarried in 1915, only after learning that her husband had died a few years earlier. Her new husband, Otto Wittpenn, shared her interest in government affairs and brought her closer to the world of state politics. Wittpenn, a businessman and real estate developer, was mayor of Jersey City at the time of their marriage. He later ran for governor and served on the Port of New York Authority and on the State Highway Commission. He also shared her commitment to woman suffrage. A lifelong interest in the public welfare undoubtedly contributed to Mrs. Wittpenn's suffragist beliefs, but her lengthy efforts, together with other women, to convince the legislature to establish a separate reformatory for women graphically demonstrated to her the need for suffrage as women sought needed reforms. In 1910 she helped to found the Equal Franchise Society at a meeting held in her home at Castle Point, and in mid-decade she joined the board of the NJWSA.

When the vote was won, Wittpenn immediately became a vice president of the state LWV, a position she held until her death. Although she had memberships on other state boards—the SFWC (she was a founder of the Woman's Club of Hoboken) and the CL—she was particularly devoted to the goals of the LWV and especially its commitment to the peace movement. A supporter of Woodrow Wilson, she believed in his vision of a world united in a league of nations. In 1921 she became chairman of the league's Committee on Limitation of Armaments, and in that capacity she spoke before various women's groups. On two separate occasions she observed:

> I think everyone will agree that the spiritual and moral results of the war have been much more disastrous than the economic upheaval. . . . The causes which led to the last war can only be eradicated by a friendly understanding and conference between the nations. The last few years have taught us that we can no longer keep to our isolated position of aloofness.[15]

Despite her clear identification as a Democrat, Wittpenn managed to remain above the political fray. Nevertheless she found herself in 1926 in a swirl of controversy with political overtones. Her decision a year earlier to quietly support a Republican relative in his quest for the gubernatorial nomination now threatened her reappointment to the State Board of Institutions and Agencies by Democratic Governor A. Harry Moore. The issue became a cause célèbre as the league and other women's groups came to Wittpenn's defense, criticizing "the injection of partisan politics into the conduct of the state institutions." The outpouring of support was testimony to the high regard in which she was held by so many. Wittpenn was not reappointed. She was returned to the board by Moore's successor, Republican Governor Morgan F. Larson in 1919.[16]

When on December 4, 1932, Wittpenn died suddenly, the tributes poured in. President Hoover sent his, as did Governor Moore and Mayor Frank Hague. Perhaps the most moving and appropriate came from the editors of the *Stute*, the student paper of Stevens Institute: "No other woman in America, no man, no human being on this globe can have given his life so unsparingly and unselfishly toward bettering the condition of humanity as this marvellous lady. Her every day was spent working for some organization whose constitutional purpose was to do good in some way to someone."[17]

Miriam Lippincott

When Miriam Lee Early Lippincott, chairman of the New Jersey Committee of the Woman's National Committee for Law Enforcement, stepped up the stand of the Senate Judiciary Committee in 1926 in its hearings on Prohibition and unfurled a huge petition bearing sixteen thousand signatures in support of the Eighteenth Amendment, her dramatic flair came easily. A graduate of Northwestern University she had been chairman of the drama department of Swarthmore College from 1906 to 1915 and in subsequent years had been involved in little theater groups as both coach and participant. She was also a prolific writer of plays and short stories.[18] Lippincott's performance before a packed house in the Senate hearing room went beyond mere histrionics, of course. She believed, as did the CFLE's national chairman, Mrs. Henry W. Peabody, that Prohibition was "the greatest reform of modern times" and that constant vigilance was required to prevent its undoing. More than this, she held, Prohibition's defense was a test for women as new citizens. Would women be content merely to go to club meetings and bridge parties and not speak out, as politicians, business men, lawyers, and judges made a mockery of the Constitution? If so, she asserted, they did not deserve the ballot.[19]

The vote was something Lippincott did not take lightly, for she had been committed to it since her youth. Growing up in her native Hightstown, she later recalled, she was converted to the suffrage cause while a student at Pennington Seminary. Her active suffrage career, however, began years later when, in 1913, she married A. Haines Lippincott, a prominent Camden surgeon, and moved to that city situated across the river from Philadelphia. After 1915, when the suffragists began to devote all their energies to passage of a federal suffrage amendment, she became congressional district chairman of the NJWSA, and she played a leading role in the final drive, in 1920, for ratification of the amendment by the state legislature.

Her talents were quickly recognized. In the spring of 1920, in anticipation of full ratification of the amendment, Lillian Feickert appointed her to represent Camden County as member-at-large of the Republican State Committee, with the charge of organizing the county's Republican women. Lippincott heralded the final suffrage victory in August, with her penchant for grand statements: "It means a great day in the history of our country. It rivals the Magna Charta of England in removing the last vestige of political bigotry."[20]

Although she remained on the State Committee for eight years (soon earning the enmity of the Republican leadership for her unyielding dry views), she saw her political connections as but one of several avenues she as a woman and other women could and must use to serve their communities, educate the public, and move the parties in the right direction. She ran for the Camden Board of Education, for example, was elected, and became the board's first woman vice president in 1924, a position she held for three years. She was probably the most devoted to the Camden Woman's Club, which she joined as a young bride and served as president from 1927 to 1930. Through the club she worked to establish the New Jersey College for Women. In the 1930s and 1940s she was a trustee of the college and of Rutgers University. In 1951, three years after her death, the Woman's Club named a scholarship in her honor to the New Jersey College for Women for a deserving freshman from Camden County.[21]

In retrospect, like so many other suffragists in the forefront of reform, Lippincott seemed to be enlisted in a series of crusades, always battling against insuperable odds. The first was in behalf of suffrage. The second was for peace; as a member of the CCCW she was a delegate to an international peace conference held in Brussels in 1935. The third was in support of strict adherence to the Prohibition laws, fighting the growing modificationist and wet sentiment in the state, never willing to concede that the conflict was anything but good versus evil. Finally, there was the crusade against cancer; after her husband's death in 1937 Lippincott gave of herself in the same way she had to her other endeavors, becoming a state organizer for the American Cancer Society. Her portrait in uniform as state commander of the society, accompanying her obituary in the *New Jersey Club Woman*, clearly revealed the woman she was and had always been: erect and alert, always ready to take on an important assignment on behalf of a better world.

Equal Righters

Mary Philbrook

At a time when most suffragists were arguing that women should be granted the vote because they were more moral than men and could therefore improve on men's political record, Mary Philbrook was insisting that men and women were basically alike. This view was the basis of her application in 1894 to be accepted to the state bar and of subsequent positions she took. In 1897, for example, in an article in the *New Jersey Law Journal*, she asserted that if women truly wanted equality, as the suffragists maintained, they had to accept the full implications of what they were demanding. Women could not wish to be considered the equal of men in some areas and still demand protection in others because of a claim of weakness:

> It must be admitted that it is time the statute was removed whereby a woman can plead ignorance of a law as a ground for dissolving an obligation—a thing which only idiots, lunatics, and infants could ever do. The custom of privileging a woman in some matters and restraining them in others, from a feeling of pity for her bodily weakness and presumed mental capacity, rather than for any more worthy reason, should be abolished. . . . My theory would be to give neither sex more privileges than the other. Place them on the same footing and by thus establishing this equality both man and woman will be better able to work intelligently in the business and professional world.[22]

Philbrook's early desires to become an attorney, despite the odds, and to work for suffrage and equal rights were clearly influenced by her family background. She was born in Washington, D.C., in 1872, the oldest of five children. Her father was a successful lawyer who subsequently practiced in New York City. Both her mother and grandmother were suffragists. Philbrook's precedent-setting effort to practice law had parental support. "My father was proud of me," she later recalled. "He encouraged me every bit of the way and was always anxious to help me in every way he could." Her mother was at her side when she made her application to the bar. So much of Philbrook's independent life seemed to have been sustained by this family encouragement. Even her suffrage activity was out of the ordinary.

Except for her involvement in the NJWSA in the 1890s, she participated very little in suffrage organizational life. Instead, she chose to
write articles in law journals about the need to equalize women's
legal status and, in 1912, to make a dramatic fight for woman suffrage
through the brief she drew up in behalf of Harriet Carpenter. Her
law practice, first in Jersey City and then in Newark, was successful.
She also practiced before the U.S. Supreme Court, the only woman
lawyer from New Jersey to do so at the time. She put her legal talents
to work as Essex County probation officer, as "special investigator for
the United States Immigration Commission," and as counsel to the
New Jersey Legal Aid Association, which she helped to found.[23]

Age was never an impediment to Philbrook. She was only
twenty-two when she sought to practice law. In 1917, at the age of
forty-five, she decided that she could be useful in the war effort. For a
short time she worked as a legal assistant for the War Trade Board in
Washington, D.C., and then spent a year in France doing legal work
for the Red Cross. In 1920 her most productive period on behalf of
equal rights was just beginning. Like many other professional women
who were educated in the late nineteenth and early twentieth century, Philbrook never married. She gradually put aside her law practice and devoted herself to winning complete equality for women by
working for the WP both at the state and national levels. Although
she believed that women's political participation was important, she
had other priorities. "I have never gone in for politics," she observed
in 1936. "I have always favored the woman's movement and found it
best to work with both parties."[24] In the latter part of the 1930s, Philbrook became a member of the NWP's National Advisory Council.
Appointed the NWP's chairman of archives in 1936, she had the important task of organizing its vast collection of papers and correspondence from the suffrage era.[25]

It was during this period that Philbrook decided to revive the
dormant campaign for a state ERA. The amendment's passage was
essential, she held, for the Depression had brought serious threats to
women's rights. "[Women] don't see what is coming," she told the
230 members of the newly organized New Jersey Women Lawyers
Club in 1936. "There are already strong forces at work to deprive
them of the rights they have."[26] The founding of several ad hoc committees in the late 1930s and the 1940s to secure a state ERA—the

Committee to Eliminate Discriminations Against Women, the Committee for Constitutional Amendment, the Women's Non-Partisan Committee Against the Proposed Revised Constitution, and the Women's Alliance for Equal Status—were to a large degree the result of her driving force and organizational ability.

Philbrook's greatest fear was that she would not live to see her dream realized. "Poor me," she wrote a fellow member of the Women's Non-Partisan Committee in 1944. "I am everlastingly on the job. Hope I shall see results before the last day comes, but the days on [sic] slipping by—yesterday I was 72 years old."[27] Philbrook lived another thirteen years. Not content to retire from active public life after adoption of the revised state constitution in 1947, she continued, in the 1950s, to serve on the NWP Advisory Council and to press for the federal ERA, which she believed was the only true guarantee of equal rights for women.

Lillian Feickert

Until she became active in the New Jersey suffrage movement, Lillian Ford Feickert lived a quiet life in Plainfield. Born in Brooklyn, New York, in 1877 into a family that dated its American forbears to 1622, she moved to her home in Somerset County after her marriage to Edward Feickert, a banker, in 1902. They had one child, who died in infancy. Feickert's appointment in 1910 as enrollment chairman of the NJWSA propelled her onto the public stage.[28]

Feickert's leadership and organizational ability grew with the job. Not only did she increase NJWSA membership from the hundreds to over a thousand in a two-year period; she gradually learned the skills of public speaking. Becoming president of the association in 1912, her commanding presence was soon commonly acknowledged. Feickert retained her position for eight years until the vote was won. Her firm, often acid comments in press statements and campaign speeches had become her hallmark. By 1920, having helped to build the state's major suffrage organization to a membership of more than 120,000 and led the suffrage campaign to victory, she was supremely confident of her own ability and of the ability of organized women to influence the direction of public affairs. She was convinced that the proper course for women was through direct involvement in politics rather than nonpartisan endeavor.

In the early 1920s as president of the NJWRC, Feickert rode the crest of confidence among women in the political parties. Women, it seemed then, truly held power in their hands, and the politicians were going to have to pay attention to their demands. In 1923 a *New York Times* reporter sought out Feickert in an attempt to find out more about this woman, whom he dubbed a "New Political General." There were actually two pictures of her, the interviewer noted. One was of "a tall graceful grayhaired woman . . . cutting asparagus" in her garden. She was still youthful, and "her blue eyes sparkled with humor." The other was of a woman "strolling through the corridors of the State House at Trenton with a leather bag bursting with paper," a picture which "strikes terror to the heart, if that heart be a political one."[29]

The latter picture seemed to be gaining dominance, for while Feickert had retained her balance and good humor during the suffrage period, she was losing it now. She was becoming angry and fanatic because events did not move in the successful progression to which she had become accustomed in previous years. In particular, the Prohibition question was one area in which she was inflexible. She simply could not accept the fact that total prohibition of alcoholic beverages was not working and that the citizenry and politicians from both parties were seeking either modification or repeal. That fact added to the one that few NJWRC bills were being passed caused her to label all those who disagreed with her as enemies.

Perhaps Feickert's stridency was due in part to the state of her personal life, for her marriage was falling apart. In his suit for divorce, filed in Nevada in 1925, Edward Feickert asserted that his wife's nonstop political activities were more than he could endure. Although he apparently accepted her role as New Jersey's foremost suffrage leader—indeed he was an active suffragist as well—he could not accept her failure to return, after 1920, to the normal womanly pursuits preferred by most intelligent suburban matrons. Edward Feickert's new wife, whom he married seven weeks later—his former secretary—better fit his image of what a wife should be.

The divorce had a decidedly negative effect on Feickert, her old suffragist friends asserted, for she became irritable and nervous. In a counter divorce suit filed by Lillian in New Jersey in 1927 on grounds of adultery, Dr. Mary Cummins testified that her friend was not the person she had known in suffrage days: "Then she was the most perfect example of health, marvellous poise. Nothing annoyed or bothered her. She was a woman you just felt you could lean on. Now you feel you want to carry her."[30]

But Feickert picked herself up and carried on. Despite her ouster from the state committee and the membership decline of the NJWRC, she still had a substantial cadre of supporters. Her decision to seek the nomination for the U.S. Senate as a dry candidate demonstrated that she had not really lost her old combative and determined quality, and she remained the Equal Righter she had always been, believing that women should seek an equal place in the political party structure. Was "she . . . running as a woman's candidate?" she was asked. "No," she replied, "I don't represent the interests of my own sex any more than I do those of the opposite sex. Those interests are not separate." She was qualified to run for this high office, she said, because of her training and background:

> My intimate acquaintance with the New Jersey Legislature has taught me how to work. I understand the passage of legislation, know how to get support for it and where to look for opposition. My insight into the working of political machinery makes me qualified as few men are qualified who run for office. Should I be elected to the Senate I propose to act just as a man would act. Why should a woman legislator be expected to be different?"[31]

As suddenly as Lillian Feickert appeared on the public scene, she disappeared. After 1932, with the election of Franklin Roosevelt and the demise of Prohibition, her recently organized State Council of New Jersey Republican Women disbanded for lack of a rallying point. Her next public appearance was not until February 1938, when the suffragists gathered at a Newark restaurant for a sentimental reunion. She was still living in Dunellen, according to newspaper accounts.[31] Feickert died in 1945 at the age of sixty-seven. Her obituary in the *New York Times* was accurate but brief. What the obituary failed to emphasize, in addition to her major contribution to the New Jersey suffrage cause, was her importance as a role model for women's initial foray into politics in the postsuffrage era.[32]

The Group Profile

As a group (see Appendix, detailing the social characteristics of ninety-three suffragists), the New Jersey suffragists can be described as relatively young (in their thirties and forties at the time of the 1915 referendum campaign), white, Protestant, and native born; they lived in the more populous northern part of the state, were married, had some college education, did not work, and were married to men who had middle class professional or managerial occupations. (A number of married suffragists had children, but not enough information is known about this aspect of their lives.) Some individual suffragists did work, of course, and those who did had occupations that were overwhelmingly professional, such as attorney, physician, school teacher, and journalist. The smaller number of suffragists who were single shared similar characteristics; they were not distinguished from the main body of suffragists in age, race, religion, nativity, or residence. A greater proportion of them had, however, a college education and professional occupation than did their married counterparts.

The six suffragists portrayed in these pages diverged but little from this broad social profile. But more can be said to sum up these six, for they shared certain observable qualities that the statistics fail to reveal. What is immediately striking about these women is their tremendous energy and willingness to work long and strenuous hours. They held leadership positions in not one organization but many. Yet they were not dabblers. Whatever these women undertook, they deemed to be important. Furthermore, they believed that their individual efforts made a difference. Even when the outlook looked bleak, for some, they were reluctant to give up their organizational burdens because they feared that they might not be shouldered by others.

Another notable feature of these suffragists is their self-assurance and seeming lack of discomfort in the public limelight. Years of experience in the suffrage drive had undoubtedly given them the confidence to organize, speak, lobby, and deal with persons in various official capacities. Nor did they appear to seek the limelight for ego gratification. Their highly public role was necessary, they believed, to achieve their varied objectives.

What follows from this is another quality: the suffragists' feminism. For underlying their myriad public activities was their contention that their sex belonged in the public sphere as a natural right. Indeed, it was for the right to become fully public persons that they had labored so long for the vote. All, Moral Prodders and Equal Righters alike, expressed the belief that they worked at what they did as women and, in addition to their other objectives, on behalf of women.

One can detect a sense of weariness in a number of these six suffragists by the 1930s. By this time, they had been in the forefront of the woman's movement for more than two decades. All knew that they would soon be supplanted by a new generation of women who had not experienced the comraderie and known the excitement generated by the fight for suffrage.

CHAPTER EIGHT

Depression Years, 1930–1940

IN the 1930s both Moral Prodders and Equal Righters continued to work for many of the goals they had each set for themselves in the previous decade. The period also witnessed the
demise of one Moral Prodder organization and one Equal Righter
group and the establishment of two new organizations committed to
the equal rights cause. What characterized the era was more than
mere continuity, however, for Depression conditions and the growing threat of global war, seemed to impart a new determination to
both groups, thus widening the gap separating the representatives of
the two philosophical positions.

The breakdown of economic conditions in the 1930s convinced
Moral Prodders that state and national problems required the careful,
unbiased study and lobbying techniques that had become their hallmark. As unemployment figures rose, as production dropped, as poverty and dependency became the experience of more and more
Americans, suffragists and their associates in the various reform organizations became doubly committed to their nonpartisan method-
ology. Indeed, the salvation of a democratic society was at stake, they
held. The revival of the economy, and the satisfaction of social needs
was not a matter of electing particular candidates or of concentrat-
ing on advancing women's political status, but of influencing public
opinion and of swaying legislators to pass the right bills. As war
clouds gathered in Europe and the Far East, suffragists in the peace
organizations declared that their proposals for international arms
control, the mediation of conflicts, and adherence to treaty obligations, among others, were the only hope of preventing a total breakdown in international order. Women, the Moral Prodders declared,
whose primary commitment was to their homes and families, must
be leaders in the effort to restore prosperity, to advance social well-
being, and to assure peace.

The Equal Righters, on the other hand, were equally convinced
that the worsening economic conditions had made women's small advances in politics, government service, business, and the professions

extremely tenuous and that the proper response was an urgent call for equal rights on the part of women. The suffragists in the political parties maintained that women must not only prevent further erosion of their political status but demand greater recognition of women in the political process. Suffragists in the NJWP, observing that the Depression had brought grave threats to the welfare of all working women—in the form of state economy bills and new protective legislation, asserted that women's right to equal access to all areas of public life must finally be guaranteed by state and federal ERAs.

But the Equal Righters, already in decline at the outset of the decade, experienced further setbacks in the 1930s. By 1940 the portrait of the suffragists that had emerged ten years after the vote was won had gained in clarity. The Moral Prodders, although fewer in number, remained the dominant group of suffragists, highly respected and praised for their impeccable credentials, while the Equal Righters had lost most of their organized support and were largely ignored.

Moral Prodders

The New Jersey League of Women Voters

Although the leadership of the NJLWV in the 1930s was no longer dominated by suffragists, as it had been in the 1920s, suffragists continued to hold important posts. The most prominent suffragist figure in this period was Lena Anthony Robbins, who assumed the presidency in 1935 and retained it until 1942. Other league suffragists were Florence Eagleton, first vice president throughout the 1930s; Helena Simmons, chairman of the Committee on Women in Industry; and Miriam Lippincott and Louise Steelman, chairmen, at different times, of the Committee on the Legal Status of Women.[1]

Suffragists and their fellow members in the NJLWV continued to work for the same five broad objectives of the 1920s and added another: improving the general economic welfare. The impact of the Depression caused the league to emphasize its first objective, governmental reform, more than ever. Here was an area of league expertise that seemed tailor made for the problems that beset the state. Somehow, both business and government had failed to keep the economy on course. Now it was the task of government to set its house in order and to restore financial health. League members believed that their methods of study and deliberation could help to uncover the causes of the state's maladies. In the early 1930s, as the growing numbers of unemployed and needy clamored for relief, the league declared that the proper remedies for the state's twin economic woes of increased debts and falling revenues were governmental economy and efficiency. In 1933, through its Department of Efficiency in Government, the NJLWV supported the recommendations of the Princeton Survey, a Princeton University study of the state government conducted the previous year at the request of Governor A. Harry Moore. The recommendations, which were subsequently put into effect, called for reduced government spending and consolidation and centralization of the state's fiscal department. In 1934 the league, with twenty-three other organizations, joined the Good Government Council, which also urged governmental economy, along with relief for property taxpayers and overhaul of the state tax system.[2]

In the mid-1930s professionalization of government service through expansion of the state civil service system became a major league priority. Asserting that the "spoils system" resulted in "appalling waste" in government, the NJLWV launched a two-year anti-patronage campaign and opposed violations of the merit system at state and local levels. In 1937 it successfully backed a civil service referendum that resulted in the creation of the five-member Civil Service Commission and provided for stringent regulations regarding "the employment, tenure and discharge of state, county, and municipal employees." Other league-backed bills authorized the voluntary use of voting machines (passed in 1935) and the establishment of permanent registration. The NJLWV also continued to defend the direct primary. In the late 1930s the league called for consolidation of the state court system, labeling it complicated and cumbersome. Finally, in 1940 it sought complete revision of the state constitution through the convening of a state constitutional convention.[3]

As economic conditions worsened, the NJLWV's second objective, improving the working conditions of women and children, ranked closely with that of governmental reform. The NJLWV observed that women were bearing the brunt of the Depression in low wages and unemployment. Governor Moore's decision in the winter of 1932 to suspend operations of the Bureau for Women and Children confirmed league fears that the welfare of working women and children had become a low government priority. Simmons, in her double capacity as chairman of the league's Committee on Women in Industry and as president of the CL, warned in December that industrial standards were breaking down in New Jersey, as they were in other states. League members saw their task clearly: to press the state legislature to pass bills that would help women and children fight economic forces that were attacking them with singular cruelty and thus to help prevent deterioration of the family unit.

In 1932 the NJLWV began to lobby for increased protective legislation. In addition to its increased support of older measures, the league backed new bills that provided for a nine-hour day and a forty-eight-hour workweek for women, prohibited the employment of minors in specified dangerous occupations (passed in 1932), and called for the establishment of a minimum wage commission which would recommend minimum wage standards for women and minors (passed in 1933). (New Jersey was one of seven states to pass a minimum wage law in 1933, all urged by the New Deal administration to do so. Wage boards authorized by the New Jersey law, however, did not receive initial funding until 1935.)[4]

In a replay of confrontations of the 1920s, the NJLWV's continued support of protective legislation brought it into conflict with the NWP and its New Jersey state branch, both of which were embarking on a new campaign to pass a federal ERA. In the late 1930s the league also clashed with a new group, the Committee to Eliminate Discriminations Against Women, over this issue. The committee, which was organized in 1938 and was composed primarily of business and professional women, sought repeal of the minimum wage and night work laws and in 1939 sponsored an ERA to the state constitution.[5]

In spite of its ongoing opposition to the principle of absolute equality between men and women that underlay the ERAs, the NJLWV's views about protective legislation were gradually being altered by national events. The passage of the federal Fair Labor Standards Act in 1938 providing for minimum wages and maximum hours for men and women engaged in interstate commerce set aside the whole notion of a minimum wage for women only. In 1939 a bill was introduced in the New Jersey Assembly, the object of which was to bring minimum wage and maximum hours standards in intrastate commerce in line with the federal standards. This bill had NJLWV support. (It was also supported by the CL and other organizations.) Significantly, the league, at its 1939 annual convention, voted to eliminate the word *women* from its support item for "legislation to improve conditions of work, wages, and hours for women workers."[6]

The league's third and newest objective, to improve the general economic welfare, was closely allied to its first two goals, as all three were designed to find means to reverse the downward course of economic conditions. Through its Public Welfare Committee the NJLWV supported bills for slum clearance and low-rent housing, for expansion of social security, and for increased unemployment and welfare relief.[7] The NJLWV, along with the majority of Americans in the 1930s, accepted the idea that government must bear the responsibility for the welfare of its citizens and that the administrations of the 1920s had failed in that task. It also believed that the Depression years raised a challenge for league members for which they were uniquely prepared. Members would study the facts and come to logical conclusions about the course that must be followed. "Wild new ideas and stale old ideas," Robbins observed in 1936, "we must challenge and test them all."[8]

The NJLWV's fourth objective, to advance the political and legal status of women, had clearly changed since the previous decade. No longer were women urged to join the political parties and to run for local office. Even the lip service paid later in the 1920s to the need for women's political participation was noticeably absent. By the 1930s the basic league position that women, because of their different point of view from that of men, could best influence the direction of public life as nonpartisan educated voters had hardened into orthodoxy. Political activity was equated with knowledgeable voting and lobbying, nothing more.[9]

On the other hand, the improvement of women's legal status remained an important league goal. Through the Committee on the Legal Status of Women, which had been established in 1927, the NJLWV worked "to secure for women a larger freedom and a true equality with men before the law." In 1933 it vigorously opposed a "married persons" clause in the newly passed State Economy Act that proposed the dismissal of married women from state employment if their husbands were similarly employed. (A comparable clause in the Federal Economy Act of 1932 required the dismissal of employed "persons" whose spouses worked for the federal government. The term was almost always interpreted to refer to women.) It also sought to secure the full equality of women in jury service. Although women were legally entitled to serve on all jury panels, a league survey in 1935–1936 revealed that a few counties still did not include women on their jury lists, a major offender being Essex County. The NJLWV publicized its findings and sought to reverse these court practices. In the beginning of 1939 Steelman, who had succeeded to the chairmanship of the Legal Status Committee, helped organize jury schools for women in several counties, the purpose of which was to inform women about the role of jurors. In October of that year she had the honor to be the first woman appointed as federal grand jury commissioner. Her task was to compile lists of prospective jurors who would serve in the four federal courts in the state, and in her role as commissioner she worked to promote women's participation in jury service.[10]

Toward its fifth objective, social reform, the NJLWV continued to press, unsuccessfully, for a sterilization measure, which it felt had become imperative as institutional costs rose and state revenues did not keep pace. In the late 1930s the NJLWV backed a measure, passed in 1939, to abolish the legal recognition of common law marriage. The intent was to insure that all marriages had the legal and medical safeguards attached to those that were formally licensed. In addition, the league, holding that society should be protected from the hazards of early and indiscriminate marriage, supported legislation to raise the legal age of marriage from fourteen to sixteen years of age for girls, from sixteen to eighteen years for boys.[11]

Finally, through its Department of International Cooperation and later its Foreign Policy Committee, the NJLWV sought, as it had before, the peaceful settlement of international disputes and gave new emphasis to the need for disarmament. In the mid- and late 1930s, as military preparations and aggressive moves by Italy, Germany, and Japan grew, the NJLWV declared its support for the policies of the Roosevelt administration designed to improve international relations and steer the nation on a neutral course: reciprocal trade agreements, neutrality legislation, and nonintervention. It continued to urge U.S. adherence to the World Court, affiliation with the League of Nations, and observance of international peace agreements. It also participated in the annual conferences of the CCCW. As war threatened to become a reality for Americans in the late 1930s, league members never wavered in their belief that women, armed with the facts, could educate the public to insist that global war must not be repeated.[12]

Although the suffragists and others in the league were working in the 1930s for many of the same objectives as in the 1920s, there was a mood about this period that was different from the previous decade. In particular, a certain feminist spirit was absent—that is, the kind of feminism that not only asserted that women should get involved in politics but also maintained that organized women should work together for issues that concerned them. In the 1930s league members not only had become impeccably nonpartisan but they had de-emphasized their joint lobbying with other women's reform organizations. Further, something of the earlier zeal to pass legislation, so evident in those few years after the vote was won, had gone out of league life. The days when a league president could call an urgent and "confidential" meeting of many of the representatives of organized women of the state, as in 1926, had long passed.

League members were not unaware that a change in outlook had taken place, but it was all to the good, they maintained. In 1940, for example, when the league's Committee on the Legal Status of Women lost its independent category and was placed under the jurisdiction of the Department of Government and Its Operation, a league officer made the following observation in the *Bulletin*: "In recent years the interests of the League members has been rather away from the traditional feminist objectives and more in the direction of governmental matters of interest to all citizens."[13]

As the twentieth anniversary of the founding of the LWV approached, the NJLWV assessed its accomplishments and was satisfied. The league had grown slowly but steadily. By 1940 there were five thousand members and thirty-two local leagues.[14] "It should reassure us to know," Robbins noted in the June 1939 *Bulletin*,

> that no group of men or women in the land is more respected for honesty and unselfishness of purpose than the League. . . .
> We find ourselves with an ever growing circle of contacts with public officials and with civic organizations, that want, like the League, to know the facts and the inner truth of a given public question or political situation.[15]

By 1940 suffragists and their associates in the NJLWV believed that the stature of the league was such that it had fulfilled the highest hopes of its suffragist founders. Robbins articulated their sentiments in the *New Jersey Voter* that June. Numerous league-backed measures had become law, of course; yet it was the quiet accomplishments that were most important. Without fanfare, without "advancing on Trenton in torchlight procession," the league did its job, which had not basically changed over the years. "The women of the League are still on the job, quietly educating the citizens and building up public sentiment. These have become their two primary functions," she observed.[16]

The New Jersey State Federation of Women's Clubs

In contrast to the considerable number of suffragists serving on the board of the SFWC in the 1920s, there were only two in the 1930s. In 1930/1931 Robbins was vice chairman of federal legislation, and in 1935/1936 Miriam Early Lippincott served as committeewoman-at-large of the Department of International Relations.[17] In many ways, the SFWC legislative program continued to parallel that of the NJLWV and the CLNJ, as it had in previous years. Through its various departments the SFWC supported measures that sought to bring economic recovery to New Jersey, provide protection to working women and children, and advance women's legal status. Peace was a major priority; throughout the decade the SFWC remained a member of the CCCW.[18]

Although the SFWC was actively working for a broad range of economic and social reform measures, many not dissimilar from those it had sponsored in the 1920s, there was a noticeable shift in outlook. Not unlike the NJLWV, the SFWC in the 1930s chose to de-emphasize its joint legislative efforts with other women's groups and retreated from its original call for political activism by club members. By the early 1930s the Women's Cooperative Legislative Bureau in Trenton, established by the federation in 1920, had died without comment. Although the SFWC maintained a legislation bureau in Trenton for most of the decade, the bureau had no apparent ties to other organizations. Second, interest in active political participation, so evident after ratification of the Nineteenth Amendment, had waned. There were still get-out-the-vote contests, and clubwomen were continually urged to know the issues so that they might be knowledgeable citizens; yet the earlier exhortations to join the parties and to run for local and county office were gone.

It even appeared improper to ask clubwomen to engage in partisan politics. Politics, it was agreed, was a dirty business, full of personal intrigue, ambition, and greed, better left to men. Nevertheless, federation leaders maintained women had a stake in public affairs. Women were consumers. They paid taxes. They were concerned, as they had always been, about those governmental matters that affected the home: education, public health and welfare, the quality of the goods they purchased, and above all, the preservation of peace.[19] The answer was not to withdraw from politics altogether but to expose it for what it was. How could club members effectively indict politics and still remain unsullied by its nastiness? The answer, said SFWC leaders, was to exercise the privilege of the ballot. For the ballot, in women's hands, as the suffragists had known so well, had the power to transform society for the better. It could elect the right men to office and turn others out. It could pass referenda and reject others. Used by women in large enough numbers, it would cause politicians to listen to women's demands and to ask for their support.[20]

Of course clubwomen might choose to go beyond simply voting and actually become active party workers, but this course was neither urged nor expected. As the editor of the *New Jersey Club Woman* observed in February 1938:

> The time has come when to get what she wants—and her motives are generally directed toward the public good—she must fearlessly be party politics conscious and, without apology, take her place in the party of her choice.

> The vote, however, is the first step and a perfectly ladylike, personally inconspicuous, even anonymous, method of control which is recognized, feared and respected. Its use should be on record one hundred per cent.[21]

What a far cry was this assurance, in 1938, that voting was perfectly "ladylike" and "inconspicuous" from President Agnes Schermerhorn's counsel in 1920 that clubwomen must take their rightful place in the political world! Why this relatively recent reluctance to become involved in political affairs? Had the absence of suffragists in prominent SFWC leadership positions in the 1930s made the difference? Partly. But the passage of time had been more influential. There was, first of all, a degree of disillusionment. Experience had shown that male legislators often ignored organized women's demands; the early high hopes that most women would pour out to vote on Election Day had not materialized. More important, clubwomen were focusing once more on their traditional concerns and interests: art, music, literature, and drama; gardening and conservation; home life; community planning; and the passage of social legislation.[22]

Having won the vote, they were, of course, obligated to exercise it. The vote remained the one channel of political activity that was deemed appropriate for women. Indeed, by the late 1930s federation leaders had elevated the ballot to a position of supreme importance, describing its power with almost reverential awe. Yet, for all the accolades the ballot received, voting was also portrayed as a duty clubwomen must perform, simply because they were citizens, the implication being that members' true interests lay elsewhere. "By her very nature woman is more sensitive to certain social wrongs than a man," the chairman of legislation and citizenship observed in the *New Jersey Club Woman* in February 1936. "The care of the sick, the aged, and the mentally defective have an appeal for every normal woman. Add to this list work for education, temperance, better government, international peace and many other movements and we catch a glimpse of the vast field of service before us."[23]

By the end of the decade the SFWC had three hundred clubs and more than thirty-three thousand members. (The state federation had lost seven thousand members over the ten-year period. The total rose again to approximately thirty-nine thousand in 1950. General Federation of Women's Clubs's membership had declined as well over a twenty-year period, from 2,500,000 in 1920 to "more than 2,000,000" in 1940.)[24] In spite of the membership decline, SFWC leaders did not doubt that the federation remained a highly esteemed body of socially minded women whose first priority was preservation of the home. In 1941 the SFWC celebrated the Golden Jubilee of the General Federation. "I wonder," mused President Helen Purdy Adams at that gala event in May, "if the most far-sighted of our pioneers or the most courageous of those leaders could ever have predicted the position that women and most especially women in powerful organizations such as the General Federation of which we are all proudly a part, would hold in the scheme of things today." Clubwomen, she declared, could be proud that they "were banded together in a common good cause." The nation and the world needed their "vision . . . and . . . courage" more than ever before.[25]

The Consumers' League

In 1930, when Helena Simmons took the reins of leadership of the CLNJ from the hands of its founder and only president, Juliet Cushing, Simmons became a major CLNJ spokesman for the 1930s. In 1935 she succeeded Katherine T. Wiley as executive secretary, a salaried post she held until her death in 1942. Other suffragists—Melinda Scott, Amelia Moorfield, Florence Eagleton, and Florence Halsey—retained board positions in this period.[26]

The deterioration of the economy undoubtedly concerned the CL more than any other woman's reform organization, for it directly affected the working conditions of women and children, the CL's sole interest. The CL contended that employers were blatantly disregarding existing protective labor laws. Women were often working more than a ten-hour day, for example, and wages paid for industrial homework had plummeted to shockingly low levels. "New Jersey has suffered, as have all other states," read a CL memorandum, "from a new type of sweat shop and fly-by-night employer."[27] A call to action was issued by Wiley at the annual convention held in Jersey City in April 1931: "Never was deliberate social planning more needed than now."[28] That year the CL, with the support of the NJLWV, the NJWTUL, the SFWC, and the YWCA, began to formulate a legislative program for the coming decade that provided for the following: a nine-hour day and a forty-eighty-hour workweek for women in industrial and mercantile occupations; a minimum wage for women and minors; a penalty clause in the night work law; regulation of industrial homework; unemployment insurance; prohibition of the work of minors in dangerous occupations; and regulation of the employment of migratory children. It also urged uniform enforcement of the New Deal National Recovery Act code provisions authorizing minimum wage and maximum hours standards for various industries in the state.[29]

Acting on a recommendation of the national CL, the New Jersey league, in December 1932, organized the Industrial Standards Committee, a statewide organization composed of more than thirty reform, labor, and church groups, of which Simmons became chairman. The committee, whose stated purpose was to reverse the breakdown of industrial standards, was committed essentially to the same legislative goals as the CL.[30] Notably, the CL's arguments on behalf of protective legislation for women were beginning to change. Although the old arguments of the 1920s remained, new positions received greater emphasis. The CL asserted that protection of working women would ultimately benefit everyone by helping to pull New Jersey's economy out of its depressed state. Reduction in women's hours of employment would "make possible more jobs," "regularize employment," and could be a first step toward limiting the hours of men as well. A shorter workday, moreover, made sense as technical advances caused productive output to rise. Similarly, the minimum wage bill was a sound means toward bringing woman's wages back to reasonable levels. Purchasing power could thus be restored to a group hardest hit by the Depression, the effect of which would immediately benefit industry.[31]

While Depression conditions had clearly influenced the CL's arguments for protection, other factors were also at work. Opposition to protective legislation was appearing, unexpectedly, from several new quarters. In the early 1930s, for example, the State Federation of Business and Professional Women's Clubs, like its parent group, proclaimed its opposition to all labor laws applying to women only. In 1932 the Women's State Republican Club, the new organization of regular Republican women chaired by Mrs. George H. Miles, announced that it would oppose the CL's forty-eight-hour bill because "working people don't want [it]." Too long, Miles said, women's clubs have accepted CL bills as "inherited mandates." In the late 1930s the Committee to Eliminate Discriminations Against Women sponsored two bills directly threatening CL interests: one to delete the word *women* from the Minimum Wage Act and another to repeal the No Night Work Law. Neither was successful. Finally, in early 1940, to the CL's considerable consternation, Congresswoman Mary Norton stated publicly that she favored the submission of the federal ERA to the states for consideration and by implication characterized many labor laws pertaining to women as restrictive. Of course the CL still had to contend with its old opponent, the state branch of the WP, which continued to protest that labor legislation on behalf of women alone was detrimental to women's employment opportunities.[32]

This growth in equal rights sentiment was relatively small, as most organized women in New Jersey supported the CL view. Nevertheless, it remained a significant threat to the CL's legislative effort throughout the decade, and it was one of several reasons why the CL seemed to be struggling against more difficult odds in the 1930s than it had in the 1920s. Another was the fact that depressed economic conditions were eroding existing labor standards, thus forcing the league to devote considerable energies to an attempt to reverse that trend. Third, the CL's legislative accomplishment in this period, in part owing to sentiment favoring governmental economy, was limited in effectiveness. Passage of a minors dangerous occupations bill was the organization's only outright victory. The complex apparatus authorized by the Minimum Wage Law in 1933 did not receive an appropriation until 1935. The Bureau for Women and Children, although not formally abolished, found itself in 1932 without funding. Efforts to add a penalty clause to the Night Work Law met alternately with heavy opposition or efforts to amend the existing law making it almost meaningless. The CL also suffered a psychological blow in September 1934 when Juliet Cushing died. "Mrs. Cushing's long years of distinguished service for the social welfare of the people of this State, makes her going from us, seem the end of an epoch," the recording secretary observed that October.[33]

With these developments as background, the CL experienced new declines in membership. In the fall of 1932 the league went through the worst crisis of its organizational existence, as it appeared that it might no longer have adequate funds to carry on. An emergency finance drive caused old friends and loyal members to rally behind the CL and come to the rescue. Nevertheless, annual membership figures reflected the harsh truth of declining support: from a high of 550 members in 1932 to a low of 289 members in 1936. Only in the late 1930s did the numbers climb slowly up to the 400 mark. (Other state CLs experienced similar, even more radical membership declines. National Consumers' League figures told that story. By 1939, its fortieth anniversary, the membership of the national league had shrunk from forty-one thousand in 1930 to a mere four thousand.)[34]

To Simmons went a great deal of credit for keeping the organization alive and for continually urging members to remember its noble purpose and do their part. "I have a sense of what a small group we are," she noted in her annual report in April 1934, "and worse still that we are not an articulate group. . . . After all, this CL is yours. . . . It is for you to decide if you want it to live or die. It is not a one woman organization." Simmons may have felt, at times, that the CL was indeed a one-woman organization, as she moved about the state with indefatigable energy, speaking before different organizations, talking on the radio, serving on various state boards (including, in 1936, the first minimum wage board), lobbying in Trenton, and then returning to Newark to oversee the CL's mundane daily affairs. Simmons was helped in these efforts by others, of course. There was volunteer secretarial help. Bills were drawn up by the CL's attorney and legislative chairman, Herman Marx. And in 1935 the presidency went to other women, and for a brief period to Marx himself. But Simmons's connection with the league was so intimate that she felt a special sense of identification with the organization, probably akin only to that which Cushing had experienced.[35]

There were occasions when Simmons found her energy and her usual optimism flagging. "There are times when I become so discouraged over the support we receive that I ask myself why struggle? Only my knowledge of the real need filled by the League keep me at work," she wrote in 1939. What sustained Simmons and her fellow board members, in spite of occasional doubts, was the belief that the league's place in public life was still vital. By the end of the decade they could realistically say that, in large measure because of league educational and lobbying efforts, working children in New Jersey no longer needed to fear for their physical safety; the first minimum wage law in the state had been passed and was finally being implemented; the legislature had, in 1934, ratified the Child Labor Amendment; and the public was becoming aware, as it never had before, of the monstrous evil of industrial homework.[36]

CL leaders remained confident that the stature of the league had not diminished and that it was, above all, because of the league's scrupulous nonpartisanship that it retained the public's high regard. As Simmons observed in her annual report in 1939:

> The public believes we are honest in our purpose and disinterested in our work. Our members go forth to try and find a unity of outlook, rather than to increase division; to increase common knowledge of factual information rather than extend propaganda, to include in our deliberations a wide range of thought rather than narrow it to a few people who think alike.

Here was the basic philosophy of a Moral Prodder. Simmons was implying that partisanship was divisive and therefore not in society's best interest. Women, she was saying, as the moral moral of the sexes, although they had won the vote, would do best to shun that course. Instead they should, like the members of the CL, examine the facts from a purely disinterested, independent point of view. "I firmly believe," she concluded, "that if peaceful solutions to our social and economic problems are to be found we must approach them in this spirit." [37]

The Peace Organizations

During the 1930s the suffragists continued their participation in the two major peace organizations in the state, the CCCW and the New Jersey branch of the Women's International League for Peace and Freedom. Notable suffragists in this period were Amelia Berndt Moorfield, who retained her position as president of the NJWIL for the entire decade; Florence Halsey and Paula Laddey, who were members of the NJWIL executive board; and Miriam Lippincott, who served as delegate from the CCCW to the first World Peace Conference, held in Brussels in 1935.[38]

The belief of the suffragists and their fellow members in the peace groups, held with such certainty at the outset of the decade, that women could be a decisive force in the creation of peace sentiment, was being challenged by the inexorable march of international events toward world war: the Japanese incursion into Manchuria in 1931, the accession of Hitler to power in 1933, the Japanese renunciation of the Washington Naval Treaty in 1934, the growing naval and armament programs of the major powers, the Italian invasion of Ethiopia in 1935, the outbreak of Civil War in Spain in 1936, in the latter part of the 1930s the gradual absorption of Central Europe into the German orbit, and the Japanese invasion of northern China.[39]

At their annual conferences and meetings, the members of both organizations discussed these threats to world peace and offered proposals to counter them. The large number of participants at many of these gatherings reflected the widespread concern among women about the ominous turn in world affairs. In April 1933, for example, approximately two thousand women representing the eleven member organizations of the CCCW gathered at McCarter Theatre in Princeton to hear Dr. Mary Woolley, President of Mount Holyoke College, speak about "Women's Part in the Settlement of International Problems": "It [is] high time women . . . take their part in the peaceful adjustment of affairs."[40]

That year, condemning the buildup of the U.S. Navy that began not long after Franklin D. Roosevelt took office, the peace advocates demanded that nations live up to their international treaty obligations. They also urged, as before, U.S. entry into the World Court. Such action was more imperative than ever before, they declared. "[The United States] is at a crucial stage in world affairs," Moorfield advised NJWIL members in April 1934 just before the organization's annual meeting in Trenton. "With militarism again gaining the ascendancy in Europe and the Far East, it behooves America to take the lead in reestablishing world peace." The peace groups also supported measures designed to strengthen cooperation between nations, such as reciprocal trade agreements, international arms control, and pacts for mutual consultation between signatory states in the event of treaty violations. They called for punishment of nations that violated the terms of the Kellogg-Briand Pact through nonrecognition, military embargoes, and the withdrawal of economic assistance. In addition, they supported efforts of the Roosevelt administration to improve relations with Latin American countries and worked to build the peace movement in that region.[41]

These positions and actions, taken at various points during the 1930s, were but the bare outlines of the peace advocates' program. The heart of that program, as always, was educational. Women, they held, had an obligation, first of all, to educate themselves, through investigation of the causes of the progressive breakdown of international order and identification of the major obstacles to peace. Armed with the facts and the right solutions, women ought, in turn, they said, to go out into the community to convince others that they must demand of their governments new policies to implement peace. In 1933, for example, the CCCW established the Leadership Institute, whose purpose was to train women to organize and lead relatively small discussion groups in their individual organizations, in the schools, and in the larger community to pinpoint the issues and arrive at group decisions. From these intimate encounters there would develop, it was believed, a ground swell of peace sentiment that could not be ignored. There was no higher CCCW priority in the 1930s than its leadership program. Its leadership chairman described this effort as "consecrated work."[42]

By the fall of 1939 events had made the world peace movement, of which the state peace groups were a part, irrelevant. As German tanks rolled into Poland, it was obvious that soon all of Europe would be drawn into the conflagration. For the peace workers in New Jersey, as in the rest of the country, the plea that nations observe earlier pledges to outlaw war had become meaningless. The next step was to prevent direct U.S. involvement. Moorfield, speaking in Newark before the United Women's Republican Clubs of Middlesex County just a little over a week after the Polish invasion, cautioned women to be true to their convictions in spite of the growing war mood. The president's "pleas for national unity" were a thinly disguised request for further discretionary war powers, she observed:

> The President wants more power but he already has all the power he needs. . . . We paid for the last party and we will never get repaid. War may make for a temporary prosperity but this would only be followed by a worse depression than the one we have experienced. Will we be stampeded again?[43]

As the decade ended, many of the suffragists and their associates in the peace groups were still actively opposing U.S. involvement in the war. In February 1940, for example, the CCCW sent four delegates to the Fifteenth National CCCW Conference being held in Washington, D.C. Throughout the 1930s the members of the peace organizations had remained a large, dynamic body of women who continued to prod their fellow New Jerseyans to remember the ultimate devastation of war and to work for its permanent banishment. But by mid-1940, as one European state after another toppled before the Nazi war machine, the peace workers, fighting to avoid U.S. entry into the war, seemed to be facing more difficult odds with each passing day.[44]

The Committee for Law Enforcement

As of 1931 suffragists continued to provide leadership for the New Jersey Woman's CFLE. The board of directors included Lippincott, president; Robbins, executive secretary; Geraldine Livingston Thompson, Lillian Feickert, Florence Randolph, and Halsey. Helen

Paul, who was also president of the Moorestown LWV, was a more recent addition. Several suffragists were also serving on the national board of the CFLE: Feickert, Lippincott, Mrs. Arthur Proal, and Mina Van Winkle.[45] Still believing that dry sentiment would prevail, Lippincott encouraged her followers to keep up their hopes and to enroll new members despite the election of Republican Dwight Morrow to the U.S. Senate. On January 8, in a letter addressed "Dear Daughters of the Constitution," she reminded members that the Eighteenth Amendment was still the law of the land. Women must be ready to defend it, she cautioned, for the battle over the Constitution was about to begin.[46]

Notwithstanding continuing setbacks, the CFLE view, that women, through education, could persuade their fellow citizens that morality must be upheld and law must be observed, remained intact. The defense of law would not be easy, for there were powerful enemies: the brewers, the politicians, the multimillionaires, and gangland. But women were up to the task because all they held dear was in the balance. "The unlimited money at the disposal of the wets," Lippincott observed in a message to CFLE members in October 1931, "is difficult to fight, but when the protection of the home and the child is at stake the real true American citizen is aroused."[47]

Lippincott's prediction that the newest, most serious, challenge to Prohibition would soon be underway was correct. By the fall of 1931 Republicans and Democrats were working in concert to end more than a decade of dry legislation in the state. On October 9 the legislature approved a resolution requesting Congress to modify the Volstead Act "so as to legalize real beer and light wines"; it was submitted in December. The Republican party was finally prepared to oppose the state prohibition law as well. At its convention in May 1932, heeding former Governor Edward Stokes's admonition that Democrats continued to win votes at Republican expense over the prohibition issue, the Republicans approved a platform plank that called for repeal of the Hobart Act, a position the Democrats had taken years earlier. By fall, the legislature had voted in favor of a referendum on the State Enforcement Act, to be held on Election Day, November 2.[48]

The suffragists and their associates in the CFLE felt both confused and isolated. They were in debt, as well. They realized for the first time that the tide of public opinion was rapidly shifting in favor of total repeal. They predicted, correctly, that the referendum would pass despite their public warnings that repeal would leave New Jersey "without any state law to protect its people against the liquor traffic."[49] Moreover, as they prepared to vote for the next president of the United States, neither candidate had any appeal for them. Roosevelt, a Democrat, was committed to national Prohibition repeal, and Hoover's support of the dry position was questionable. Was Hoover a dry or a wet? The members of the CFLE could not be sure.

Lippincott was admittedly discouraged. "Why I keep on with this thankless job I do not know," she wrote Robbins in the fall of 1932. Nevertheless, she would persevere. Somehow, she said, she still believed that the amendment, the hope of all women who truly understood the protection it gave the home, could be saved through "two years of intensive educational work."[50] But CFLE and national committee plans for a vast educational campaign barely had a chance to begin. The passage of the state referendum and the election of Roosevelt spelled final defeat for the defenders of Prohibition. In February 1933 the new Democratic Congress quickly voted repeal of the Eighteenth Amendment and modification of the Volstead Act. New Jersey legislators were only too eager to have state law conform to federal regulation. On April 7, wine and 3.2 beer became legal in New Jersey, as in many other states. On December 5 the Twenty-First Amendment, nullifying the Eighteenth, was formally ratified. "The end of an era of national prohibition, most controversial legislation since the founding of the republic, has been written into history," observed the *Newark Evening News* a few weeks earlier. As the most recent amendment became part of the Constitution, the CFLE passed into history as well.[51]

Equal Righters

The suffragists, and many other women who entered the political parties in the early 1920s, had hoped that over the next two decades more and more women would run for office and would hold elective and appointive positions. This had not occurred. Initially, in the first few years of women's enfranchisement, the prospects for political equality looked hopeful. The number of women running for state and county office was increasing; a specific number of women on the state boards of education and health had been mandated by law; and a few women were being appointed to county election and tax boards. But by the early and mid-1930s it had become apparent that the number of women in major public office would not proceed in a slow but steady upward progression. Indeed, the record showed that women's political status was not improving, and in some areas it had worsened.

In the 1930s, for example, the number of women running for state and county office on the major party tickets had decreased over the previous decade. In the 1920s the number of women running for these offices as Democrats and Republicans had risen from seven in 1920, to highs of seventeen and eighteen in 1925, 1926, and 1927. But after that date, these figures gradually declined (with the exception of 1935) to lows of twelve and thirteen. (The number of women running for state and county office on third party tickets in the 1930s actually increased over the previous decade—from a total of sixty-seven in the 1920s to a total of 163 in the 1930s. Third party candidates running at these levels, though, both male and female, never won office.)[52]

Fewer women won state office, as well. In the 1920s the number of women who won seats in the sixty-member assembly rose from two in 1920 to a high of nine in 1926, declined to a low of four in 1931, and in the latter part of the 1930s never rose above five and six, approximately 10 percent of the total membership. In addition, the number of women serving on county boards of freeholders remained small and stable; each year, between 1925 and 1931, a total of three women in the state served on freeholder boards. In the 1930s this number never exceeded four (reached in 1935).[53]

Further, women, in the 1930s continued to be excluded from many political posts. No woman, for example, had ever won office as state senator, surrogate, coroner, or county clerk. Only one woman, Mary Norton, had been elected to Congress, a position she continued to hold in this period. Although women were appointed to state boards and commissions traditionally viewed as appropriate for women, such as Institutions and Agencies, health, and education, they were absent from others, such as the State Highway Commission, the Civil Service Commission, and the Department of Conservation and Development, to name a few. There was one notable exception. In 1932 Thelma Parkinson, a Democrat from Cumberland

County, was appointed by Governor A. Harry Moore to the State Board of Tax Appeals and was reappointed in 1938.[54]

There was another exception to the otherwise perceptible erosion of women's political status. By the 1930s women were gradually becoming an accepted presence on county election boards. In 1927, for example, thirteen women were serving on election boards out of a total of eighty-four positions, approximately 16 percent. By 1935 that figure had risen to twenty-six, or 30 percent of the total. Women were rarely appointed, however, to the other major county board, the tax board. In 1927, for example, there were five women on tax boards out of a total of sixty-three positions, approximately 8 percent, and in 1935 there were still only five.[55]

It was against this background, then, of failed hopes, that the suffragists and other women in the political organizations began in the 1930s to place a greater emphasis on increased representation for women in elective and appointive office and continued to press for increased recognition in the party apparatus. A number of suffragists were serving in prominent positions in the women's party organizations, and several held state appointive posts. Only three held selective office. Florence Haines served her last and fifth term in the assembly in 1932. Thompson was returned once more to the Republican State Committee in 1933, from Monmouth County (she remained a member until 1961). Edith Hyde Colby was elected Essex County freeholder in 1934 and was reelected in 1937.[56]

Republican Women

The NJWRC, reorganized in December 1930 as the State Council of New Jersey Republican Women, had been replaced as the official women's Republican organization by the Women's State Republican Club (WSRC), but it was still a factor in Republican party life. The exact number of members in the State Council (SC) is not known, but Feickert, its founder and president, still drew a significant following of women who believed in the organization's firm Prohibition stand. The SC may have lacked the power of earlier days, but the fiery independence which characterized its former self had not died. On March 25, 1931, at its first "annual" luncheon in Trenton, at which featured speakers were Katherine Wiley of the CL, Nina Frantz of the

WCTU, and Lippincott representing the CFLE, the SC passed two resolutions, one demanding greater recognition of women in the Republican party organization and another urging inclusion of a strong law enforcement plank in the 1931 party platform. It also endorsed the policies of Herbert Hoover. "We are behind President Hoover," Feickert declared. "We are reasonably certain that Mr. Hoover will seek reelection on a dry platform and his will be our platform."[57]

The equal rights demands of the SC surely came as no surprise to Republican party leaders in light of the point of view of its predecessor, the NJWRC; but when the organized regular party women proved no less pliant, it was unexpected. Several suffragists were now allied with the new state organization, having recognized that Feickert's group no longer had influence. Thompson, for example, was WSRC vice president; Colby was on its board of governors; and Margaret Laird and Haines, each president of sizeable women's Republican organizations in Essex County, had chosen to affiliate with the "regulars." When the WSRC, of which Georgianna S. Miles was president, held its first annual luncheon on April 7, 1931, in Trenton, it passed resolutions strikingly similar to those of the SC, demanding greater recognition of women legislators in party caucuses and the appointment of women to posts not generally viewed as "women's positions": "as juvenile court judges; as members of the Joint Conference Committee of the Legislature . . . as members of the county boards of election and county tax boards; as motor vehicle agents and as members of the legislative and State Commissions." The featured speaker at the luncheon was none other than Feickert, who applauded the WSRC stand and suggested that if the party did not respond positively, the club should threaten a voting "strike."[58]

Within two weeks a committee of twelve appointed by Miles to draw up these resolutions in final form met with party leaders in Trenton. Present were former U.S. Senator David Baird, Jr. (the old foe of the suffragists), who was seeking the Republican nomination for governor that May; U.S. Senator Hamilton F. Kean; and Republican Chairman Bertram E. Mott. The committee submitted a list of specific appointments the WSRC sought and elaborated club complaints. A major problem, it maintained, was the caliber of county chairmen, many of whom were unconcerned about women's interests. A number needed to be replaced by "men of finer character."[59] Miles, who was also present, warned Baird that he might well lose women's votes in the May primary if some positive action was not taken before then. As the years went by, she said, women were gradually losing confidence that the party really meant to fulfill its promises to accept women as equals in the party apparatus. Indeed, women might turn to the Democrats, whose record was far better. "The intelligence, efforts and loyalty of the Republican women cannot be questioned," she declared. "They must now be brought into the full confidence of the party in all conferences pertaining to government in the state, and have representation by appointments and support of leaders for elective positions in order to hold their valuable interest in the Republican party."[60]

The confrontation of the organized Republican women and the political establishment received considerable newspaper coverage, and there was speculation that the Republican leadership might make some concessions. But by mid-May, following Baird's nomination, it became clear that it would not. In a letter to the WSRC Baird praised the women for their past accomplishments in political life, reminded them that the Republican party had always promoted women's participation in party affairs, and gave vague assurances that their demands would receive the highest consideration.[61] But what Baird proposed to do, it was learned from other party sources, was refer the matter to the state committee and dissociate himself from the whole affair. It would be difficult, these officials noted, for even the state committee to accede to the women's demands. It was unrealistic to call for the ouster of certain county leaders, who were, after all, elected by the voters. Nor could promises regarding appointments be made to one specific group.[62] The Republican party leadership was responding once more to the political facts it learned years earlier. The leaders of the organized women might make demands, might subtly threaten reprisals, but the average female party office holder, party worker, and registered voter cared more about party loyalty than equal rights issues. Demands and ultimatums could thus be safely circumvented and compromised.

The members of the WSRC proved, ultimately, to be loyal party women, too. Miles and others held fast to their position for awhile. But a more conservative faction, with close ties to the party organization, led by Helen Berry, Margaret Baker, and Thompson was urging accommodation. By the time of the Republican convention in early June, the issue had been resolved, and Baird was assured that he had the club's support. WSRC leaders had been convinced by party chiefs that their proposals were "unworkable" and had settled instead for a vaguely worded platform plank that "pledg[ed] the Republican party of New Jersey to a full and deserved recognition of the women of our State in the appointment to office and in party councils."[63]

The SC, meanwhile, had gone its own way, unhampered by the need to assure its members that it would support the party ticket. In June 1931 Feickert announced that the SC would not support Baird because of the "vicious political machine" he had built in Camden County, "the shabby treatment" accorded women workers of the party, and his anti-Prohibition stand. The SC's support, she noted, might eventually go to the independent dry candidate, Edmund R. Halsey.[64] Feickert's declaration, of course, was not a significant threat to either Baird or A. Harry Moore, the Democratic candidate (and the winner in November), both of whom favored Prohibition repeal, as did most of New Jersey's voters. The SC had become, by that time, relatively impotent. Indeed, in a little over a year the SC disappeared from the political scene. The council survived through 1932 only because it actively campaigned for Hoover. Hoover, in fact, respecting the council's ability to attract dry votes in New Jersey for the national ticket, accorded an SC delegation that included Feickert, Mrs. Charles Woodruff, and Lippincott a cordial reception at the White House in April of that year. But with the election of Roosevelt in November, what had become the SC's major reason for being had ended. It is doubtful that it lasted much beyond this date. Having backed itself into a pro-Prohibition corner, the organization that had once represented those suffragists who demanded equal rights in politics disappeared from view.[65]

The WSRC remained loyal to the state Republican party, but it had not totally capitulated. In the ensuing years it continued to press for greater recognition of women in party affairs. Early in 1932, for example, before the Republican national convention, the club unsuccessfully urged that the twenty-eight-member New Jersey delegation be equally composed of men and women and that three of the delegates-at-large be women. (At the 1928 Republican convention, it was noted, New Jersey women had "only three votes.") In 1935 it authored the plank on women in public office that was included in the party platform. In the name of "the women of the Republican Party," the plank sought the appointment of a woman to the State Civil Service Commission and of women to state and county tax boards and requested that "responsible Republican Party leaders throughout the state . . . promote the position of Republican women of outstanding ability so that they may become logical candidates for elective offices." This plank was reinserted in the 1936 platform. Never again, however, was there a period like that in the spring of 1931 when the organized women literally threatened to withhold their votes if their demands for equal rights were not recognized. After that, the Republican women were reduced to suppliants who hoped that their wishes would be granted. They were not.[66]

Other Efforts

During the 1931 gubernatorial campaign, the Democrats, much as they had almost a decade earlier, relished comparing the dissension in Republican ranks with the good will evident in their own party. At rallies and in public statements, they pointed out, over and over, that Democratic leaders kept their promises to women, while the Republicans did not.[67] Much of this effusive praise of the party was campaign oratory, however. While Republican women were prepared to acknowledge that their Democratic sisters did receive a greater number of political appointments, the facts were, of course, that the political status of women in neither party was impressive nor improving, and this became more apparent with each passing year.

Democratic Congresswoman Mary Norton, who once had been so optimistic that women would eventually become a potent force in political life, was more realistic about the status of women in both parties. By 1935 she was sorely dismayed by the evidence. Women, she said, not only in New Jersey, but in the nation at large, had "during the last few years . . . made little progress in political work. . . . In the last national election, fewer women were elected to office than in any previous elections." The reason for this unfortunate state of affairs? Norton's analysis was perceptive. By implication, Norton admitted that she no longer believed, as she had in 1926, that ultimately "there will be no need for special campaigns to place women in office" and that male politicians would welcome seasoned female political workers into their inner councils. The men had proved more resistant than she had anticipated. But Norton refused to blame the male political establishment. The fault lay, she said, with women themselves. They chose to work "behind the scenes" instead of getting directly involved in political work. "Women are not being taken seriously in politics," she asserted. "They never will be until they make themselves felt. We get discouraged too easily. Our motives are fine and have a good influence, but we have influenced others to act instead of assuming full responsibility ourselves."[68] Norton, clearly, was referring to women's preference for the role of Moral Prodder to that of Equal Righter; it reflected the course chosen by most of the New Jersey suffragists as well.

In April 1932 a state branch of a new national organization committed to promoting women's political equality—the Organized Women Legislators (OWLs) of New Jersey—appeared on the political scene. Its founder and first president was suffragist Assemblywoman Florence Haines. The OWLs membership was limited to all past and present women members of the state legislature. Its purpose: "to encourage and help new women legislators; to support desirable legislation . . . and to promote election and appointment of a greater number of qualified women to public office."[69] In the mid-1930s, as it became clear that fewer women were running for elective office on the major party tickets, the OWLs decided to focus its efforts on reversing this trend. In 1936 and 1937 it embarked on a major campaign to persuade county committee chairmen to place women on their primary slates, especially in those counties where chances of winning were good. In particular, it urged that this course be followed by Republican leaders in Union, and Democratic leaders in Camden, Middlesex, and Mercer, counties, where the parties had largely ignored women as primary choices. Several chairmen promised that as soon as there were openings on the party slates, women would fill these slots. The OWLs also sought the appointment of more women to state boards and commissions. In May 1938 an OWLs delegation visited Governor Moore (reelected in 1937) for this purpose. Moore indicated that he had difficulty finding qualified women to fill many state posts but that he would make every effort to comply.[70]

Yet despite the promises of several county chairmen and the assurances given by Governor Moore, the political standing of New Jersey women remained at its low ebb. Both major parties continued solemnly to pledge in their platforms that women would be assured equal opportunity in public service, but nothing changed. In May

1939 the OWLs decided to publicize the failure of women to win public office to any significant degree by holding its "first annual 'Empty Chair' luncheon." At the gathering held in East Orange, "Empty Chairs" were dedicated to an absent "women Governor, state senator, member of the Civil Service Commission, and a 'lady from Union,' the only large New Jersey county which has never elected a woman legislator." The following year the OWLs held a second "Empty Chair" luncheon at which these same chairs were re-dedicated.[71]

By the end of the decade the OWLs had become the sole spokesman for the Equal Righters in the political parties. As the WSRC, discouraged and disillusioned, no longer sought special planks on women in public office, the OWLs remained the lone voice urging both parties to remember their repeated promises to women. By 1940, then, twenty years after the vote was won, suffragist hopes for political equality had virtually died. In retrospect, it appears that the further decline of women's political standing in the 1930s was brought about, in large measure, by two factors. The first was the Depression. The stock market crash in late 1929 and the ensuing collapse of the economy, which persisted for most of the 1930s, ushered in a new mood for New Jerseyans and for all Americans. Gone was the general optimism of the 1920s, a period in which businessmen and consumers believed that technology would bring about a utopia of plenty for all.[72] The mood of the 1930s, by contrast, was rational and pragmatic. The prime objective in this period was the restoration of economic health. In this changed atmosphere those new women voters who had hoped to become equal partners with men in political life suffered. They encountered a new indifference in the male political establishment to their aspirations. The former willingness of male politicians to welcome women into the political party structure, to experiment with the new idea of "political woman," which was so apparent at the outset of the 1920s had waned visibly in the climate of economic failure. The Depression, moreover, affected women's prospects in another way. Political jobs were, at bottom, just that: jobs, that paid a salary, some better than others. As jobs became harder to find, it was predictable that male political leaders would think of men, the traditional family providers, as their first choices for political appointment.

The second factor, and the more important one, was the inability of women to convince male politicians that women could unite around the issue of equal rights and use their ultimate weapon, the vote, to press their demands. Women's lack of unity on other issues had been observed, of course, in earlier years. In the 1930s the Equal Righters, suffragists and others, remained a small minority of women in the political parties and lacked a following among most women voters and party workers. But even the Equal Righters did not have persistence and clarity of purpose. They could be diverted by their desire for party loyalty. Thus, by the end of the decade, their calls for meaningful political recognition were met with party promises of "parity and equal opportunity for all"—and then dismissed.[73]

The Woman's Party

By the late 1920s the NWP was gradually shifting its attention from its activities in the states toward concentration on passage of the federal ERA, which read: "Men and women shall have Equal Rights throughout the United States and every place subject to its jurisdiction. Congress shall have power to enforce this article by appropriate legislation." The work of the state branches, the NWP held, to improve women's legal status and to pass state ERAs, was proceeding far too slowly. Only a federal amendment could permanently guarantee equal rights to all women in the nation.[74]

In the early 1930s Depression conditions accelerated this change in emphasis. The NWP declared that women's economic status was being threatened by newly passed federal and state economy acts forbidding the employment of married women in government service and by decrees issued by numerous local municipalities and school boards prohibiting the employment of married teachers. Furthermore, the position of married working women in the private sector was in equal jeopardy. "From coast to coast, the dismissal of married women from their jobs, just because they are women and are married, continues," a NWP official observed in *Equal Rights* in January 1932.[75]

The national organization's decision to direct all its energies toward passage of the ERA had important consequences for the New Jersey state branch, for it brought about a sharp diminution in the NJWP's decade-long campaign to eliminate state legal discriminations against women. After 1931 the flow of correspondence between

Chairman Leila Enders and Burnita Shelton Mathews of the national Legal Research Department came to an abrupt halt. Finished, too, were long-range plans to introduce equal rights bills into the legislature. Instead, over the next five years there were isolated instances of lobbying for and against specific bills. In 1931, for example, the NJWP worked unsuccessfully for the passage of a bill that made the legal age of marriage the same for men and women and successfully opposed another bill that sharply restricted the wife's dower rights, guaranteed by the existing Dower and Curtesy Law. In 1934, together with the NJLWV, it lobbied on behalf of a bill that "would make it mandatory to place an equal number of women's and men's names in the box from which juries are drawn" (not passed). In 1936 it successfully opposed a bill that sought to extend the 1932 Economy Acts prohibition of the employment of husband and wife in state jobs to all public jobs. In the main, however, the state branch's activities in the 1930s revolved around the NWP congressional campaign and opposition to all attempts to pass state protective legislation.[76] During this period most of the suffragists who had been active in the state branch in the 1920s were still in prominent posts. Minnie Karr and Margaret Laird remained vice chairman and legislative chairman, respectively. Mary Philbrook, Agnes Campbell, Caroline Delany, Mary Dubrow, Bertha Irving, Paula Laddey, and Grace Osgood were members of the State Advisory Council. Enders, a nonsuffragist, remained chairman.[77]

In early 1932 the NJWP leadership began a lobbying campaign against two CLNJ-sponsored bills: one to establish a forty-eight-hour workweek for women and another to add a penalty to the Night Work Law. It sought to amend the forty-eight-hour bill by substituting the word *person* for *female*. This so-called protective legislation, it declared, was totally inappropriate, for it only made women's job chances more difficult, in difficult times. The central problem, Helen Caldwell, NJWP industrial chairman, observed, was finding decent jobs for all, but unfortunately, it was not being addressed. "I think all will agree," she said, "it is work we want not useless legislation."[78] The following year the state branch sought, without success, to amend the pending minimum wage bill so that it would apply equally to both sexes. A minimum wage law would set a dangerous precedent, Enders warned. "Once New Jersey admits a minimum wage bill for women in industry the 'next step backward' would be a minimum wage for women in the teaching profession." It was due to NJWP efforts in 1925, she pointed out, that discrimination based on sex in the employment of teachers was forbidden by law. It was a worthy principle that should be extended to all areas of employment.[79]

With these ongoing, albeit limited, efforts in the early and mid-1930s to improve women's legal status and to oppose protective legislation, the suffragists and their fellow members in the NJWP, along with the Equal Righters in the political parties, helped to keep the public aware of the goal to achieve full equality for women in every sphere of endeavor. As they hammered away at the overriding need to pass the ERA, they publicized the fact that women in many states of the nation still suffered glaring legal inequality. Yet, in spite of the worthy activity of the NJWP, something was clearly amiss, for its existence was coming to an end. By late 1936, or 1937, it had, in effect, disbanded. If it existed beyond these years, it was in name only, for in January 1940, when the NWP considered reactivating the organization, it noted that there were only four individuals on the state branch list.[80]

Without further information, the downward course of the NJWP, can only be conjectured, but reasons for the party's demise are not difficult to find. The NJWP's failures, not as apparent in the 1920s, had become blatant in the 1930s. As the state legislative campaign to improve women's legal status was de-emphasized and as the NJWP's primary focus shifted to passage of the federal amendment, the differences between the state branch and the large number of women in the reform organizations were magnified. Instead of moving positively, as it had a decade earlier, to pass equal rights legislation, the NJWP's new activities were essentially negative—against protective legislation and against other organized women. In these Depression years, when the Moral Prodders believed that working women were more likely than ever to be overworked, underpaid, or unemployed, and thus in need of protection, the NJWP appeared insensitive to their valid concerns. Equally important, the failure of Enders, Karr, Laird, et al., to hold periodic elections had ossified the NJWP leadership and widened the gulf separating the executive board from the general membership. (The parallels between the experience of the state branch and that of the national organization are arresting. By the 1930s the NWP was undergoing similar declines in membership—from a party claim of ten thousand in the 1920s to a mere five or six hundred in 1933. Nancy Cott, in her essay on the history of the NWP in the 1920s, attributes the decline to the organization's exceedingly narrow aims, its authoritarian leadership, particularly that of Alice Paul, and its failure to cooperate with various women's groups with labor concerns.)[81]

Furthermore, by mid-decade the state branch was no longer the only organization dedicated to the equal rights cause. The campaign against protection was being taken up by other groups, such as the New Jersey Federation of Business and Professional Women's Clubs and the newly formed New Jersey Women Lawyers' Club (organized in 1936). As the NJWP increasingly appeared to be nothing more than an appendage to the national body, members undoubtedly lost interest or drifted away to more innovative organizations with similar goals.

The Committee to Eliminate Discriminations Against Women

In 1938 an attempt was made to rally the forces that supported the equal rights cause and to coordinate their efforts. In January of that year Philbrook, who had recently become chairman of the Congressional Committee of the NWP, called a meeting of a handful of representatives of the New Jersey Women Lawyers' Club (NJWLC) and the New Jersey Federation of Business and Professional Women's Clubs (NJFBPWC) and formed the Committee to Eliminate Discriminations Against Women (CEDAW), with Philbrook acting chairman. The CEDAW had two main objectives: to remove two state protective laws from the record books and to secure the passage of an ERA to the state constitution. Within a short time of founding, it consisted of close to one hundred women, primarily from the defunct NJWP, the NJWLC, and the NJFBPWC. Suffragists who joined, in addition to Philbrook, were Haines, Karr, and Laddey.

The CEDAW's first action was to draw up two bills, one to amend the minimum wage law by deleting the word *woman* and another to repeal the Night Work Law. Constance Hand, Republican Assemblywoman from Essex County, who was present at the meeting, agreed to introduce these bills in the next session of the legislature. "With these two discriminations against women removed," Philbrook subsequently observed, "the women of New Jersey will stand almost wholly on a basis of equality with men. The few remaining inequalities are negligible and no difficulty will be encountered in removing them at a later session."[82] The CEDAW won the endorsement of Hand's bills from several groups: the 5,000-member NJFBPWC, the approximately 230-member NJWLC, and several municipal and county women's Republican and Democratic clubs in northern New Jersey.[83]

That fall the committee began to lay the ground work for its next legislative drive. It petitioned both political parties to include planks favoring a state ERA in their platforms being drafted for adoption that October. Writing to party chairmen, Philbrook observed that, in light of the recent passage for the federal Wage-Hour Law providing for fair labor standards for both sexes, it was appropriate that the state of New Jersey declare its support for the principle of equality. These efforts were partially successful. Although the 1938 and 1939 Democratic platforms merely noted the party's opposition to "discrimination on the ground of sex," planks in the Republican platforms in both these years contained a pledge that read in part: "that no law shall be enacted which discriminates against any person on account of sex. We favor a suitable amendment to our constitution to accomplish this purpose if the same is deemed necessary."[84] The Republican plank did not contain an outright endorsement of an ERA, but the committee chose to consider it as such. In early 1939 Hand, acting on behalf of the committee, introduced an ERA into the legislature which read: "Men and women shall have equal rights throughout the State." The amendment was subsequently defeated and was reintroduced the following year.[85]

Hand's bills relating to the minimum wage law and the Night Work Law met with immediate opposition from numerous labor groups and women's reform organizations and were eventually defeated, but prospects for the state ERA were better. Although the ERA was also opposed, support for the concept of a written guarantee of equal rights appeared to be growing. In 1938, for instance, a committee of women lawyers of the New Jersey Bar Association appointed to study the legal status of women in New Jersey recommended that the association attempt to repeal existing protective legislation and that it support the federal ERA. In January 1940 the SFCWC pledged support of the federal amendment. And on March 20, 1940, the committee scored a significant victory when Governor Moore issued a statement endorsing both the federal and state amendments. "I feel," Moore declared, "that their adoption will be effective in removing discriminatory laws and will clear the way for women to work out their own salvation, especially in the industrial world."[86]

A few months earlier Congresswoman Norton, who now held the powerful post of chairman of the House Committee on Labor, wrote to Philbrook that she favored submission of the federal ERA to the states for a vote. "The time has come," she observed, "to submit this question, which has been agitating women for so long, to the states for consideration . . . you and I know that there is much discrimination against women and although this may never be cured by amendment or otherwise, I can see no reason why the question should not be given an airing." Norton, however, was careful not to commit herself to support the amendment.[87]

The committee used all of these pledges, endorsements, and statements to develop its case that the demand for a state ERA had reached overwhelming proportions. But of course it had not. By 1940, in spite of the Republican party planks favoring an amendment "if the same is deemed necessary," few Republican legislators in either house had shown any willingness to support such a proposal. (Democratic support was more forthcoming, however.) The majority of women's organizations, including women's political clubs from both major parties, either opposed the amendment or chose not to endorse it. Unionized women, and organized labor in general, were among the amendments most outspoken opponents.[88]

Nevertheless, this small group of Equal Righters had not totally failed. In the two short years of its existence, the CEDAW, under Philbrook's dynamic leadership, had succeeded in keeping alive the demand for equal rights in all areas of public and private life and had won the endorsement of that principle from major public figures. These efforts would be rewarded, to a degree, at a future date.

The Postsuffrage Portrait Completed

By 1940 the portrait of the suffragists was relatively complete. It was not only similar to that of 1930 but could be painted in deeper tones. The Moral Prodders remained dominant. The NJLWV had continued to grow and solidify its position as a highly regarded group that carefully studied the facts before reaching any public position; the SFWC, thirty-three thousand strong and the largest woman's organization in the state, was known for its dedication to the preservation of home life and the advancement of the public welfare; the CL was still the same small band of highly committed women who were in the forefront of the fight to protect working women and children; the peace groups represented thousands of women from numerous organizations who sought to persuade their fellow citizens that U.S. involvement in the European and Asian conflicts would only bring disastrous consequences. Upon careful scrutiny, however, the profile of the Moral Prodders had changed over the ten-year period. As a group, they were now supremely nonpartisan, shedding any earlier enthusiasm for political activism. These suffragists, who maintained that women had loftier motives than men, now had a sharply etched identity, clearly separate from those men and women who were active in the political parties.

The Equal Righters, on the other hand, were in disarray. The State Council had dissolved. The organized Republican women had failed to win any substantive response from party officials to their demands for greater political recognition. Democratic women, though far less militant, had not fared any better in terms of their degree of representation in elective and appointive office. The NJWP, only ten years earlier the leader of the effective drive to improve women's legal status, had disbanded for lack of an organized following. The efforts of the newly formed CEDAW to pass a state ERA had, thus far, not been successful. Yet, despite the further reverses the Equal Righters experienced in the 1930s, sentiment for equal rights was alive and well. In the next decade that issue would be debated once more, and suffragists would still be an important factor in that debate.

CHAPTER NINE

Equal Rights and the State Constitution, 1940–1947

T HE history of the activities of the suffragists in the years between 1940 and 1947 is an important epilogue to this study
of the outcome of the New Jersey suffrage movement. Although their participation in public affairs diminished considerably
during the 1940s, the suffragists played a significant role in the
outcome of one major public question, the adoption of a new
constitution.

At the outset of the decade the Moral Prodders, led by the
NJLWV, spearheaded the drive to revise the nearly one-hundred-
year-old Constitution. The Equal Righters, on the other hand,
fought the adoption of any new document that did not include an
equal rights clause—a position that the Moral Prodders opposed.
Here, then, was a renewal of a two-decades-old clash. The resolution
of this conflict in 1947 was a small but significant advance for the
equal rights cause, for which one segment of the suffragists could
legitimately claim significant credit.

When the NJLWV was approached in late 1940 by several organizations and individuals to promote the idea of revising the state constitution, a few suffragists still held important posts. Lena Anthony
Robbins was president and would remain in office until the following June. Florence Eagleton was honorary first vice president, and
Louise Steelman was advisory counselor. With board approval it was
Robbins who set in motion the revision movement by appointing a
committee to plan a course of action.[1]

On February 24, 1941, Robbins chaired a meeting held in Newark and attended by approximately two hundred representatives
of interested groups, among them the league, the CL, the SFWC,
the WTUL, the American Association of University Women, the
NJFBPWC, the NJWLC, the New Jersey State Chamber of Commerce, the New Jersey Education Association, the Democratic

Women's Luncheon Club, the Non-Partisan League (CIO), and the New Jersey Taxpayers Association. A twenty-six–person executive committee was created, which called itself the New Jersey Committee for Constitutional Convention, to which Steelman was appointed. Robbins was elected committee chairman.[2]

The time was ripe for consideration of complete overhaul of the Constitution. Knowledgeable individuals had pointed out for years that the office of governor needed to be strengthened, the terms of the legislators ought to be extended, and the state court system, which was termed "antiquated and intricate," required reorganization. A constitution drawn up when the state's population was overwhelmingly rural and totaled 373,000 was described as inadequate and inappropriate for a primarily urban state with a population exceeding 4 million. Newly elected Democratic Governor Charles Edison, moreover, had pledged in his recent campaign "to urge upon the legislature with all the force at my command, the necessity for the calling of a constitutional convention." In September 1941 both Democratic and Republican platforms had planks calling for constitutional revision.[3]

Here was the league's greatest opportunity to render nonpartisan service to the citizens of New Jersey. Not only had it worked for governmental reform for the past twenty years, but it had proven that it was free from partisan bias. Further, it had favored constitutional revision for two years and was knowledgeable about the defects in the present system. "Organizations and individuals have indicated that the league is an ideal group to lead such a movement," a board member observed in early 1941.

> The movement should not come from a political party but from all political parties and all partisan groups and should not be left to any special interest group. We should be very proud as a group that we are interested in good government from a non-partisan standpoint. It is a chance for us to prove and work for the promotion of good government and the education of citizens.[4]

While the league and the Committee for Constitutional Convention proceeded with their educational campaign to create sentiment for a constitutional convention, the legislature also acted by creating, on November 18, 1941, the Commission on Revision of the

New Jersey Constitution, charging it "with the duty of inquiring into the subject of constitutional revision and of suggesting in what respects the Constitution of New Jersey should be changed and make recommendations to provide for the more effective working of present-day representative processes." The seven-person commission, which was headed by State Senator Robert C. Hendrickson of Gloucester County, included nonlegislators. In its deliberations, the commission heard proposals for changes in the constitution from the NJLWV and other civic groups and individuals. In May, 1942, it reported that it "unanimously recommended a revised Constitution," to be drawn up by legislative bill.[5]

In November 1943 the citizenry voted in the affirmative on a referendum that empowered the legislature to draw up a revised constitution. The newly elected Republican governor, former Senator Walter E. Edge, immediately appointed a thirty-member advisory joint legislative committee, chaired by State Senator Howard Eastwood, Republican of Burlington County, to fulfill the voters' mandate. By the fall of 1944 the electorate was preparing to vote on a referendum to adopt the newly drafted constitution.[6] The NJLWV was understandably proud of its role. "The League has worked for many years to bring about this modernized Constitution," noted a board member in the October *Bulletin*, "and is actively urging acceptance as one of the outstanding issues of this election."[7]

The newly revised constitution, prepared by the Joint Legislative Committee and incorporating most of the recommendations of the Hendrickson Commission on Revision, did not meet with broad public approval as the NJLWV hoped. By early 1944 strong opposition was being voiced by representatives of veterans, farmer, and labor groups, who appeared at scheduled hearings of the Joint Legislative Committee. The veterans' spokesmen declared that it was inappropriate for revision to take place during wartime when so many servicemen were overseas; farm spokesmen charged that the proposed abolition of the dedicated highway fund threatened rural road construction; labor representatives expressed dissatisfaction with the failure to include a clause providing for periodic revision of the charter by referendum and with the fact that the new document did not spell out labor's right to collective bargaining. Opposition also came from two other groups that became unlikely allies. One was a new equal rights group organized by Mary Philbrook, called the Women's Non-Partisan Committee Against the Proposed Revised Constitution. The other was the Democratic party, with its powerful party leader, Mayor Frank Hague of Jersey City.[8]

For the previous four years Philbrook had been devoting all her energies toward securing an ERA to the state constitution. In early 1940 she had resigned as chairman of the CEDAW because she felt its emphasis on repeal of protective legislation and passage of equal rights bills only diluted the ERA effort. Thus, while CEDAW carried on with its program, Philbrook, in the spring of 1941, formed the Women's Consultative Committee on Constitutional Amendments, which had as its sole objective adoption of a state ERA. Members of this twenty-three woman committee included Emma Dillon, president of the NJFBPW, and Constance Hand, who was still serving in the assembly. In June the Committee voted to support the ERA which had been introduced once again by Hand in the assembly and by Hendrickson in the senate. The following January it petitioned the legislative Commission on Revision to include an ERA in its proposals, but without success.[9]

By 1942, with the entry of the United States into the war, Philbrook had become encouraged to believe that a growing number of individuals viewed protective legislation as an anachronism. As women plunged into demanding war work and enlisted in the women's branches of the armed services, the whole notion of protecting the "health and morals" of women indeed seemed outdated. Moreover, the legislature appeared to agree, for on December 12, 1941, only days after Pearl Harbor, it passed an hours bill for women that permitted the governor to suspend the Night Work Law "in time of war or other serious national emergency." (CEDAW and the NJFBPWC called for complete repeal of the law, rather than suspension, while the NJLWV and NJCL urged a one-year limitation.)[10]

The SFWC seemed to be reconsidering its long-held position favoring protective legislation. At any rate it was ready to listen to other viewpoints, for it asked Philbrook to write a two thousand–word article on the subject, which appeared in the *New Jersey Club Woman* in February 1942. Marion Cox, SFWC chairman of legislation, promptly wrote Philbrook that her article had caused her to change her opinions about the ERA. Her earlier views about the need for protective legislation had obviously been faulty, she said:

Probably many perfectly well-intentioned persons will be astonished to learn that their efforts on behalf of women workers have created serious dislocations and outright hardships for the very ones whom they were seeking to protect. In any case, your exposition of the true state of affairs should be an eye-opener for many of us, myself included.[11]

There were other signs in the early 1940s that equal rights sentiment in New Jersey was flowering in the climate of war. Besides the calls for the permanent rescinding of all protective laws, bills were introduced for complete equality for women in their jury status and for equal pay for equal work. In addition two CEDAW-sponsored bills were passed in this period. On June 30, 1941, a "working wives" bill, introduced by Assemblywoman Mattie Doremus of Passaic, was passed; it prohibited "discrimination against citizens in public employment based on sex or marital status." On June 19, 1942, another was passed "concerning the compensation of teachers in the public schools," which provided that female teachers receive equal pay with their male counterparts "holding similar positions and employments." To the surprise of feminists, a third bill, without their sponsorship, was approved on November 18, 1941, that permitted female attorneys who married to retain their maiden name if they so elected, or to add their married name to their maiden name with a hyphen between the two.[12]

Between 1942 and early 1944 Philbrook and the Committee on Constitutional Amendments sought to assure the inclusion of an ERA in the preparation of a revised constitution. The effort was primarily Philbrook's. She wrote regularly to Republican State Chairman H. Alexander Smith, for example, chastising the Republicans for their failure to support the ERA, pointing out that the Democrats had been far more sympathetic to the equal rights demands of women. Philbrook also sought Hague's endorsement of the ERA but did not receive it. In mid-1943 she received an evasive reply in which the mayor, simply noted that he was a long-time advocate of equal rights, that it was through his efforts that the Hudson delegation had voted for ratification of the federal suffrage amendment in 1920, and that he "believed that women today enjoy equal rights with men."[13]

When, in March 1944, Philbrook and some of her fellow members of the Committee on Constitutional Amendments learned that the revised constitution drawn up by the Joint Legislative Committee did not contain an equal rights clause, they decided to regroup as the Women's Non-Partisan Committee Against the Proposed Revised Constitution. The new committee of fourteen women was cochaired by Emma Dillon, a Republican, and Mrs. Howard Height, president of the New Jersey Women's Democratic Luncheon Club. Other committee members included past and present presidents of the New Jersey Education Association of Newark, the New Jersey Nurses Associations of Newark and Elizabeth, the United Women's Republican Clubs of Monmouth County, the Business and Professional Club of Westfield, the Realtors Club of Camden, and several attorneys.[14] The committee began to issue press releases, distribute broadsides, and speak throughout the state, warning that all of women's advances over the past one hundred years could be wiped out if the legislature so chose because the proposed constitution lacked a permanent guarantee of those rights. One broadside, for example, urged citizens to vote no on the referendum in November because women were still "regarded as a 'special class' and will be given only such rights as the Legislature will dole out to them." "A 'special class' is a subjective class," the broadside read. "*Don't vote to keep yourself in* subjection!"[15]

Hague and other influential leaders of the Democratic party had other reasons to oppose the revised constitution. First, the proposed enlargement of the powers of the governor threatened to diminish those of the powerful county committee chairmen. Indeed, Governor Edison, no ally of Hague, had openly declared that he hoped such might be the result. "There is a rumor around New Jersey that the present Democratic Governor is independent of the State's self-chosen Democratic boss," Edison noted in a speech in November 1941. "I believe I can confirm that rumor . . . a careful rewriting of the Constitution would make it more difficult for political bosses to ply their trade at Trenton." The passage of the referendum in 1943, empowering the legislature to draft a new constitution, was viewed as a victory for Edison and a defeat for Hague, who campaigned vigorously against the referendum.[16] Second, by the spring of 1944 Hague and many Democrats viewed the proposed constitution in purely partisan terms, and with good reason. Instead of being drafted by a bipartisan constitutional convention, as most revision advocates had originally proposed, the task had been granted to the legislature, which by 1944 was heavily Republican. Indeed, the Joint Legislative Committee, appointed by a Republican governor, was composed entirely of Republicans. A yes vote on the constitution in November could well be claimed a Republican victory.[17]

Although Hague had not been willing to commit himself to an endorsement of a state ERA in 1943, he saw real profit in doing so in 1944. When the Women's Non-Partisan Committee approached Democratic leaders and asked for the party's support, it received it with alacrity. The Democratic platform, adopted on May 29, which had a plank opposing adoption of the revised constitution because it was not drawn up by a constitutional convention, also included a plank on women: "The proposed Revised Constitution will take away every advantage that women had gained since 1844." It called instead for a state constitutional amendment "which will guarantee forever the full equality of rights to women under the law, without abridgement on account of sex." The Hague organization also charged that adoption of the proposed constitution would result in a tax giveaway for the railroads. The *Jersey Journal*, which supported Hague editorially, helped link the mayor's assertions with those of the Women's Non-Partisan Committee in the public mind. "Charges by the [Women's Non-Partisan Committee] that the draft is a concoction designed among other things to reduce women's rights," a *Journal* editor observed, "fits in and supplements the claims of taxpayers and rentpayers that the constitution is so drawn as to give the railroads a definite assurance of preferential treatment in taxes."[18]

Political expediency had thus aided the equal rights cause. The Equal Righters had won from the Democratic party the commitment they had sought as early as 1940, when Governor A. Harry Moore lent his support and Mary Norton held out the promise of hers. But the proposed constitution had to be defeated before a newly drafted one could include that long-sought provision.

The NJLWV, the SFWC, the CL, and other organizations, having satisfied themselves that the new constitution contained all the revisions they had hoped for, were now working for passage of the referendum as the New Jersey Committee for Constitutional Revision. (The committee had been organized in the fall of 1943.) Robbins was no longer committee chairman, but she was still an active committee member. The SFWC had voted in favor of the principle of constitutional revision in 1941 and had been represented on the Committee for Constitutional Convention since that time. The CL, noting that in the past it "repeatedly found itself hampered in its work for legislation in the interests of working people," voted in May 1944 to endorse and work for the new constitution because of the beneficial changes that had been made over the old document. The NJLWV declared that ratification was its first priority and sought to counter the Women's Non-Partisan Committee's assertion that women's rights were endangered by the proposed constitution. It stepped up this effort in the fall. "The new Constitution is infinitely better than the old," a league official noted in the October *Bulletin*. "In no respect has it changed for the worse. . . . The *status of women* in this state under the new Constitution *has not* in any way been impaired."[19]

The league's president, Jane Barus, and the state presidents of the American Association of University Women, the New Jersey Council of Jewish Women, and the SFWC issued a joint statement in support of the new constitution, terming the campaign of the Non-Partisan Committee "propaganda" based on untruths. "There is not the slightest risk that under the new Constitution women would lose any rights and privileges they now hold," they declared. The Committee for Constitutional Revision distributed broadsides assuring the voters that "Women's Rights Are Protected!" The CL, in its October *News Letter*, charged that women who were working for an ERA were "trying to sabotage the proposed constitution."[20]

What is significant about the debate over the constitution is that equal rights had become a public issue as never before. Previously, Moral Prodders and Equal Righters had clashed primarily over the passage of protective legislation. Their differences of opinion had been aired in legislative hearings and within their own ranks. But by the fall of 1944 the entire voting public was being asked to consider whether women's civil and legal rights should be spelled out and guaranteed in a new, modern constitution. The Equal Righters, led by Philbrook and Dillon, had seized the opportunity, as an outmoded constitution was being discarded, to force the entire electorate to consider this question. And as the old arguments for protective legislation were weakened, the proposal for an equal rights provision indeed seemed attainable.

As important as the equal rights debate was to various women's organizations, other factors were ultimately far more influential in the voters' final decision. Only weeks before Election Day the Hague organization began a barrage of campaign advertisements, press releases, and messages warning voters and political leaders that a yes vote on the constitution would aid the railroad lobby, challenge the tax exemption of churches, and threaten the pension and tenure rights of public employees, including school teachers. Moreover, lay and religious leaders of the Catholic church and various civil service organizations vigorously echoed Hague's warnings. On the eve of election Governor Edge sought to blunt the Democratic blitz, calling the Jersey City mayor "one of the few old-line political bosses still at large" and charging that the Hague campaign was an effort "to stir up class against class."[21]

The ultimate defeat of the referendum by more than 155,000 votes—a defeat that analysts subsequently attributed primarily to the Hague effort, to the religious issue, and to the partisan nature of the revision method—was also a defeat for the NJLWV, which had consistently been in the forefront of the fight for revision. "It is not only a blow to our hopes," Barus wrote in the November *Bulletin*; "it is a serious setback in the long struggle for efficient and democratic government in New Jersey. . . . The opportunity will come again," she noted. Barus's accusation that "a vicious campaign of slander, appeals to narrow selfish interests, [and] the arousing of fantastic peers without the slightest foundation in fact" appeared to be aimed not only at Hague but at the Women's Non-Partisan Committee.[22]

The committee, of course, was jubilant. Philbrook and Dillon were convinced that the equal rights issue had been decisive. Although they granted that various groups had opposed the revised constitution for many other reasons, they asserted that these groups also agreed that the Equal Righters' demands were justified. Moreover, they held, the alliance to defeat the referendum had resulted in a new awareness of women's need to protect their rights. "The many men and women who helped us present the proposition to the voters are now all more conversant with the status of women in New Jersey," Dillon wrote Philbrook the day after the election. Philbrook declared that the election results showed that the voters were now ready to pass a state ERA and recommended that the amendment be introduced once more in the coming legislative session.[23]

Philbrook's hopes for prompt passage of a state ERA proved to be overly optimistic. Legislative interest in equal rights for women had to wait upon revival of the question of constitutional revision, which did not occur for another two years. In his inaugural address on January 21, 1947, the new Republican governor, Alfred E. Driscoll, sparked the effort by calling for constitutional revision by the convention method, a proposal that met with immediate bipartisan approval.[24] Within weeks, the groups involved in the revision movement in 1944 came to life. The Committee for Constitutional Revision, which had been meeting on an annual basis, reconvened to prepare its recommendations once again. Philbrook (now seventy-five years old) reorganized the various organizations committed to the equal rights cause as the Women's Alliance for Equal Status. Among the member groups of the alliance were the NJFBPWC, the NJWLC, and the state branch of the WP, a small group now headed by Gussie Vickers. Vickers (now eighty years old) and Rosemary Carroll were named cochairmen of the alliance, and Philbrook assumed the post of legislative chairman. There were now only three suffragists active in the revision effort: Vickers, Philbrook, and Geraldine Livingston Thompson (now seventy-five years old), who had just been appointed chairman of the Woman's Committee of the New Jersey Committee for Constitutional Revision. Helena Simmons, Lena Anthony Robbins, and Louise Steelman had all recently passed away, and Amelia Moorfield had just retired from her long-held position as treasurer of the CL.[25]

As both political parties were now prepared to endorse a revised state charter, events moved rapidly. The legislature passed a bill calling for a constitutional convention, to which eighty-one delegates equally divided among both parties were to be elected on a county-wide basis, and this proposition was passed by the voters at a special election held on June 3. On June 12 the constitution opened at Rutgers University in New Brunswick, with instructions to complete its task by September 12.[26]

In the ensuing weeks the NJLWV and the Committee for Constitutional Revision appeared at all the public hearings of the subcommittees of the convention, making recommendations based on their earlier investigations. The Women's Alliance sought out the committees on rights and privileges and on rules, urging the inclusion of a clause that read: "No distinction shall be created between the rights of men and women to vote, to hold office, or to enjoy equally all civil, political, religious and economic rights and privileges." In their statement before the Committee on Rights and Privileges, Vickers and Carroll declared that women were entitled to constitutional recognition of the rights they had assumed in the years since the adoption of the Constitution of 1844. They pointed out that a similar declaration offering women's equality with men could be found in the Preamble of the Charter of the United Nations.[27]

Through Philbrook's efforts, the alliance also endeavored to win the endorsement of the SFWC, then wavering, if only unofficially, in its support of protective legislation. The State Federation had consistently opposed both the federal and state ERAs, despite the General Federation board's almost unanimous endorsement of the federal ERA at its May 1943 meeting. SFWC president Elizabeth Maddock cast one of the two negative votes at the time. (In September of that year the SFWC board supported Maddock by formally voting to oppose the ERA.) To Philbrook's disappointment the SFWC remained opposed to an equal rights provision in the new constitution and so stated at the convention hearings.[28]

The alliance had more success with the New Jersey Bar Association, which lent the full weight of its support on June 13, after considering the recommendations of its Committee to Study the Status of Women. "If we are to have a modern Constitution," the committee's report stated, "and avoid confusion respecting the legal status of women, the legal status that women have attained must be established and safeguarded. . . . There is no way by which women can achieve equal status as citizens and be brought out of this subject class, except by Constitutional provision." Then on June 28 the Organized Women Legislators of New Jersey voted to endorse the Bar Association report (which had been submitted to the convention's Committee on Rights and Privileges) and appeared the next day before the Rights and Privileges Committee to register its support.[29]

Not unexpectedly, as the committees on Rights and Privileges and on Rules considered changes in the Constitution's Bill of Rights and in Article X of the General Provisions, the CL and various labor groups opposed any alteration in wording that could be interpreted to grant blanket equality to men and women. (Although the NJLWV had consistently opposed a state ERA in the past, it remained notably silent on the equal rights question, perhaps reflecting the fact that its members were no longer in total agreement on this issue. In its statement before the Rights and Privileges Committee, the NJLWV simply urged retention of all sections of the Bill of Rights, with a few minor exceptions.) The CL argued that retention of the earlier provisions would serve women best by keeping all the statutory rights women had gained over the past intact while retaining protective laws as long as they were needed. A prime example of much needed protection, it noted, was the minimum wage law that currently covered women workers in several intrastate trades untouched by the provisions of the Fair Labor Standards Act. These arguments struck a responsive chord among committee members, for despite the changes in women's economic and legal status brought about by the war, by the Fair Labor Standards Act, and by the increased unionization of women, most still believed that protective labor legislation was valid.[30]

Given the obviously divided opinion among women about the question of equal rights, the committees might have chosen to leave the original article sections unaltered, had not a new and ingenious approach been devised. Backed by their organization, a team of four women, all attorneys, of the NJFBPWC—Marguerite Carpenter, Myra Blakeslee, Libby Sachar, and May Carty—proposed to the Committee on Rights and Privileges that wherever the word *men* appeared in the Bill of Rights, the word *person* should be substituted. They noted, further, that the word *person* should be explicitly stated to refer to both sexes. It was not sufficient to assume that the term *men* applied to women as well, they observed. The fact that protective legislation had been passed solely for women demonstrated that women could be singled out as a special class. "Sex is not a matter of choice or right," they maintained. "It is a matter of birth and should be so regarded." The claim that women were the weaker sex had been exposed as a myth by women's activities in the world war. Women were fully capable of competing with men both mentally and physically.[31]

The NJFBPW believed that if its recommendation was acted upon, the Constitution would, in effect, guarantee equal rights, but it skirted use of that term. "It was not without guile that the words 'equal rights' were not used," the federation's first vice president Margaret Warner later observed:

> We knew too well that those two words might prove a call to arms to the groups—some of them made up of women—who do not share our convictions with respect to equality of rights,

and that a controversy on the convention floor would again make this unfortunate division of opinion among women an excuse for delay.[32]

The reaction of the committee was favorable. In spite of the NJFBPW statement labeling protective laws "discriminatory," the committee judged that the proposal granted women equal rights yet did not threaten the protective laws on the books. It noted that even the CL had argued that where the word *men* appeared in the Constitution, the courts had always interpreted it to include women. Making that interpretation crystal clear, it concluded, would not challenge the interpretation of the CL.[33]

The "solution" was successful, for as Election Day approached, it brought no objections from the Moral Prodder organizations. The NJLWV, for example, chose to ignore the change. In its summary of the new constitution in the October 1947 *Bulletin*, it simply noted that the Bill of Rights prohibited discrimination based on "religious principles, race, color, ancestry or national origin." The SFWC also disregarded the new wording. But the CL interpreted it to its satisfaction. The use of the word *persons*, it noted in its summary of changes in the new constitution, "[gives] constitutional recognition of the rights which have been won by women since the drafting of the old Constitution in 1844."[34]

The Women's Alliance realistically chose not to oppose the New Jersey federation's proposal. It saw that its efforts to win an equal rights clause were destined to fail. But some members of the alliance, particularly those in the NJWP, viewed the reworded articles as an interim compromise, for protective legislation remained intact. "We felt that the compromise Art. 10, Sec. 4, which was finally adopted," Vickers subsequently wrote in 1953, "was of psychological value but we never thought for a moment that it would achieve complete equality for the women of N.J." The WP's objective, she said, remained what it had always been: passage of the federal ERA.[35]

When the Constitution was approved on November 4 by a majority of approximately 468,000, both Moral Prodder and Equal Righter groups rejoiced. Most of the suffragists were no longer around to join in the celebration. But the adoption of a new, efficient, more democratic constitution was the culmination of the Moral Prodders' long-term, nonpartisan effort for governmental reform, in which the suffragists had played such a vital part. The Equal Righters were also able to declare that a significant advance had been made in the fight for equal rights.[36]

Women, of course, had not won true equality. Their political status had not markedly changed. During the 1940s the OWLs continued to urge that more women be appointed to state boards and commissions, but without noticeable effect. The number of women in state elective office did not rise. Nevertheless, something significant had occurred. Although the new constitution did not contain an equal rights clause, women's right to equality was now legally recognized. "Under the proposed Constitution," it was noted in the official summary of the Constitution prepared before Election Day, "New Jersey will be the first state to give equal constitutional rights to women."[37] The new constitution now began with these words: "All persons are by nature free and independent, and have certain natural and unalienable rights." "Happy day!" Vice President Warner exulted in the NJFBPWC's publication, *Independent Woman*. "It has happened here, and in the state of New Jersey, we women are now persons." It was a goal the suffragists had sought since the early beginnings of the suffrage movement in the nineteenth century. It had remained an objective for almost one hundred years. This public recognition of women's basic equality as human beings was due, in large measure, to their efforts.[38]

CHAPTER TEN

The New Jersey
Suffragists in Retrospect

T HE New Jersey suffragists, though relatively united as they campaigned for the vote, held two basically different views about women's proper role in society and divided along these lines in the postsuffrage era. The ideological underpinnings of these two philosophical positions were the two suffrage arguments, that of justice and expediency, the heart of which were, respectively, that women were the same as men in their common humanity and that women were different from men in their basic natures, interests, and concerns. Although the overwhelming majority of the suffragists used both arguments (though basically contradictory) in the suffrage campaign, they divided after 1920 into two discernible groups, or types, each emphasizing one argument over the other, translating it into a guide for women's proper role as voting citizens. Those suffragists who gave greater weight to the expediency argument (the Moral Prodders) joined the nonpartisan reform organizations, while those who stressed the justice argument (the Equal Righters) joined the political parties and the WP. The former accepted women's traditional role as moral guardians of the family; the latter sought to break out of that traditional mold to assert women's right to equal opportunity in political and economic life. The experiences of these two suffragist groups over the next two decades differed markedly. The Moral Prodders grew stronger and became dominant; the Equal Righters declined and lost influence. This outcome had important positive results, but in the main it spelled defeat for those suffragists who hoped for political equality and for equal rights in general.

Several important questions arise from the foregoing account: Why did some suffragists choose the path of Moral Prodder and others that of Equal Righter? Why did the Moral Prodder view prevail, and why was the Equal Righter view less successful? Finally, how did this development impinge upon the suffrage movement's failures and successes?

First, what were the motivations and self-perceptions of those suffragists who endorsed the Moral Prodder view? Why did the suffragist view that men and women had different spheres of interest and that women were the more moral sex (a view that appears strikingly similar to the Victorian doctrine of the separate spheres) continue to be a satisfactory definition of the role of women for so many suffragists after 1920? Certainly the fact that the majority of women were not in the paid labor force, even by 1940—that most women indeed had separate spheres of activity from men—helps to explain why this perception endured. Between 1920 and 1940 the proportion of women who worked had risen only slightly—from 23.3 percent to 25.7 percent. Moreover, the majority of women workers were "the young, the single and the poor." By 1940 married women made up only 35 percent of the female work force. In that year 15.2 percent of married women were in the paid labor force, a figure that reflected the fact that approximately one-quarter of married black women worked for wages and 11.9 percent of their white counterparts did so.[1]

These facts alone, however, do not adequately help one to understand the self-perception of this large body of suffragists. It is helpful, I suggest, to trace the origins of that outlook by looking at the suffrage period. I therefore pose another question: why had the justice argument, as well as the broad equal rights demands of the early women's rights leaders, lost ground by the end of the nineteenth century? Several historians who have studied the suffrage movement from a national standpoint have offered valid explanations. William O'Neill maintains that the earlier women's rights advocates were more perceptive than the later suffragists in their analysis of the cause of women's unequal and repressed state, for they argued that the lack of the vote was only one of women's many grievances—"that the heart of the woman question was domestic and not legal or political; that woman's place in the family system was the source from which her inequities derived." By contrast, O'Neill observes, the later suffragists had lost this bold perspective and not only accepted woman's place in the family but had enshrined it and ennobled it. Having placed woman back on the moral pedestal she had been assigned by the earlier Victorians, the suffragists focused on the lack of the vote as their main grievance and saw the vote as the sole means by which all problems, both women's and society's, would be solved. Their exaggerated claims for the ballot grew out of their strong desire to win adherents to their cause and to succeed.[2]

Carl Degler, in his history of women and the family, sounds a similar pragmatic role. The later suffragists, he suggests, realized that the earlier suffrage argument, appealing as it did to women's "individuality [and] their sense of self-interest," was not succeeding because suffrage appeared to be a threat to women's traditional place in the family. They therefore took a new, more acceptable tack, arguing that suffrage would merely widen women's sphere into the larger world without altering it. Another reason the later suffragists did not care to challenge women's position in the family, Degler observes, was that they found it basically satisfactory. Throughout the nineteenth century women had been gaining greater autonomy within the family, he points out. Women were responsible for the moral guidance of their children; they were the loving companions of their husbands; they could choose to limit their fertility; and they could, if they wished, decide to sever their marital ties or not marry at all.[3]

Aileen Kraditor proposes that the shift from justice to expediency as the basis of the suffrage argument occurred because of changes in the political and social environment. The appeal to justice in the antebellum period, she points out, reflected the widely held faith of the Jacksonian era that the nation's democratic ideals of equality for all could be realized. But by the late nineteenth century, as the problems arising from industrialization and immigration brought about a "declining faith in democracy," the suffragists linked their demand for the vote with explanations of how woman suffrage would help solve these problems. Kraditor observes that the very fact that women had won many rights by the end of the century contributed to the decline of the justice argument: "It was no longer necessary to prove what was now obvious . . . once the abstract equality of the sexes had been established beyond public dispute, the difference could be spelled out in greater detail without fear of inference being drawn therefrom that women were inferior to men."[4]

Kraditor's analysis seems most compelling for understanding the later suffragists' role perception. These suffragists were no longer rebelling against stifling domesticity, as had their Victorian predecessors. As women attained property rights and rights to their own earnings, as the barriers to higher education and the professions gave way, and as middle class women joined the numerous organizations that flourished in the Progressive Era, women formulated a new definition of themselves as public and private persons. Contributing to this new perspective was women's improved position in the family. Most middle class women, including those who joined the suffrage cause, still defined themselves essentially as wives and mothers. Nevertheless, they also saw themselves as assertive individuals actively concerned about the welfare of their families and the welfare of the wider community. Their moral frame of reference—seeing women as the more moral and humane sex—enabled them successfully to ally their activist stance with their traditional sex role viewpoint. It was in this context that the later suffragists, and the great mass of women who eventually supported them, could argue that women needed the vote primarily to effect reforms to benefit the family and the larger society.

It is thus easy to see the transition of larger numbers of middle class women from active suffragist to Moral Prodder. Their perception that women were different from men did not alter simply because the vote was won. In their view, the winning of the vote, though a major achievement, did not portend radical changes in their lives. Although as suffragists they had argued, in a secondary way, that women should be granted the vote because they were men's equal, they were not prepared nor did they wish to assume the role of political equal that followed from that argument. (Few men were willing to view women in such a light either.) Neither did they seek to become men's equal in other respects. In particular, they held, women needed protection in the workplace because they were physically weaker than men and because they had special burdens as mothers and potential mothers. They believed, however, that a new era was dawning in which politicians would have to pay more attention to women's demands. Women had an obligation to become informed voters and a responsibility to educate all citizens about the issues, a concern generally ignored by male politicians. The nonpartisan reform organizations, including the newly formed LWV, were ideally suited to meet these objectives. Entry into politics was acceptable, but partisanship, which ran counter to the public good, was not, for the core of political life, totally lacking in ethical content, appropriately remained a male province.

Why did some suffragists choose the path of Equal Righter

while most others eventually did not? Socioeconomic factors do not account for the preference, for the members of both groups were almost all white, native-born, middle class Protestants. Nevertheless, family environment was a factor. A number of suffragists grew up in families in which women were raised to believe that their sex was entitled to the same advantages as men; in which one or more parent believed in equal suffrage, and in which women were encouraged to go on to higher education. A family like that of Mary Philbrook serves as an example. Philbrook's mother and grandmother were suffragists. Her precedent-setting effort to practice law had parental support. Philbrook also moved in a world of activist, achieving women. She was acquainted with the early woman's rights leaders and knew Antoinette Brown Blackwell and Elizabeth Blackwell, both pioneering professional women. Such individuals were important role models.[5]

A major factor was the impact of the justice argument itself. Although the justice argument had declined in importance by the late nineteenth century, it had remained an integral part of the demand for the vote. More than a reflection of women's belief that they were innately equal with men, the argument also operated to remind and persuade women, both as they campaigned for the vote and after winning, that their existing status in the marriage relationship and in economic and political life was far from satisfactory. The message of the justice argument was carried on by the suffragists and their fellow members in the New Jersey state branch of the WP, who led the drive to improve women's legal status; by their successors in CEDAW and the Women's Non-Partisan Committee Against the Proposed Revised Constitution, who respectively opposed protective legislation and sought a state ERA; and by those who joined the political parties.

The impact of the justice argument on a substantial, though ultimately smaller, segment of the suffragists in the postsuffrage period has been minimized or overlooked by historians who have examined the suffrage movement from a national standpoint. They have characterized the divisions that arose between organized women after 1920 as a clash between the WP and the nonpartisan reform groups over the passage of the ERA. Less attention has been paid to the activities of the suffragists, and other women, in politics and to the degree to which political women's perspective differed from that of their counterparts in the reform organizations. The suffragists who chose to join the WP clearly did so on equal rights grounds, but the same could be said for those women who enthusiastically entered the political parties. The latter believed that women, as voters, should take their place as equals on the party committees, should have a say in the development of party policy, and should hold office. The decision to enter politics was different and dramatic, and most important, it ran counter to woman's traditional place in society, as wife, mother, and social reformer.

Equally important in winning adherents to the Equal Righter view was the suffrage campaign. The women who enlisted in the suffrage cause learned to be assertive, independent, and political. They ran their own organizations, lobbied regularly in Trenton and Washington, and even made periodic trips to see the president of the United States. They shared ideas with one another at state and national conventions. They mounted campaigns respectively to support and defeat friends and foes of suffrage running for office. Organization, lobbying, publicity, and vigorous campaigning ultimately paid off. The fact that the political parties and male voters listened to their arguments and became convinced of the validity of their cause proved to many suffragists that women could ultimately be accepted as political equals and indeed as equals in every other regard.

Why did the Moral Prodders emerge as the more dominant and successful group and the Equal Righters experience disappointment and disarray? Both the social and political environment in which the suffragists operated as well as the suffragists' own tactics and methods explain this outcome. The Moral Prodders' efforts on behalf of governmental reform, improvement of working conditions of women and children, and support for maternal and infant care; their attempts to deal with the problems of the saloon and alcoholism; and their grand coalition to assure world peace were but a continuation of the social feminist activities that epitomized their public endeavors before 1920. As nonpartisan reformers and as well-informed voting citizens, the suffragists and their associates did not seek to alter women's traditional place in society, and they left unchallenged the traditional view that politics was a male preserve. The Moral Prodders' slow but steady efforts to improve the world beyond their homes, but in behalf of their homes and children, thus won approval from men and women alike and advanced their organizational well-being.

The Equal Righters, on the other hand, were entering uncharted political territory and demanding fundamental changes in women's position in society. They sought an equal place in politics and complete equality in their economic and legal status. The response from male political leaders, from legislators, and from most organized women ranged from conditional approval to outright hostility. Nevertheless, there was a potential for concrete change, for events had helped to create an atmosphere in which real change was feasible. The Equal Righters, however, made some major strategic errors. The suffragists who entered the political parties were political neophytes and had unrealistic expectations about their political role. They wanted to be accepted as political equals, but they refused to play the political game. They were not willing to compromise; they were uninterested in party loyalty; and they set themselves above party jobs, the traditional party reward. Their conviction that women had a moral obligation to keep the parties on the right course alienated politicians and eventually undercut their political effectiveness. The suffragists and their fellow members in the WP were initially successful in their legislative campaign to advance women's legal status, but their subsequent narrow focus on the ERA and their refusal to compromise on that issue contributed to the organization's demise. The euphoria after winning the vote had fueled the activities of the Equal Righters, but as the years passed, the expectations about women's political influence declined, and the confidence that women would work together for a federal ERA proved false. By the 1930s the effort in behalf of equal rights had lost its substantial base of support and was sustained by only a small group of committed women.

How, then, does one judge the New Jersey suffrage movement in this final analysis? The vote was won, but the suffragists had hoped for far more: to become equals with men in political life, to pass needed legislation, to create a more ethical society, to improve women's legal and economic status. Certainly a theme of failure runs throughout this study as it recounts opportunities lost by both groups of suffragists. The strengthened position of the Moral Prodders in the 1920s and 1930s indirectly contributed to the failure to win political equality, for it spelled defeat for the view that women, as voters, should focus their energies on direct political involvement. The Moral Prodders' assertion that women had different concerns than men is understandable given the reality of their lives, but their insistence that men and women operated in sharply differentiated worlds—that of the former related to money and power, the latter to people and human values—must be faulted. The vote, by implication, was intended to broaden women's lives, to bring women more fully into the public realm, and to give added weight to their relatively new concerns about the problems of the world beyond their homes. But, in the long run, the Moral Prodders did not take sufficient advantage of their newly won right to bring this about. Their initial enthusiasm for political activism was admirable but proved temporary. The LWV—literally the child of the suffrage victory— with its initial emphasis on political participation, was the one reform organization that promised to be different. But by the 1930s it seemed to have lost sight of this goal and, like its fellow reformers, was stating its distaste for politics (though its position was more subtle) and asserting that women's most important contribution to public affairs was devotion to the facts and strict impartiality. The eventual dominance of the Moral Prodders had another less obvious result. It encouraged male politicians to believe that most women, even activist women, were not interested in sharing political power and that the parties need not fear women as a political force.

The Equal Righters, particularly those suffragists who joined the political parties, contributed more directly to the failure to win political equality. Male politicians, both Republicans and Democrats, were certainly not eager to share power, and it may be that whatever the suffragists' tactics, the male political establishment would have found ways to bar women from the inner circles of political influence. But the suffragists, particularly those in the NJWRC, must also bear responsibility for women's ultimate political decline. Clearly, these women must be praised for recognizing that winning the vote implied political responsibility and offered political opportunity. They rejected the Moral Prodder course and chose to enter the political system. Furthermore, it is to their credit that they sought to retain their identities as women and refused to be swallowed up or taken for granted by the parties. They entered the political arena asserting boldly that they had something to contribute. They expected their insights about social problems and their views about necessary legislation to be heeded.

To their discredit, however, they failed to see that the contribution of male politicians was equally valid. Certainly, men and women enriched and enhanced the political realm working together far more than they could if they excluded one another. But the suffragists assumed that the male element in politics acted out of self-interest and that women had a monopoly on concern for the public interest. The suffragists also assumed that the average female voter and party worker agreed with their position and was prepared to defeat candidates who did not live up to their expectations. Both assumptions proved fatal to their hopes for political influence. The Republican party leaders' disenchantment by mid-decade with the methods of the NJWRC and their observation that the club lacked broad support among party women led to the deliberate replacement of the "independent" women with "regular" Republican women in the party apparatus. This proved to be a crucial turning point, not only for the suffragists in the political parties, but for women in New Jersey politics in general. In particular, the party leaders' growing awareness that women were not united—that most women cared more about party loyalty than equal rights and other issues—was important in establishing a long-term climate in which politicians were no longer prepared to treat seriously women's demands for increased recognition.

The suffragists and their associates in the WP must be faulted in terms of politics as well, for despite their stated belief in political equality, they gave scant attention to the practical effort to improve women's political status by entering the parties. Their approach to politics was purely legal. Passage of the ERA, they came to believe more and more, was the only means by which women could win equality, not only in the political arena but in all areas of life. The NJWP must also bear the responsibility for exacerbating the dissension between organized women over the ERA and the issue of protective legislation. Its reference, throughout the Depression years, to the nonpartisan reformers as meddling "philanthropists" who sought to impose outworn ideas about protection on unwilling women workers revealed its insensitivity to the real concerns of the reformers for the plight of working women in desperate times. The NJWP might have compromised, for example, on the minimum wage issue and accepted minimum wage legislation for women as a stopgap measure until such time as basic wages were guaranteed to men and women alike. Indeed, by 1938 the Fair Labor Standards Act had done just that for interstate trade, and the reformers thereafter sought to have it applied to intrastate trade as well, indicating that they could support equal rights measures on a selective basis. By the 1930s, however, the NJWP had lost the broader outlook and willingness to work with other women's groups that had characterized its efforts a decade earlier and, like its parent body, had become rigid and doctrinaire.

Despite the foregoing rather lengthy indictment, there are other measures of the New Jersey suffragists' success, and their accomplishments are significant and considerable. First, the suffragists, particularly the Moral Prodders, helped women make the transition to voting citizen. They organized citizenship schools, distributed voting information, and ran get-out-the-vote contests. Exuding their tremendous enthusiasm after the suffrage victory, they encouraged women to vote, to join the parties, to run for office, and to press for specific legislation. After 1920 the suffragists and their fellow members in the nonpartisan organizations lobbied for their causes with a new vigor. They felt a responsibility to examine the issues carefully, to discuss their special concerns with one another, and to educate the public about the issues.

Second, their efforts produced results both tangible and otherwise. The suffragists did not "abolish . . . cruelty and injustice," as many of them had hoped, but they had helped to heighten public awareness of the threats to world peace and of pressing social problems and governmental needs, and they were responsible, in substantial measure, for the passage of a number of related laws: The City Manager Enabling Act; the Night Work Law; the pure food laws; the act prohibiting the work of minors in dangerous occupations; the act establishing the Bureau for Women and Children; the Minimum Wage Act; the Voting Machines Act; the Civil Service Act; and the Industrial Home Work Act (passed in 1941), to name an important few. The revision of the state constitution and its approval in November 1947 was the capstone of the Moral Prodders' reform efforts.[6]

Third, and contrary to historians' judgment of the suffrage movement in the nation as a whole, the suffragists' successful campaign for the vote and their postsuffrage endeavors had made a perceptible difference to women and had helped to enlarge women's perception of their proper areas of interest. There were no radical changes, it is true, and the suffragists, both Moral Prodders and Equal Righters, could have done far more with their new political weapon; but after 1920 women's lives were no longer quite the same. Although the Moral Prodders insisted that men's and women's interests were basically different, they helped influence the movement of large numbers of women into the male-dominated public world; and it was owing to the efforts of the suffragists and particularly the Equal Righters that women's political, legal, and economic status had been measurably altered.

The suffrage victory established a climate in which New Jersey legislators and political leaders accepted the fact that women were entering the public realm. There was a tacit understanding that certain old rules governing male and female behavior no longer applied. As soon as the Nineteenth Amendment was adopted, legislators realized, for example, that if women were entitled to vote, they were also entitled to hold office, both elective and appointive, and to serve in a variety of government posts. A law was passed in 1921 making this absolutely clear. Politicians understood that women expected to become participants in party life and governmental affairs. To the Equal Righters' credit, they saw the opportunities and grasped them. Those suffragists who joined the political parties demanded and won equal representation for women at all levels of the party apparatus (matched, as of 1940, in only eight other states), appointments on the boards of education and health, and equal jury status. The suffragists did not gain the political influence they had hoped for, but women had entered the party structure; they were running their own political organizations; and they were holding office at all levels of local and state government. Women's newly won jury rights (matched, as of 1940, in fewer than half of the states in the nation—twenty) meant that men no longer regarded women as too frail and delicate to sit on jury panels where they might hear unpleasant and even shocking testimony.

The suffrage victory made a difference to women in another way. Numerous laws relating to married women now appeared outmoded. The suffragists had sought to improve women's legal status since the nineteenth century, but once the vote was won they mounted a well-organized campaign to bring this about and found a receptive audience in the State House. The nonpartisan reform groups enthusiastically supported this effort, but the state branch of the WP, as part of the NWP campaign to eliminate legal discriminations against women, led the drive and made it its number one priority. Relying on the expertise of the NWP's Legal Research Department, the NJWP selected the laws it wished to see passed and educated the legislators and the public as to how women, particularly married women, were unjustly treated by the law. The unprecedented success of this drive was perhaps the most important concrete achievement of the suffragists on behalf of women, for by 1930 the passage of a substantial body of laws had advanced New Jersey women's rights more than the vote itself and more than the movement into the political parties. Women were now considered mature and responsible adults in the eyes of the law. Married women, like single, could now draw up contracts, execute deeds, and convey their own real estate without a husband's signature; could act as administratrix, guardian, or trustee; could retain their own wages and earnings resulting from work done for a third party in their homes; were considered equal guardians of their children; were entitled to equal inheritance rights; could establish separate domiciles from their husbands for such purposes as voting, officeholding, and taxation; and if attorneys, could retain their maiden names. In addition, fathers of illegitimate children were now legally responsible for the support of these offspring. In 1897 Mary Philbrook had declared, "It is time the statute was removed whereby a woman can plead ignorance of the law as a ground for dissolving an obligation—a thing only idiots, lunatics, and infants could ever do." More than thirty years later this came about; in 1929 a law was passed making a married woman "solely responsible for her torts."[7]

By the early 1940s the suffragists' campaign for legal equality had also helped to advance women's economic status. Women in public employment, namely, school teachers and those in government service, were the main beneficiaries. A law passed in 1925 and another in 1942 forbade discrimination on account of sex in the compensation of teachers in the public schools (including those at the university level), and one passed in 1941 prohibited discrimination among public employees because of marital status.[8]

Fourth, a segment of the suffragists had helped to keep alive the demand for equal rights for approximately two and one half decades after the vote was won. Those suffragists who fought for a state ERA in the 1930s and 1940s helped to bring about the recognition of women as "persons" who had "certain natural and unalienable rights" in the new state constitution—a significant achievement in the long-term drive to advance women's rights as individuals.

Does the New Jersey suffragist experience have relevance for American women today? At first glance it does not, for a great deal has changed. A number of factors seem to have tipped the balance in favor of the Equal Righter position. Women's economic status has considerably improved. According to the 1980 census figures, 50 percent of all women over sixteen years of age now work, and married women make up 57 percent of the female work force. A number of laws prohibit discrimination based on sex in federal and private employment: the Equal Pay Act of 1963, the Civil Rights Act of 1964, and various executive orders issued in the late 1960s and early 1970s. Women are entering professional schools in increasing numbers and proportions, and women are becoming visible, active participants in political life. The number of women holding political office at all levels—local, county, state, and federal—rose dramatically in the 1970s. By 1980 women held 10 percent of all offices in the nation, more than double their proportion in elective office a decade earlier.[9]

Societal attitudes support this movement of women into the public sphere. In 1972 the ERA was at long last passed by both houses of Congress. As of 1978 a majority of Americans approved of its passage. (The time limit for ratification of the ERA ran out in 1982. The amendment fell three states short of the thirty-eight required for ratification. It was reintroduced in Congress in 1983.) A survey in 1972 and another in 1978 respectively revealed that approximately 83 percent of Americans were willing to vote for a qualified woman for Congress and 80 percent would vote for a qualified woman for president of the United States. Symbolic of the national support for equal rights for women is that, for the first time, a woman now sits on the U.S. Supreme Court and in 1984 a woman was nominated for the office of vice president by a major political party.[10]

Contributing to the change in women's political and economic status since 1940 have been the impact of World War II and the woman's movement of the 1960s. The war brought millions of women into the work force, expanded job opportunities for women, and permanently changed the composition of the work force. After 1945 the average woman worker was no longer "young, single . . . and poor" but "married and over thirty-five." Despite a resurgence in the late 1940s and 1950s of the belief that woman's proper place is in the home (bolstered by the return of servicemen to civilian life, a postwar psychology of "getting back to normal," and the revival once again of domesticity with the move to the suburbs), the proportion of women who worked continued to rise. The woman's movement, which flowered in the climate of rebellion in the 1960s—against the Vietnam war and against racial discrimination—was a product most of all of the reality that women were moving out of their private sphere into the public world. The woman's movement gave women a new awareness of their need to be regarded as more than full-time wives and mothers who found total fulfillment in cooking, cleaning, and childrearing. Women demanded greater options in their lives: to advance their education, to combine work with family obligations, and to be able to work in any area of endeavor, not only in jobs deemed appropriate for women.[11]

Although the concept of the separate spheres and the sharp division between the Moral Prodder and Equal Righter views now seem outmoded, a number of parallels can be drawn between the deeper issues which confronted the suffragists and those facing women today. Most notably, the underlying and conflicting meanings of the justice and expediency arguments are still relevant. Women continue to be pulled in the same opposing directions as the suffragists: toward seeking full equality because of their belief in their innate similarity to men; toward a recognition that in many ways their life experiences as wives and mothers are different from those of men. This double pull toward greater individual fulfillment and toward family responsibilities, Degler aptly terms "woman's dilemma," which has yet to be resolved. Indeed, as long as women bear children and nurture them in their earliest years, it is doubtful that men's and women's participation in the world of work and politics can ever be identical.

Another similarity is that the campaign for equal rights, a priority of one segment of the suffragists, still continues, for it is far from won. First, women have yet to achieve economic equality. Although women are now a significant portion of the work force, most are still concentrated in specific occupations which are female-intensive and for which they receive considerably lower pay than men. Thus women are found primarily in clerical jobs, in service industries, in retail trade, and in those professions usually chosen by women: teacher and nurse. In 1981 the median weekly earnings of full-time employees in occupations with total employment of fifty thousand or more was $347 for men and $224 for women. Analysts have concluded that the earnings gap between men and women can be attributed to both occupational sex segregation and sex discrimination. They have also pointed out that we live in a technological society and that if American women are to participate in the workplace on an equal basis with men and share its rewards, they must consider technological careers such as science, medicine, and engineering, which they do rarely. Feminists thus seek to impress upon young women that their occupational choices must be far broader and to impress upon employers and university administrators that women are able to handle numerous fields heretofore considered appropriate for men only.

Women are also far from men's political equals. As Ruth Mandel observes in her study of female candidates for political office in the 1970s, women are still a small minority of officeholders and continue to be regarded as "outsiders" by the male political establishment. Women, Mandel notes, have two major political disadvantages. They generally lack access to financial backing enjoyed by men through their business, labor, and fraternal connections and so crucial to mounting an effective political campaign. They also must prove to party leaders and the general electorate that they are fit to hold public office—not only that women rightfully belong in the political sphere but that in seeking to enter it they are not neglecting their duties at home, to husband and children.[12]

The contemporary effort to win political equality reveals yet another significant parallel with the suffragist experience. That effort still has a tendency to be couched in moral terms. Female aspirants to office appropriately suggest that their active participation in political life can make a difference. Much as the suffragists who joined the political parties in the 1920s asserted that their insights about social problems and needed legislation were necessary to the political process, female candidates and legislators now maintain that women are particularly alert to problems that concern women. They list the following as examples: "day care facilities, nursing home care, battered

wives, the problems of divorced women and displaced homemakers";
"developing objective job evaluations based on the principle of equal
pay for equal worth"; "property rights of married women, pension
and insurance equity for widows and divorced women . . . and reform of statutes dealing with rape and related sexual offenses."[13] But
some proponents of women's participation in politics depart from
this constructive agenda and propose that women can bring far more
to politics. One political analyst, for example, suggests that because
"women have a distinct moral language . . . one which emphasizes
concern for others, responsibility, care, and obligation, hence a moral
language profoundly at odds with formal, abstract models of morality defined in terms of absolute principles," they can bring "a trans-
formed vision of the political community" to political life.[14] Other
supporters of women in politics theorize that women may bring
about a revolution of the entire public realm. They speculate that
women's influence may someday result in a concern for human welfare rather than success, for people rather than profit, and that the
whole frantic tempo of life may be slowed to a more reflective pace.[15]

The vision of these proponents implies, of course, that women
can succeed in creating a better society where men have failed. Such a
position has its risks. If the New Jersey suffragist experience has any
relevance, it is that women assert their moral superiority over men to
their peril, for it guarantees that they will remain outside the circle
of political power and influence. It was their moral viewpoint that
caused so many suffragists to hold themselves aloof from direct political involvement, and it was their assertion that they knew what
was best for the political parties that caused another group of suffragists to be ousted from positions of potential political power. The
assumption that women have a special concern for human values calls
into question men's sensitivity to human needs as well. The interests
of women and society as a whole are more effectively served by a
view that sees men and women living and working together, contributing their unique and similar insights and talents.

Social Characteristics of Ninety-three Suffragists, 1910–1920

	Number	Percentage	Number of single women
Age groups (as of 1915)			
Below 40	15	16	4
40 to 49	13	14	5
50 and over	5	5	3
Unknown	60	64	15
Race			
White	91	98	27
Black	2	2	0
Religion			
Protestant	33	35	8
Catholic	2	2	0
Jewish	3	3	2
Unknown	55	59	17
Nativity			
Native born	30	32	9
Foreign born	3	3	0
Unknown	60	64	18
Residence			
Northern	67	72	17
Central	7	8	5
Southern	10	10	5
Unknown	9	10	0
Marital status			
Married	66	71	
Single	27	29	
Education			
High school or less	11	12	2
Some college or graduate	17	18	8
Unknown	65	69	17

	Number	Percentage	Number of single women
Occupation			
Professional	13	14	9
Industrial worker	1	1	1
Did not work	40	43	17
Unknown	39	42	0
Husband's occupation			
Professional and managerial	32	49	
Unknown	34	51	

Notes

Introduction

1. See Eleanor Flexner, *Century of Struggle: The Woman's Rights Movement in the United States*, rev. ed. (Cambridge, Mass., 1975) and Aileen Kraditor, *The Ideas of the Woman Suffrage Movement 1890-1920* (New York, 1965) for their analyses of the period up to 1920. The presuffrage and post-suffrage eras are discussed in William L. O'Neill, *Everyone Was Brave: A History of Feminism in America* (Chicago, 1969); Lois W. Banner, *Women in Modern America: A Brief History* (New York, 1974). William H. Chafe, *The American Woman: Her Changing Social, Economic and Political Roles, 1920-1970* (New York, 1972) concentrates on the period after 1920. For her analysis of historians' treatment of post-1920 feminism, see Estelle B. Freedman, "The New Woman: Changing Views of Women in the 1920s," *Journal of American History* 61 (September 1974): 372–393.

2. As far as I know, there are only three major state studies of the suffragists in the period after 1920, one on Connecticut and two on Texas. See Carole Nichols, *Votes and More for Women: Suffrage and After in Connecticut* (New York, 1983), and the unpublished doctoral dissertations of Emma Louise Moyer Jackson, "Petticoat Politics: Political Activism among Texas Women in the 1920s" (University of Texas at Austin, 1980) and Judie Karen Walton Gammage, "Quest for Equality: An Historical Overview of Women's Rights Activism in Texas, 1890–1975" (North Texas State University, 1982). Other relevant theses and books are Paul Taylor, "The Entrance of Women into Party Politics: The 1920s" (Harvard, 1966); Marian Roydhouse, "The Universal Sisterhood of Women: Women and Labor Reform in North Carolina, 1900–1932" (Duke University, 1980); Anne Firor Scott, *The Southern Lady: From Pedestal to Politics, 1830–1930* (Chicago, 1970); J. Stanley Lemons, *The Woman Citizen: Social Feminism in the 1920s* (Urbana, Ill., 1973). Lemons credits the "social feminists" with continuing the reforms begun earlier by the social justice wing of the Progressive movement. The experience of the National Woman's Party after 1920 is examined in Susan D. Becker, *The Origins of the Equal Rights Amendment: American Feminism between the Wars* (Westport, Conn., 1981) and Nancy F. Cott, "Feminist Politics in the 1920s: The National Woman's Party," *Journal of American History* 71 (June 1984): 43. For her consideration of the hypothesis that feminism failed after 1920 owing to the decline of female separatism, see Estelle B. Freedman, "Separatism as Strategy: Female Institution Building and American Feminism, 1870–1930," *Feminist Studies* 5 (Fall 1979): 512.

3. Becker, *Equal Rights Amendment*.

Chapter 1: The Demand for the Vote, 1857–1920

1. *New Jersey Minutes of Assembly* (New Jersey Legislative General Assembly). Minutes of votes and proceedings of the 81st General Assembly of the state of New Jersey, convened at Trenton, January 13, 1857, pp. 552–554.

2. The text of this letter can be found in Elizabeth Cady Stanton, Susan B. Anthony, and Matilda Joslyn Gage, eds., *History of Woman Suffrage*, vol. 1: *1848–1861* (New York, 1881), p. 450. There are a total of six volumes covering the period 1848 to 1920. Stanton, Anthony, and Gage also edited vol. 2, *1861–1876* (New York, 1882), and vol. 3, *1876–1885* (Rochester, 1887). Volume 4, *1885–1900* (Rochester, 1902) was edited by Susan B. Anthony. Volumes 5 and 6, 1900–1920 (New York, 1922) were edited by Ida Husted Harper.

3. For a brief biography of Lucy Stone, see the four-page pamphlet New Jersey Broadsides, "Pilgrimage to the Home of Lucy Stone, Orange, New Jersey, August 13, 1915," Special Collections, Alexander Library, Rutgers University. See also Alice Stone Blackwell, "Lucy Stone: New Jersey Pioneer Suffragist," *Civic Pilot* 2 (September 1923): 8, 21–24. For portraits of Lucy Stone and Henry Blackwell, see *Dictionary of American Biography*.

4. For her excellent study of the origins of nineteenth century feminism, see Ellen Carol DuBois, *Feminism and Suffrage: The Emergence of an Independent Women's Movement in America, 1848–1869,* (Ithaca, 1978). The Declaration of Sentiments is Document no. 172 in Henry Steele Commager, ed., *Documents of American History* 9th ed. (New York, 1973), pp. 315–316.

5. Eleanor Flexner, *Century of Struggle: The Woman's Rights Movement in the United States,* rev. ed. (Cambridge, Mass., 1975), p. 83.

6. For their discussion of the role of women in antebellum America, see Barbara Welter, "The Cult of True Womanhood: 1820–1860," *American Quarterly* 18 (Summer 1966): 151–174; Carroll Smith-Rosenberg, "Beauty, the Beast and the Militant Woman: A Case Study in Sex Roles and Social Stress in Jacksonian America," *American Quarterly* 23 (1971): 562–584; DuBois, *Feminism and Suffrage,* pp. 16–22, 46–47; Nancy F. Cott, *The Bonds of Womanhood: "Woman's Sphere" in New England, 1780–1835* (New Haven, Conn., 1977); Carl N. Degler, *At Odds: Women and the Family in America from the Revolution to the Present* (New York, 1980), pp. 26–29, 50, 74.

7. For a background of the early woman's rights movement, see Flexner, *Century of Struggle,* pp. 71–102, 145–158. See also Aileen Kraditor, *The Ideas of the Woman Suffrage Movement, 1890–1920* (New York, 1965), pp. 1–3; William L. O'Neill, *Everyone Was Brave: A History of Feminism in America* (Chicago, 1969), pp. 3–48.

8. The Constitution of 1776 provided that "all inhabitants of this Colony of full age, who are worth £50 . . . and have resided within the county, in which they claim a vote, for twelve months immediately preceding the elec-

tion," were entitled to vote. A copy of the Constitution of 1776 may be found in Charles R. Erdman, Jr., *The New Jersey Constitution of 1776* (Princeton, 1929), pp. 145–151. See also Lucy Stone and H. B. Blackwell, "Woman Suffrage in New Jersey" [1867], pamphlet, in New Jersey Pamphlets, Special Collections.

9. Edward Raymond Turner, "Woman Suffrage in New Jersey, 1790–1807," *Smith College Studies in History* 1 (1916): 167, 170–173, 181–185. Women would show up at the polls, particularly in closely contested elections. Contemporary newspapers were often critical of female voters, suggesting that changes should be made in the election law. An important vote in the county of Essex in 1806 to decide the location of a new courthouse brought about just that result. Voting irregularities throughout the county caused the state legislature in 1807 to write a new election law which strictly limited the franchise to free white men.

10. Stone and Blackwell, "Woman Suffrage in New Jersey"; Blackwell, "Lucy Stone: Pioneer Suffragist," p. 8. See also Stanton, Anthony, and Gage, *History of Woman Suffrage*, 3 : 476–478; Anthony, ibid., 4 : 830.

11. Lucy Stone, "Reasons Why the Women of New Jersey Should Vote, as shown from the Constitution and Statutes of New Jersey," New Jersey Woman Suffrage Association (NJWSA) pamphlet, Vineland, N.J., March 1, 1868, in Special Collections. Stone listed six laws that made women inferior to men: (1) Widows did not share with widowers the rights to the deceased spouse's real estate, if there was no will. Widows were entitled by their dower interest to only one-third of the deceased's real estate, while the widower's curtesy interest was one hundred percent. (2) A married woman could only administer an estate by taking out a bond with her husband. She could only write a will by obtaining her husband's written consent, which could be withdrawn by him at any time. Husbands needed no bond as administrators and could write their wills without the wife's consent. (3) The husband had sole custody of the child and could give custody of the child to someone other than the mother, who had no legal recourse. (4) A child under seven years of age might be given to the care of the mother by the court if husband and wife separated, but the father had preference regarding custody of older children. (5) The estate of a deceased adult child who left no will went automatically to the father. (6) A wife guilty of adultery lost her dower interest; a husband guilty of adultery did not lose his curtesy interest.

12. Kraditor, *Ideas of the Woman Suffrage Movement.* For her discussion of the two types of suffrage argument, see chap. 3.

13. Blackwell, "Lucy Stone: Pioneer Suffragist," p. 8, 21; Stanton, Anthony, and Gage, *History of Woman Suffrage*, 3 : 80.

14. Anthony, *History of Woman Suffrage*, 4 : 822, 828, 830; Flexner, *Century of Struggle*, p. 176.

15. Flexner, *Century of Struggle*, pp. 185–189. The Woman's Christian Temperance Union (WCTU) worked for prison reform, improved care of the sick, and the elimination of prostitution, among other projects. For the relationship of the WCTU to the feminist movement, see Joseph R. Gusfield, *Symbolic Crusade: Status Politics and the American Temperance Movement* (Urbana, Ill., 1963), pp. 88–91. A short but excellent summary of the NJWCTU's suffrage activity can be found in the four-page pamphlet "A Suffrage Quiz," prepared by Mrs. M. E. Lawrence of Salem, New Jersey, the NJWCTU state superintendent of franchise, in 1915, in New Jersey Pamphlets, Special Collections.

16. Anthony, *History of Woman Suffrage*, 4:820. For biographical information on these women see "Early Women Leaders," typed copy of autobiographical notes in Folder 1, Box 1, Mary Philbrook Papers, New Jersey Historical Society, Newark; *Dictionary of American Biography*. The establishment of new local societies is noted in *New Jersey Woman Suffrage Association Minute Book, 1894–1898*, New Jersey Woman Suffrage Association Papers, New Jersey Historical Society.

17. O'Neill, *Everyone Was Brave*, pp. 19–30, 47–48.

18. Anthony, *History of Woman Suffrage*, 4:820–822, 830–831. See also Opinion of the attorney general, *New Jersey Law Journal* 17 (1894): 229.

19. *Suffrage Association Minute Book*. The work of the Committee on Laws Relating to Women is recorded in the minutes of January 25, 1895.

20. Anthony, *History of Woman Suffrage*, 4:828–829; *Laws of New Jersey: Acts of the One Hundred and Nineteenth Legislature of the State of New Jersey and Fifty-First under the New Constitution* (Camden, 1895), p. 366.

21. "Admission to the Bar, 1895," typed copy of autobiographical notes, in Folder 1, Box 1, Philbrook Papers; quotation in *New York World*, February 22, 1894 newsclipping, Philbrook File, Federal Writers' Project, New Jersey Women's Archives (hereafter NJWA), 1890–1953, New Jersey Historical Society, Newark, New Jersey. "In the Matter of the Application of Mary Philbrook to an Examination as an Attorney at Law," *New Jersey Law Journal* 17 (1894): 202–203. See also "A Woman Asks Leave to Practise Law," ibid., p. 93; "She Knocks at the Bar," newsclipping, newspaper unknown, January 27, 1895. Scrapbook 3, Box 4, Philbrook Papers; "Miss Philbrook Wins," newsclipping, June 6, 1896, ibid.

22. Anthony, *History of Woman Suffrage*, 4:823–824. Suffragists blamed the outcome on the failure of urban voters, who had no experience with female school suffrage, to vote for the measure.

23. Harper, *History of Woman Suffrage*, 6:413–414.

24. See Flexner, *Century of Struggle*, pp. 162–166, 180–181, 263–270.

25. An excellent summary of activities of the New Jersey suffrage movement from 1900 to 1920 may be found in Harper, *History of Woman Suffrage*, 6:412–433. See also "Report of the New Jersey Woman Suffrage Association,

November, 1912," Box 3, New Jersey League of Women Voters (hereafter NJLWV) Papers, Ac. 1937, Special Collections.

26. Women's Political Union of New Jersey, "Votes for Women" Campaign Year Book, 1914, Box 1, Amelia Berndt Moorfield Papers, New Jersey Historical Society. Flexner, *Century of Struggle*, pp. 249–253; New Jersey Women's Political Union, 1913, "Minutes of the Suffrage Convention," written by a delegate, headquarters, 79 Halsey Street, Newark, Box 3, NJLWV Papers.

27. Harper, *History of Woman Suffrage*, 6:416–418; quotation from "Jersey Suffrage Growth," *New York Evening Post*, May 15, 1911, newsclipping in Elizabeth Pope Scrapbook, New Jersey Historical Society, Newark.

28. Harper, *History of Woman Suffrage*, 6:420, 431–434; *Manual of the Legislature of New Jersey: One Hundred and Thirty-Eighth Session, 1914* (Trenton, 1914), pp. 183, 185. The founding of the Men's Anti-Suffrage League is reported in *Jersey Journal*, January 28, 1914.

29. Harper, *History of Woman Suffrage*, 6:432.

30. The early background of Alice Paul is described in Inez Haynes Irwin, *The Story of the Woman's Party* (New York, 1921), pp. 6–13.

31. *Suffragist*, November 15, 1913, pp. 5, 10.

32. Irwin, *Story of the Woman's Party*, pp. 40–42, 47–48.

33. *Suffragist*, November 15, 1913, p. 5.

34. "New Jersey Women Have Right to Ballot," *Jersey Journal*, November 12, 1911, newsclipping in Pope Scrapbook.

35. "Carpenter vs. Cornish: Harriet F. Carpenter Petitions for Right to Register to Vote. Miss Mary Philbrook for Relator. New Jersey Supreme Court, April 11, 1912," *New Jersey Law Journal*, 35 (July 1912): 212–216.

36. Mary Philbrook, "Suffrage (2)," typed copy of autobiographical notes, Box 1, Philbrook Papers.

37. Harper, *History of Woman Suffrage*, 6:422–423.

38. Flexner, *Century of Struggle*, pp. 269–280.

39. "Suffragists Will Demand Ballots," *Newark Star*, November 4, 1911, newsclipping in Pope Scrapbook.

40. Lillian F. Feickert, "Should New Jersey Adopt Woman Suffrage," *New Jersey Bulletin* 1 (October 1916): 4–5; see four-page pamphlet "Better Babies," published by National Woman Suffrage Publishing Company, Plainfield, Box 1, NJLWV Papers.

41. Melinda Scott, "Working Woman and the Ballot," *Woman Voter*, 6 (June 1915): 6.

42. See broadsides of Women's Political Union (WPU) of New Jersey and NJWSA in Box 1, Moorfield Papers.

43. See, for example, "The New Jersey Campaign," *Suffragist*, November 15, 1913, p. 5; ibid., October 23, 1915, p. 4; ibid., September 2, 1916; ibid., January 30, 1918.

44. Kraditor, *Ideas of the Woman Suffrage Movement*, chap. 3. The distinctions between those suffragists who stressed sameness and those who stressed difference do not always line up exactly. As Kraditor points out, Elizabeth Cady Stanton, for example, acknowledged woman's role as "mother, wife, sister, daughter" and woman's biological difference, but she argued for equal rights because, above all, women were individuals and had the natural rights of all citizens.

45. The broadsides of the New Jersey Association Opposed to Woman Suffrage and the Men's Anti-Suffrage League of New Jersey are in Box 1, Moorfield Papers.

46. *Elizabeth Journal*, October 24, 1913; quotation from *New York Times*, October 13, 1915. The suffragists were supported by the editors of the *New Brunswick Home News*, the *Trenton Times*, the *Jersey Journal*, as well as the editors of the *New York Evening Post* and the *New York Globe*, both New Jersey residents. See Broadside, published by WPU of New Jersey, Box 3, NJLWV Papers.

47. "Wilson Tells Why He Will Vote for Woman Suffrage," *Newark Evening News*, October 5, 1915. See, for example, Editorial, *Jersey Journal*, October 4, 1915.

48. See scrapbook "Conventions in Newspaper Clippings from 1894–1920," New Jersey State Federation of Women's Clubs Papers (hereafter NJSFWC Papers). SFWC headquarters, New Brunswick. See also *Woman's Journal*, May 15, 1915, p. 155; Joseph F. Mahoney, "Woman Suffrage and the Urban Masses," *New Jersey History* 87 (1969): 160.

49. The suffragists blamed the referendum defeat on fraud perpetrated by the political machines; the fact that the election occurred on a Registration Day preventing verification of voters; the shabby tactics of the liquor interests; the lies of Nugent, Baird, and the antisuffragists in general; and the failure of the immigrant voters in the cities to favor woman suffrage. For referenda results, see Flexner, *Century of Struggle*, pp. 270–271. For evaluations of the results see, for example, *New Republic* 6 (March 11, 1916): 150–152; "The Defeat of Woman Suffrage in New Jersey," *Independent* 84 (November 1, 1915): 168–169; *New York Tribune*, October 21, 1915. In "Urban Masses," Mahoney evaluates the election results in the major New Jersey cities and finds that urban immigrant voters did not stand out as voting differently from other urban voters.

50. *Suffragist*, October 23, 1915, p. 4; Flexner, *Century of Struggle*, pp. 286–292.

51. *Woman's Journal*, December 18, 1915; ibid., August 5, 1916. See also "Proceedings of the Forty-Eighth Convention of the NJWSA, 1916," Box 3, NJLWV Papers; Harper, *History of Woman Suffrage*, 6:426–427.

52. Harper, *History of Woman Suffrage*, 6:426; *Paterson Morning Call*, November 4, 1913.

53. The activities of the state branch of the Congressional Union (CU) are reported in *Suffragist*, March 1916, p. 9; ibid., July 1916, p. 10. For background of both Mr. and Mrs. J. A. H. Hopkins, see Irwin, *Story of the Woman's Party*, pp. 226–227, 267, 300. See "Call to Mid-Atlantic State Conference," CU for Woman Suffrage, Box 1, Moorfield Papers.

54. Irwin, *Story of the Woman's Party*, pp. 124, 193–219, 225–228, 249–255. See also Flexner, *Century of Struggle*, pp. 292–298.

55. "Important Suffrage Meeting, Militants—Soldiers Club—and Antis Discussed," Publicity Department, NJWSA, Plainfield, for release August 15 [1917], Box 3, NJLWV Papers; Lillian Feickert, "Confidential Political Situation," October 19, 1918, memorandum, ibid.

56. The NJSFWC vote to endorse suffrage is reported in Ada D. Fuller, historian, *A History of the New Jersey State Federation of Women's Clubs, 1894– 1927* (Newark, 1927), p. 38, NJSFWC headquarters, New Brunswick; see *New Jersey State Federation of Women's Clubs Year Books*, 1915–1919, in state federation headquarters, New Brunswick (hereafter *NJSFWC Year Book*).

57. The details of the origin of the black federation can be found in the federation pamphlet with caption title "New Jersey State Federation of Colored Women's Clubs, Incorporated," the federation's Carver Center, Trenton. For background of the black club movement, see Gerda Lerner, "Early Community Work of Black Club Women," *Journal of Negro History* 59 (April 1974): 158–167; Alfreda M. Duster, ed., *Crusade for Justice: The Autobiography of Ida B. Wells* (Chicago, 1970). See also Gerda Lerner, ed., *Black Women in White America* (New York, 1972), chap. 8; figures cited on the size of the National Association of Colored Women may be found on p. 437.

58. SFWC membership figures may be found in *NJSFWC Year Book*, 1917–1918. Black federation membership figures as of 1919 are reported in "Elated Over Political Outlook," *Woman Citizen*, July 26, 1919. Membership figures of NJWSA are reported in "Important Suffrage Meeting," Publicity Release, August 15, 1917, Box 3, NJLWV Papers, Ac. 1937.

59. For a discussion of the change in sentiment toward suffrage exhibited by the political machines in several states, see John D. Buenker, "The Urban Political Machine and Woman Suffrage: A Study in Political Adaptability," *Historian* 33 (1970–1971): 264–279.

60. For Governor Edge's position see "Both New Jersey Senators Favor Federal Amendment," NJWSA Publicity Release, January 15, 1918, Box 3, NJLWV Papers; "Confidential to Suffragists," NJWSA, March 6, 1918, ibid. See Flexner, *Century of Struggle*, pp. 291–293; "Jersey Women Fight Sub-Cellar Politics," *Woman Citizen*, October 26, 1918, pp. 438–439.

61. See broadside "The Case against Senator Baird: An Appeal to New Jersey Voters," distributed by the NJWSA, Box 3, NJLWV Papers.

62. "Beat Baird in New Jersey," *Suffragist*, November 9, 1918; "NJWSA

Organizes Fight against Nugent," Press Release, October 23, 1918, Box 3, NJLWV Papers.

63. See "An Urgent Call to Action," typed copy of letter from Margaret K. Basset, president, to membership of New Jersey Association Opposed to Woman Suffrage, August 1918, Box 3, NJLWV Papers; the electoral outcome is reported in Harper, *History of Woman Suffrage*, 6:428.

64. *Jersey Journal*, September 17, 1919; ibid. October 1, 1919.

65. See "Elated over Political Outlook" (see n. 58). For a listing of officers and cooperating organizations, see New Jersey Suffrage Ratification Committee, Box 3, NJLWV Papers.

66. See "New Jersey Campaign," *Woman Citizen*, December 27, 1919. See also Irwin, *Story of the Woman's Party*, pp. 433–439.

67. Harper, *History of Woman Suffrage*, 6:430. See also Buenker, "Urban Political Machine," p. 273.

68. See Irwin, *Story of the Woman's Party*, pp. 418–463, for a detailed account of the chronology of ratification. See also Flexner, *Century of Struggle*, pp. 315–324.

69. "The Memorial Idea," extract from the address of Mrs. Carrie Chapman Catt, president of the National American Woman Suffrage Association, at St. Louis, March 1919, proposal for the organization of the League of Women Voters, Box 3, NJLWV Papers.

70. Citizenship Schools, Newark Women's Political Union, Box 5, NJLWV Papers. See also "New Jersey Campaign" (see n. 66).

71. Harper, *History of Woman Suffrage*, 6:431. See also "Suffrage League Directors Chosen," *Newark Evening News*, April 24, 1920.

72. "Suffrage League Directors Chosen."

Chapter 2: Moral Prodders I

1. "The New Jersey State League of Women Voters: A Branch of the National League of Women Voters Organized in 48 States," pamphlet published by NJLWV, 13 Central Avenue, Newark, Box 7, NJLWV Papers, Ac. 1937, Special Collections, Alexander Library, Rutgers University.

2. Board Minutes, April 30, 1920, New Jersey League of Women Voters, Box 1, ibid.

3. "Annual and Final Meeting of the Women's Political Union," May 24, 1920, ibid. The membership figures of the Newark LWV are cited in the file of the Child Welfare Committee, Box 2, ibid.

4. For citation of the number of suffrage societies in 1916, see Ida Husted Harper, *History of Woman Suffrage* (New York, 1922), 6:426. The number of local leagues and affiliates is reported in Board Minutes, October 25, 1921, Box 1, NJLWV Papers. Membership figures for 1930 are cited in Cor-

respondence, National League 1931–1935, ibid. See also league pamphlet, "Our Tenth Birthday Issue, 1930," Box 3, ibid.

5. Carrie Chapman Catt, "The Memorial Idea," Box 3, NJLWV Papers.

6. League presidents in the period 1920–1930 were: *Agnes Anne Schermerhorn (1920–1921); *Florence Halsey (1921–1923); *Helena Simmons (1923–1925); Mabelle S. Davis (1925–1926). In 1927 Harriet T. Cooke served less than six months owing to family illness. The presidency was resumed by *Helena Simmons (1926–1929); Olive C. Sanford (1929–1931). * = suffragists.

7. J. Stanley Lemons, *The Woman Citizen: Social Feminism in the 1920s* (Urbana, Ill., 1973), pp. 52–53.

8. Constitution and By-Laws, Board Minutes, May 21, 1920, Box 1, NJLWV Papers.

9. "Citizenship Schools Held by LWV of the Oranges, Jersey City LWV, LWV of Plainfield and North Plainfield," Box 5, ibid.

10. Lemons, *Woman Citizen*, p. 50.

11. *Manual of the Legislature of New Jersey: One Hundred and Forty-Fifth Session, 1921* (Trenton, 1921), p. 147.

12. Ibid., pp. 148–149.

13. *Newark Evening News*, September 15, 1920; ibid., September 25, 1920; ibid., September 30, 1920; ibid., November 3, 1920.

14. Ibid., September 14, 1920. See also *Jersey Journal*, September 13, 1920; ibid., September 14, 1920.

15. *Jersey Journal*, September 15, 1920; *Newark Evening News*, September 15, 1920; see editorial "The Women's Vote," *New York Times*, October 25, 1932.

16. Letter from Mrs. Percy Ingalls, chairman of the Get-Out-the-Vote Committee, for general mailing, August 14, 1924, Box 6, NJLWV Papers.

17. Board Minutes, December 17, 1920, Box 1, ibid.

18. Lillian F. Feickert to the Directors of the NJLWV, January 17, 1921, Box 3, ibid.

19. Ibid.

20. Ibid.

21. See the pamphlet "New Jersey State League of Women Voters" (see n. 1); see also "President's Address by Miss Florence Halsey," *Woman's Age* 1 (June 3, 1922).

22. "Tentative Programme for Citizens League," June 15, 1922, Box 3, NJLWV Papers. These citizens leagues never developed as hoped. Little was heard about them after 1922.

23. See E. C. H. Schroers, "Should Women Run for Office," *Civic Pilot* 1 (November 1922): 30.

24. William H. Chafe, *The American Woman: Her Changing Social, Economic and Political Roles, 1920–1970* (New York, 1972), pp. 27–29, 34–35. See also Lemons, *Woman Citizen*, pp. 55–56. By 1925 Congress had passed the fol-

lowing bills: Sheppard-Towner Maternity and Infancy Protection Act (1921); Packers and Stockyard Act (1921); Cable Act (1922); Lehlbach Act, "upgrading the merit system in the Civil Service" (1923); Child Labor Amendment to the Constitution (1924); Federal Prison for Women (1924). The ten organizations representing ten million women on the Woman's Joint Congressional Committee were as follows: National League of Women Voters, General Federation of Women's Clubs, National Council Jewish Women, Women's Christian Temperance Union, National Women's Trade Union League, National Consumers' League, National Congress of Mothers and Parent Teachers Association, the Association of Collegiate Alumni, the American Home Economics Association, the National Federation of Business and Professional Women's Clubs.

25. "Suffragists Will Demand Ballots," *Newark Star*, November 4, 1911, newsclipping in Elizabeth Pope Scrapbook, New Jersey Historical Society, Newark. Board Minutes, March 18, 1921, Box 1, NJLWV Papers. See also *NJSFWC Year Book*, 1917/1918, SFWC headquarters, New Brunswick, p. 39; ibid., 1920—1921, pp. 90—91. The Women's Bureau of the Legislative Department of the SFWC was founded in 1917. It was reorganized in 1920, as the Women's Cooperative Legislative Bureau.

26. *Laws of New Jersey: Acts of the One Hundred and Forty-Fifth Legislature of the State of New Jersey and Seventy-Seventh under the New Constitution* (Trenton, 1921), pp. 17—20, 33, 50, 70—71, 866.

27. Lemons, *Woman Citizen*, p. 65. See also "Married Women's Rights," *Woman Citizen*, July 1, 1922.

28. Ullilla S. Decker and Florence Halsey to Committee Chairmen, February 2, 1922, Box 2, NJLWV Papers; NJLWV Report on Legislation, February 7, 1922, ibid.; Report of Women in Industry Committee, March 1922, ibid.

29. Records of Committees on Women in Industry (1920—1926) and Legislation (1921—1925), ibid.; *Laws of New Jersey*, p. 510.

30. "Brief History of the Committee on Women in Industry NJLWV 1919—1930," Box 2, NJLWV Papers.

31. See records of Committees on Efficient Government, Committee on Production and Distribution of Commodities, and Legislation (1920—1926), ibid.

32. Margaret Porch Hamilton, "The Primary under Fire in New Jersey," *Civic Pilot* 4 (March 1926): 5. See also records of Committee on Efficient Government, Box 2, NJLWV Papers.

33. See records of Committee on Social Hygiene, Committee on Social Welfare, and Legislation, Box 2, NJLWV Papers. See also "What the 148th Legislature Achieved," *Civic Pilot* 2 (March 1924): 16—17; Louise S. Steelman, "Your Affairs at Trenton," ibid. 3 (April 1925); quotation is cited in Louise S. Steelman, "Checking Up on Legislation," ibid. 5 (May 1927): 3.

34. See, for example, Board Minutes, January 17, 1922, January 4, 1923, June 21, 1923, and May 22, 1924, Box 1, NJLWV Papers.

35. See *Manual of the Legislature* (1920–1926), Democratic party platforms, for the evolving Democratic party position: in 1919 outright opposition to the Eighteenth Amendment; following the amendment's ratification, support for "honest enforcement"; after 1923 the "modification" of the Volstead and Hobart acts.

36. See records of the Committee on Limitation of Armaments, later called International Cooperation, 1920–1926, Box 2, NJLWV Papers; Board Minutes, November 15, 1921, January 15, 1925, February 19, 1925, and November 19, 1925, Box 1, ibid. See also *Civic Pilot* 5 (April 1927): 5 for profiles of Florence Halsey, president of the northern branch of the New Jersey International League for Peace and Freedom, and Amelia Berndt Moorfield, president of the State International League for Peace and Freedom.

37. "What the 148th Legislature Achieved," *Civic Pilot* 2 (March 1924): 16–17.

38. Records of Committee on Legislation, 1920–1926, Box 2, NJLWV Papers.

39. Louise Steelman, "Your Affairs at Trenton," *Civic Pilot* 3 (April 1925).

40. The minutes and papers of the 1926 meetings, which were officially called the Legislative Conference of Women's State Organizations Interested in Legislation, can be found in Legislation, 1926–1929, Box 2, NJLWV Papers.

41. Ibid.

42. Ibid.

43. Board Minutes, June 10, 1926, Box 1, ibid.

44. Margaret Porch Hamilton, "Women and Legislation in New Jersey," *Civic Pilot* 4 (June 1926): 8–9.

45. Ibid.

46. Helena N. Simmons, "Putting the League to Work," address delivered at the state convention, *Civic Pilot* 5 (July 1927): 13–14. For Simmons's views on application of the league training in the political parties, see idem, "How the League Stands on Active Politics," ibid. 6 (October 1928): 3.

47. *Newark Evening News*, April 20, 1926; Board Minutes, April 21, 1927, October 20, 1927, November [n.d.] 1927, and May 16, 1929, Box 1, NJLWV Papers. Quotation is cited in *Newark Evening News*, April 23, 1926.

48. Louise S. Steelman, "Efficiency in Government Program for Study and Legislation," *Civic Pilot* 7 (July-August 1929): 14–15.

49. See Second Region, NJLWV Regional Letter 3, Series of 1928–1930, August 10, 1929, Box 1, NJLWV Papers. See also Louise S. Steelman, "The League's Legislative Program," *Civic Pilot* 13 (February 1930): 3–4; Lydia Sayer Walker, "Women in Industry," ibid. 14 (December 1930): 5–6.

50. Steelman, "League's Legislative Program." See also "Some of the

Achievements of the New Jersey League of Women Voters 1923–1939," Historical Statements, Box 3, NJLWV Papers.

51. The first reference to the "spider-web campaign" can be found in Board Minutes, June 9, 1924, Box 1, NJLWV Papers. Simmons remarks to the state convention can be found in Simmons, "Putting the League to Work." Historian Stanley Lemons notes that the "substantial ties" of American women "to an international feminist effort for women's rights and peace" increased in the period after World War I and "alarmed anti-feminists, extreme nationalists, anti-pacifists, and preparedness proponents." The attacks by a group calling themselves the Woman Patriots were aimed at the Women's International League for Peace and Freedom, the National Women's Trade Union League, the Woman's Joint Congressional Committee, and the National Council of Women. See Lemons, *Woman Citizen*, pp. 211–214.

52. "Who Are the Patriots?" New Jersey League of Women Voters, 1927, Publications, Box 7, NJLWV Papers.

Chapter 3: Moral Prodders II

1. Ada D. Fuller, *A History of the New Jersey State Federation of Women's Clubs, 1894–1927* (Newark, 1927), pp. 5–6, 72–78, quotation on p. 6; *A History of the New Jersey State Federation of Women's Clubs, 1894–1958* (Caldwell, New Jersey, 1958), p. 7, NJSFWC headquarters, New Brunswick.

2. See Eleanor Flexner, *Century of Struggle: The Woman's Rights Movement in the United States*, rev. ed. (Cambridge, Mass., 1975), pp. 182–196, for her discussion of the growth of women's organizations.

3. *NJSFWC Year Books*, 1898–1900, SFWC headquarters.

4. See various newsclippings in the scrapbook "New Jersey State Federation of Women's Clubs—Conventions in Newspaper Clippings from 1894–1920," SFWC headquarters, New Brunswick. This antisuffragist position was written by a clubwoman in 1916. See M. E. Swift, "Suffrage for Women a Handicap in Civic Work," *New Jersey Bulletin*, 1 (October 1916): 3, published in the interests of the SFWC.

5. *New Jersey Bulletin* 4 (February 1920): 10. The General Federation of Women's Clubs membership figure cited is in *Woman Citizen* 5 (March 12, 1921): 1066. For reference to SFWC in "Saving the Palisades," see *NJSFWC Year Books*, 1907–1908, 1910–1911; Lydia S. Osborne, "The Part Taken by Our Federation in Saving the Palisades," *New Jersey Club Woman* 1 (July 1927): 3. An account of the SFWC role in establishing the New Jersey College for Women can be found in *History of the NJSFWC, 1894–1958*; and "A Memorial to Mabel S. Douglass," *New Jersey Club Woman* 10 (February 1936): 13.

6. See *NJSFWC Year Books*, 1917–1930.

7. Ibid., 1917–1922.

8. Ibid., 1920–1921, quotation on pp. 19–21.

9. Ibid., 1921–1929.

10. Ibid.

11. Ibid., 1920–1921, p. 19.

12. *Newark Evening News*, May 9, 1930.

13. Cited in ibid., March 14, 1927. See also "Pending Legislation in Trenton, 1930," Lena Anthony Robbins Papers, Box 4, NJLWV Papers, Ac. 1937, Special Collections, Alexander Library, Rutgers University.

14. See *New York Times*, May 12, 1928, and *NJSFWC Year Book*, 1930/1931.

15. NJSFWC Get-Out-the-Vote Campaign, 1924, Box 6, NJLWV Papers.

16. Membership of the CL executive committee in the 1920s is noted in various Minutes, Box 1, Consumers' League of New Jersey (hereafter CLNJ) Ac. 1811, Special Collections, Alexander Library, Rutgers University. Reference to Melinda Scott as "organizer of the United Textile Workers of America" is in Minutes of Executive Committee, December 2, 1921, ibid. Very little is known about the New Jersey Women's Trade Union League (NJWTUL), other than its joint activities with other women's organizations. Scott, "president of a small hat trimmers union in Newark," had organized the NJWTUL in 1917. She had served as president of the New York Trade Union League from 1914 to 1917; see Nancy Schrom, "The Women's Trade Union League of New York, 1903–1920" (Ph.D. diss., University of Wisconsin, 1974), pp. 8, 87–88.

17. William L. O'Neill, *Everyone Was Brave: A History of Feminism in America* (Chicago, 1969), pp. 95–96; see the pamphlet based on the recollections of Miss Cornelia Bradford of Whittier House, Jersey City, "A Historical Souvenir of the Consumers' League of New Jersey, Twenty-Five Years, 1901–1926," Box 1, CLNJ Papers, Ac. 1811; quotation stating CL objective in "Constitution of Consumers' League of New Jersey," ibid. See also the pamphlet "Thirty Years of the Consumers' League of New Jersey," Box 5, ibid.; Susanna P. Zwemer, "History of the Consumers' League of New Jersey," (1900–1950), ibid.

18. "State Legislation Sponsored by the Consumers' League of New Jersey Since Its Founding in 1900," Box 5, CLNJ Papers, Ac. 1811; "State of New Jersey—Department of Labor," Scrapbooks, ibid. See also *Laws of New Jersey: Acts of the One Hundred and Thirty-Third Legislature of the State of New Jersey and Sixty-Fifth under the New Constitution* (Paterson, 1909), p. 221; *Laws of New Jersey* (Trenton, 1912), p. 337; ibid., 1914, pp. 99, 488, 523, 529, 456.

19. Minutes of the Executive Committee, February 20, 1923, Box 1, CLNJ Papers. See also "Memorandum on the Present Organization of the CL of NJ," ibid. National Consumers' League figures are cited in Sophinisba Breckinridge, *Women in the Twentieth Century: A Study of Their Political, Social and Economic Activities* (New York, 1933), p. 65.

20. CL statement that industrial women lack "time, money, [and] influ-

ence" may be found in Minutes of Executive Committee, October 7, 1921, Box 1, CLNJ Papers, Ac. 1811. Reference to handicaps of the industrial woman is in Annual Report of the Executive Secretary, February 1, 1924, ibid.; Scott's statement is in Annual Report of the CL of NJ, February 1, 1924, ibid.

21. "The Night Work Bill Again," *Bulletin* [of the CLNJ] 1 (January 1928), in Scrapbooks, Box 4, ibid.

22. Number of women working at night cited in "When Women Disagree," Box 9, ibid. The 1920 census figures showed that 296,000, or 23.9 percent of all women, were gainfully employed in New Jersey. See Annual Report, March 1928, Box 1, ibid. Reference to the state Labor Department Women's Bureau report, as well as a report of the federal Labor Department Women's Bureau, may be found in Minutes of Annual Meeting, February 20, 1923, ibid.

23. For a history of the night work bill, see "There Is in New Jersey Law," *Bulletin* (October 1927), in Scrapbooks, Box 4, ibid.

24. Ibid. See also "Employers Defy Law Prohibiting Employment of Women at Night," *Union Labor Advocate*, February 1925, typed copy in Federal Writers' Project, New Jersey Women's Archives, Legal Rights, Box 5, New Jersey Historical Society, Newark.

25. "In New Jersey a Law" (see n. 23).

26. "When Women Disagree" (see n. 22).

27. For a full report on the findings of the Women's Bureau, see Henry Raymond Mussey, "Law and a Living for Women," *Survey Graphic* 61 (November 1, 1928): see also 156–158, 194–195. See also "Does Legislation Prevent Women in Industry from Getting Jobs?" *Bulletin* (January 1929), in Scrapbooks, Box 4, CLNJ Papers, Ac. 1811; Annual Report of the Executive Secretary, April 26, 1929, Box 1, ibid.

28. See Report of the Executive Secretary, June 2, 1922, Box 1, CLNJ Papers, Ac. 1811; Minutes of the Executive Committee, June 2, 1922, ibid.; Minutes of the Executive Committee, October 6, 1922, ibid.; Annual Report, February 20, 1923, ibid.; Minutes of Annual Meeting, February 20, 1923, ibid.; Annual Report of the Executive Secretary, February 1, 1924, ibid.; Report of the Executive Secretary, March 14, 1924, ibid.

29. For background of CL activities regarding industrial homework, see Zwemer, "History of the Consumers' League."

30. Report of the Executive Secretary, June 6, 1924, Box 1, CLNJ Papers, Ac. 1811; Annual Report of the Executive Secretary, 1925, ibid.; "An Industrial Health Hazard: Industrial Poison," *Bulletin* (April 1928), in Scrapbooks, Box 4, ibid.; Report of the Executive Secretary, June 11, 1926, Box 1, ibid.

31. *Newark Sunday Call*, October 25, 1925; *Newark Evening News*, October 24, 1927; Minutes of the Executive Board, October 2, 1925, October 11, 1928, and October 11, 1929, Box 1, CLNJ Papers, Ac. 1811; Annual Report of the

Executive Secretary, April 26, 1929, ibid.; "Memorandum on the Present Organization of the CL of NJ, ibid. See also Report of the Executive Secretary, 1927–1928, CLNJ Papers, Ac. 2705.

32. Minutes of the Executive Board, May 5, 1930, Box 1, CLNJ Papers, Ac. 1811; Minutes of the Executive Committee, May 7, 1926, and February 25, 1927, ibid.

33. "Thirty Years of the Consumers' League," Box 5, ibid.

34. "The Consumers' League of New Jersey for the Celebration of Its Thirtieth Anniversary Invites You to Be Present at a Dinner," ibid.

35. *Newark Evening News*, November 5, 1930.

36. "Story of the Year," Report of the Executive Secretary, April 9, 1930, Box 1, CLNJ Papers, Ac. 1811.

37. Fuller, *History of the NJSFWC 1894–1927*, p. 5.

38. "Pilot Publishing Company Elects New Officers," *Civic Pilot* 5 (April 1927): 5.

39. Gertrude Carman Bussey, *Women's International League for Peace and Freedom, 1915–1965* (London, 1965), pp. 7, 20–21.

40. "Report of the Conference on the Cause and Cure of War, Held in Washington, D.C., January 18, 1925," New York, Special Collections, Alexander Library, Rutgers University.

41. See pamphlet "New Jersey State Conference on the Cause and Cure of War," Upper Montclair Woman's Club, January 21, 1926, Robbins Papers.

42. Ibid. See also Board Minutes, January 15, 1925, February 19, 1925, Box 1, NJLWV Papers, Ac. 1937; Report of International Relations Committee, *NJSFWC Year Book*, 1929/1930, p. 98.

43. Ibid. See also "Fourth National Conference on the Cause and Cure of War, Washington," *Civic Pilot* (February 1929): 6.

44. *Civic Pilot* 2 (September 1923): 10.

45. "Report of the Conference on the Cause and Cure of War" (see n. 40).

46. Halsey quotation in Committee on Education for Peace, *NJSFWC Year Book*, 1922/1923, p. 98; "N.J. State Conference on the Cause and Cure of War, January 21, 1926," Robbins Papers.

47. William E. Leuchtenburg, *The Perils of Prosperity, 1914–1932* (Chicago, 1958), pp. 113–114, 117–118.

48. *Jersey Journal*, November 13, 1928.

49. "New Jersey Woman's Committee for Law Enforcement, Miriam Lee Earley [sic] Lippincott, Chairman," *Civic Pilot* 2 (June 1924): 13–14.

50. *Manual of the Legislature of New Jersey: One Hundred and Forty-Fourth Session, 1920* (Trenton, 1920), p. 249.

51. Warren Edward Stickle, "New Jersey Democracy and the Urban Coalition: 1919–1932" (Ph.D. diss., Georgetown University, 1971).

52. *Manual of the Legislature: 1922*, pp. 110–120, 122–123. See also "Dry

Law the Issue in Jersey's Battle," *New York Times*, November 8, 1921; *Laws of New Jersey*, 1921, pp. 171–193.

53. *Jersey Journal*, November 17, 1921. See also *Laws of New Jersey*, 1922, pp. 615–626.

54. *Newark Evening News*, October 1, 1923. See also *Manual of the Legislature: 1924*, pp. 123–124.

55. *Newark Evening News*, October 1, 1923.

56. "The Churches in Action against the Liquor Traffic," Anti-Saloon League of New Jersey, Newark, Elwood Hollingshead, president, December 1925, Robbins Papers.

57. "Statement by the Executive Committee of the Woman's National Committee for Law Enforcement Adopted November 19, 1930," ibid.

58. "Prohibition Facts," Woman's National Committee for Law Enforcement, 1928," ibid.; "A Call to the Convention," New Jersey Committee for Law Enforcement, April 1926, ibid.

59. "Prohibition Facts."

60. "New Jersey Committee of Woman's National Committee for Law Enforcement, February, 1926," ibid.

61. *Jersey Journal*, April 13, 1926.

62. "Plan War on Wet Aspirants," *Newark Evening News*, June 21, 1927; *Jersey Journal*, May 13, 1927.

63. *Manual of the Legislature: 1928*, p. 135. See also "Bills Introduced in the Legislature," 1928, Committee for Law Enforcement, Robbins Papers; *Newark Evening News*, February 21, 1928.

64. "Mrs. Garrison Reveals Why She Regards Prohibition as Needing Sane Modification," *Newark Evening News*, October 2, 1929.

65. Ibid., November 11, 1929.

66. Referencde to the "know your courts" campaign can be found in *Newark Evening News*, November 11, 1929. The campaign was begun in 1925. Women were urged "to know their courts in general, their judges, prosecuting attorneys, district attorneys, juvenile courts, police courts, juries."

67. *Jersey Journal*, May 9, 1930.

68. *Manual of the Legislature: 1931*, p. 137.

69. "Jersey Women Rally to Aid Fort," *New York Times*, May 23, 1930. See also "A Statement by Mrs. Lewis S. Thompson," 1930, Robbins Papers.

Chapter 4: Equal Righters I

1. *Newark Evening News*, September 10, 1920.

2. *Jersey Journal*, September 3, 1920.

3. Gerald Pomper, "Electoral Trends," in Alan Rosenthal and John Blydenburgh eds., *Politics in New Jersey* (New Brunswick: Rutgers University

Press, 1975), p. 34; Alan Rosenthal, "The Governor, the Legislature, and State Policy," ibid., p. 155.

4. Richard P. McCormick, "An Historical Overview," in Rosenthal and Blydenburgh, *Politics in New Jersey*, pp. 13–16, 23–25. See also League of Women Voters of New Jersey, *Spotlight on Government* (New Brunswick: Rutgers University Press, 1969), pp. 5–6.

5. *Jersey Journal*, May 13, 1920; ibid., April 28, 1921; *Manual of the Legislature of New Jersey: One Hundred and Forty-Fifth Session, 1921* (Trenton, 1921), pp. 147–148; see Warren Edward Stickle, "New Jersey Democracy and the Urban Coalition, 1919–1932" (Ph.D. diss., Georgetown University, 1971), pp. 68–71, for his observation that upper middle and upper class neighborhoods voted Republican.

6. Quotation is cited in *New York Times*, April 15, 1928, sec. X. See also ibid., May 27, 1923, sec. VIII, for a similar comment.

7. *Jersey Journal*, May 13, 1920; ibid., September 2, 1920; ibid., September 11, 1920. For Stokes's comment see ibid., September 22, 1920.

8. *New York Times*, May 14, 1922; ibid., May 27, 1923, sec. VIII.

9. *Manual of the Legislature: 1921*, pp. 144–145, 148–149; *Jersey Journal*, May 8, 1920; ibid., September 23, 1920.

10. Louise M. Young, *Understanding Politics: A Practical Guide for Women* (New York, 1950), p. 83. See also Emily Newell Blair, "Women in the Political Parties," *Annals of the American Academy* 143 (May 1929): 218; Marguerite J. Fischer, "Women in the Political Parties," ibid. 251 (May 1947): 90.

11. Blair, "Women in the Political Parties," pp. 217–218; Sophinisba Breckinridge, *Women in the Twentieth Century: A Study of Their Political, Social and Economic Activities* (New York, 1933), pp. 279–282.

12. Four suffragists were elected to the assembly in the 1920s: Jennie Van Ness (1920–1921), Margaret Laird (1920–1922), Agnes Anne Schermerhorn (1922–1923), and Florence Haines (1928–1931). Information was gathered from official returns filed with the secretary of state in the State Library, Trenton, for unpublished paper, Felice Gordon, "Women in New Jersey Politics: Running for Elective Office, 1920–1934." See also *Manual of the Legislature*, 1920–1930.

13. Gordon, "Women in New Jersey Politics"; *Newark Evening News*, September 15, 1920; ibid., September 25, 1920; *Jersey Journal*, September 16, 1920; *Manual of the Legislature: 1922*, pp. 130–131.

14. Stickle, "New Jersey Democracy," pp. 68–71.

15. *Jersey Journal*, April 28, 1921; *Manual of the Legislature: 1922*, pp. 116, 119, 120, 129–130.

16. *Jersey Journal*, April 5, 1922; "The New Jersey Republican," vol. 1, no. 3, April 1923, published by the New Jersey Women's Republican Club, Plainfield, New Jersey, in Lena Anthony Robbins Papers, Box 4, NJLWV Papers, Ac. 1937, Special Collections, Alexander Library, Rutgers University.

17. *Jersey Journal*, ibid.; *New York Times*, May 14, 1922.

18. *New York Times*, May 27, 1923; *Manual of the Legislature: 1923*, p. 128; "New Jersey Republican," April 1923.

19. Quotation in *Jersey Journal*, May 12, 1923.

20. Ibid., September 18, 1923; ibid., September 26, 1924; ibid., September 27, 1924.

21. Ibid., September 20, 1923.

22. *Newark Evening News*, November 7, 1923; *Jersey Journal*, April 12, 1924.

23. *New York Times*, December 15, 1923; ibid., March 19, 1924.

24. Rosenthal and Blydenburgh, *Politics in New Jersey*, p. 114.

25. *Jersey Journal*, April 16, 1926; ibid., April 22, 1927.

26. Ibid., May 11, 1923.

27. Lillian F. Feickert to the Board of Governors, Supporting and Associate Members, and Presidents and Voting Members of Units, June 27, 1925, New Jersey Women's Republican Club, in Robbins Papers.

28. Ibid. See also *New York Times*, July 3, 1925.

29. "Why I Am a Democrat" and "Why Women Should Vote," extension of Remarks of Hon. Mary T. Norton of New Jersey in the House of Representatives, Thursday, April 1, 1926, Speech File Box 5, Mary T. Norton Papers, Special Collections, Alexander Library, Rutgers University.

30. *New York Times*, November 5, 1924; *Jersey Journal*, April 7, 1926.

31. *Jersey Journal*, April 7, 1926.

32. See *Newark Evening News*, October 15, 1924, for statement of Bessie Mention, of Princeton, who had succeeded Florence Randolph to the chairmanship of the New Jersey Colored Republican Women Voters: "I am still for Mrs. Feickert 100 percent," she declared in late 1924, "and I shall continue my state activities in organizing the women of my race as zealously as before."

33. See, for example, *Jersey Journal*, April 5, 1926; ibid., April 14, 1926; *Newark Evening News*, October 25, 1926.

34. Quotations in *Jersey Journal*, April 14, 1926; *Newark Evening News*, November 3, 1926.

35. William H. Chafe, *The American Woman: Her Changing Social, Economic and Political Roles, 1920–1970* (New York, 1972), pp. 27, 29.

36. Emily Newell Blair, "Why I Am Discouraged about Women in Politics," *Woman's Journal* 16 (January 1931): 21.

37. William O'Neill adds a third issue, sexual morality, around which women rallied. See O'Neill, *Everyone Was Brave: A History of Feminism in America* (Chicago, 1969), pp. 264–65.

38. Stickle, "New Jersey Democracy," pp. 353–354. See also *Manual of the Legislature, 1923–1930*; *Jersey Journal*, April 24, 1928; *Newark Evening News*, May 16, 1927.

39. See *Manual of the Legislature, 1927–1930*.

40. *New York Times*, June 18, 1926; *Newark Evening News*, October 25, 1926; ibid., November 5, 1926.
41. *Newark Evening News*, October 25, 1926.
42. "New Jersey Republican," March-April 1926.
43. *Newark Evening News*, April 29, 1927; "New Jersey Republican," March-April-May 1927.
44. Quotation in *New York Times*, January 28, 1928; *Jersey Journal*, April 25, 1928. See also the following broadsides: "Why You Should Vote for Lillian F. Feickert for United States Senator in the Republican Primary May 15, 1928," New Jersey Political Broadsides, Special Collections, Alexander Library, Rutgers University; "Lillian F. Feickert, Candidate for U.S. Senator: A Personal Record," ibid.; "Five Reasons Why Believers in Prohibition Should Vote for Lillian F. Feickert for United States Senator in the Republican Primary May 15, 1928," ibid.
45. *Newark Evening News*, April 14, 1928; *New York Times*, April 15, 1928.
46. *New York Times*, May 8, 1928; *Newark Evening News*, May 9, 1928; ibid., April 28, 1927. See also Lillian Feickert's obituary in *New York Times*, January 22, 1945, for Edward Feickert's comment.
47. See *Manual of the Legislature: 1928*; *Jersey Journal*, April 6, 1929.
48. *Newark Evening News*, November 6, 1929, and ibid., November 9, 1929, for Feickert's comments.
49. Ibid. See also Georgiana B. Miles, president, the Woman's State Republican Club of New Jersey, Inc., to Miss Katherine G. T. Wiley, of the Consumers' League, March 30, 1932, for reference to formation of the new Republican women's organization, Box 1, CLNJ Papers, Ac. 1811, Special Collections, Alexander Library, Rutgers University.
50. *Newark Evening News*, May 28, 1930; *New York Times*, March 25, 1931.
51. See *Manual of the Legislature: 1930*.
52. Thompson, an outspoken dry and a loyal supporter of Feickert, had managed to work amicably within the party framework. She had served on the Republican National Committee until she voluntarily withdrew in 1927, to be succeeded by Margaret Baker.

Chapter 5: Equal Righters II

1. The National Woman's Party (NWP) stated these goals, among others, in its Declaration of Principles, adopted November 11, 1922. A copy of the declaration may be found in *Equal Rights*, February 17, 1923, p. 5.
2. "Historical Sketch of the National Woman's Party," *National Woman's Party Papers, 1913–1974*, Guide to the Microform Collection (North Carolina, 1979), p. 1.
3. Ibid., pp. 1–3; J. Stanley Lemons, *The Woman Citizen: Social Feminism in the 1920s* (Urbana, Ill., 1973), p. 84; *Equal Rights*, September 23, 1922, p. 1.

4. See NWP Press Release, June 20, 1921, Reel 158, National Women's Party (hereafter NWP) Papers, Alexander Library, Rutgers University; see also letterhead of NWP in 1922, listing Mary Philbrook as New Jersey temporary state chairman, Correspondence, Reels 12–16, ibid.; Emma Wold to Paula Laddey, January 4, 1923, Correspondence, Reel 21, ibid.; *Equal Rights*, February 17, 1923, p. 3; *Newark Evening News*, November 16, 1928.

5. "Historical Sketch," pp. 1–3; *Equal Rights*, February 17, 1923, pp. 2–4; NWP Press Release, June 20, 1921.

6. Wold to Mrs. Charles D. Karr, February 24, 1923, Reel 21, NWP Papers; Correspondence, Wold to Mrs. Elizabeth W. Vrooman, February 26, 1923, ibid.

7. Vrooman to Wold, February 27, 1923, ibid.; Vrooman to Alice Paul, March 7, 1923, ibid.; see also *Equal Rights*, March 10, 1923, p. 24.

8. *Equal Rights*, November 23, 1929, p. 336.

9. See Leila Enders to Burnita Shelton Mathews, March 16, 1925, Correspondence, Reel 29, NWP Papers, for example, for names of suffragists who served on the NJWP board.

10. *Equal Rights*, February 17, 1923, pp. 5–6.

11. Ullilla S. Decker, legislative chairman, and Florence Halsey, president, to local legislative chairmen, February 2, 1922, Box 2, NJLWV Papers, Ac. 1937, Special Collections, Alexander Library, Rutgers University; Report on Legislation, February 7, 1922, Legislation 1921–1925, ibid.

12. *Equal Rights*, May 5, 1923, p. 90.

13. Ibid., October 20, 1923, p. 3.

14. "New Jersey Branch Demands Industrial Equality," ibid., December 26, 1925, p. 367.

15. See, for example, *Equal Rights*, February 24, 1923, p. 15; ibid., April 7, 1923, p. 60; ibid., December 22, 1923, p. 356; ibid., June 14, 1924, p. 141.

16. For a description of the characteristics of women in the work force in the early twentieth century and in the post–World War II period, see William H. Chafe, *The American Woman: Her Changing Social, Economic, and Political Roles, 1920–1970* (New York, 1972), pp. 68–69, 76–79, 87, 144–145. For an extended discussion of the history of protective legislation and the arguments of its proponents, see Alice Kessler-Harris, *Out to Work: A History of Wage-Earning Women in the United States* (New York, 1982), chap. 7.

17. See *Equal Rights*, February 24, 1923, p. 16.

18. Enders to Mathews, September 15, 1925, Correspondence, Reel 30, NWP Papers; Enders to Mathews, March 3, 1925, Correspondence, Reel 29, ibid.

19. Wold to Minnie S. Karr, July 17, 1924, Correspondence, Reel 27, ibid. Paul's statement in *Equal Rights*, February 17, 1923, p. 2.

20. Wold to Laddey, January 4, 1923 (see n. 4).

21. *Laws of New Jersey: Acts of the Seventy-Sixth Legislature of the State of*

New Jersey, and Eighth Session under the New Constitution (Somerville, 1852), p. 407; *Laws of New Jersey: Acts of the Eighty-Eighth Legislature of the State of New Jersey and Twentieth under the New Constitution* (Newark, 1864), p. 698. See Channing W. Gilson, "Legal Status of Women in New Jersey," *Civic Pilot* 14 (February 1931): 3–4, 12; Paula Laddey, "The Legal Status of Women in New Jersey," *New Jersey Club Woman* 11 (February 1937): 8–9, 23; Louise S. Steelman, "The Legal Status of Women in New Jersey," ibid. 14 (February 1940): 7, 14.

22. "How New Jersey Laws Discriminate against Women," NWP, 1926, pamphlet in Special Collections, Alexander Library, Rutgers University; see also *Equal Rights*, December 24, 1926, for verbatim copy of the leaflet.

23. See *Equal Rights*, March 24, 1928, p. 53; quotation in ibid., May 5, 1928, p. 101; ibid., May 18, 1929, p. 116; ibid., March 1930, p. 48.

24. Ibid., May 5, 1929, p. 101; quotation in ibid., August 24, 1929, p. 226; ibid., January 18, 1930, p. 339; Mathews to Enders, December 16, 1924, Correspondence, Reel 29, NWP Papers.

25. The NJWP bills passed by the Legislature were the following:

"An act prohibiting discrimination on account of sex in the employment of teachers." *Laws of New Jersey: Acts of One Hundred and Forty-Ninth Legislature of the State of New Jersey, and Eighty-First under the New Constitution* (Trenton, 1925), p. 669.

"An act giving the father and mother equal rights to the services and earnings of their minor children." *Laws of New Jersey*, 1926, p. 333.

"An act to amend an act entitled, 'An act respecting the Orphan's Court, and relating to the powers and duties of the ordinary and the Orphan's Court and surrogates.'" Women both married and single, were given the same right as men to be executors and trustees. Ibid., p. 186.

"An act to amend an act entitled 'An act to amend the law relating to the property of married women.' A married woman gained the same right to bind herself by contract with any person as though she were married." *Laws of New Jersey*, 1927, p. 33.

"An Act concerning the domicile of a married woman. Women were given an independent domicile 'for the purposes of voting, office-holding, testacy, intestacy, jury service, taxation.'" ibid., p. 325.

"An Act to amend an act entitled 'An act to amend the law relating to the property of married women.' All wages and earnings for work performed by a married woman for third persons were deemed her sole and separate property." *Laws of New Jersey*, 1928, p. 422.

Women were given the same rights as men to secure a dissolution of the marriage for want of age. Ibid., p. 139.

Mothers were given equal rights with fathers as to appointing guardians for minor children by will. Ibid., p. 16.

"An Act concerning the support and education of children born out of wedlock." "Any child born out of wedlock is entitled to support and education from its father and mother to the same extent as if it had been born in lawful wedlock." Mothers of illegitimate children may require the fathers of such children to contribute equally to the children's support. *Laws of New Jersey*, 1929, p. 265.

"An Act to amend an act entitled 'An Act exempting mothers of minor children from serving on juries.' Mothers who had actual physical care and custody of a minor child were exempted from jury duty. All others were equally liable for jury service with men." *Laws of New Jersey*, 1930, p. 1091.

The NJLWV, the SFWC, and the NJWRC had regular articles on the legal status of women in New Jersey and listed these laws as advances for the equalization of women's legal status. See note 21. See also "The New Jersey Republican," February 1926, Lena Anthony Robbins Papers, Box 4, NJLWV Papers.

26. Mathews to Enders, November 4, 1927, Correspondence, Reel 37, NWP Papers; for Mathews congratulatory statement see Mathews to Enders, July 17, 1928, Correspondence, Reel 39, ibid.

27. Burnita Shelton Mathews, "Report of Legislative Work from 1921 to 1929," *Equal Rights*, January 4, 1930, pp. 379–381.

28. Minnie S. Karr to Mabel Vernon, March 7, 1929, Correspondence, Reel 41, NWP Papers; R. Gussie Vickers to Vernon, March 9, 1929, Correspondence, Reel 41, ibid.; *Newark Evening News*, November 14, 1928.

29. Reported in *Equal Rights*, May 18, 1929, p. 116.

30. Declaration of Principles (see n. 1).

31. For reference to the 1924 Women in Congress campaign, see *Equal Rights*, September 13, 1924, p. 244; ibid., October 18, 1924, p. 176.

32. *Newark Evening News*, November 7, 1928; Lemons, *Woman Citizen*, p. 191.

33. See Gilson, "Legal Status of Women," pp. 3–4.

Chapter 6: After Ten Years

1. Report on March 26 Suffrage Anniversary Celebration, April 9, 1930, Box 3, NJLWV Papers, Ac. 1937, Special Collections, Alexander Library, Rutgers University; *New York Times*, March 3, 1930; ibid., March 27, 1930.

2. Alice Kessler-Harris, *Out to Work: A History of Wage-Earning Women in the United States* (New York, 1982), chap. 8, quotation on p. 248. The characteristics of the female labor force in the 1920s are also discussed more briefly in William H. Chafe, *The American Woman: Her Changing Social, Economic and Political Roles, 1920–1970* (New York, 1972), chap. 2.

3. For these nineteenth century views of women, see, for example, Ann Douglas [Wood], "'The Fashionable Diseases': Women's Complaints and Their Treatment in Nineteenth-Century America," in Mary Hartman and Lois W. Banner, eds., *Clio's Consciousness Raised: New Perspectives on the History of Women* (New York, 1974); Caroll Smith-Rosenberg, "Puberty to Menopause: The Cycle of Femininity in Nineteenth-Century America," ibid.; Rosalind Rosenberg, *Beyond Separate Spheres: Intellectual Roots of Modern Feminism* (New Haven, Conn., 1982), chap. 1.

4. Chafe, *American Woman*, pp. 100–107. See also William L. O'Neill, *Everyone Was Brave: A History of Feminism in America* (Chicago, 1969), pp. 308–313.

5. Anne Rogers Hyde, "Women Walking on Their Hind Legs," *Harper's* 162 (May 1931): 680–690.

6. Paula Fass, *The Damned and the Beautiful: American Youth in the 1920s* (New York, 1977), pp. 22–23, 80–81.

7. Dorothy Dunbar Bromley, "Feminist—New Style," *Harper's* 155 (October 1927): 554–562.

8. Fass, *Damned and the Beautiful*, pp. 318–322, 328–334.

9. *Newark Evening News*, March 27, 1930.

10. See Oliver McKee, Jr., "Ten Years of Woman Suffrage," *Commonwealth* 12 (July 16, 1930): 298–300; "Ten Years of Suffrage," *Survey* 63 (January 15, 1930): 454; Florence E. Allen, "The First Ten Years," *Woman's Journal* 15 (August 1930): 5–7, 30–32.

11. Emily Newell Blair, "Why I Am Discouraged about Women in Politics," *Woman's Journal* 16 (January 1931): 20–22, 44–45.

12. "Equality in Party Organization," *Equal Rights* 17 (June 13, 1931): 150; *Newark Evening News*, October 11, 1926.

Chapter 7: Six New Jersey Suffragists

1. Helena N. Simmons, "Putting the League to Work," *Civic Pilot* 5 (July 1927): 14.

2. *Bulletin of the New Jersey League of Women Voters* 7 (June 1938): 5.

3. Helena N. Simmons, "How the League Stands on Active Politics," *Civic Pilot* 6 (October 1928): 3.

4. Ibid.

5. Annual Report of the Executive Secretary, May 1939–May 1940, Box 1, CLNJ Papers, Ac. 1811, Special Collections, Alexander Library, Rutgers University.

6. See papers of Consumer Interest Committee, New Jersey Defense Council, Box 3, ibid.

7. President's Report, *Bulletin of the New Jersey League of Women Voters* 8 (June 1939): 2.

8. *Newark Star Ledger*, May 3, 1940; Obituary, *New York Times*, September 7, 1945.

9. Lena Anthony Robbins, "Could Women Rule New Jersey?" *New Jersey Voter*, June 1940.

10. "Women's Part in Lawmaking," newsclipping, 1928, Lena Anthony Robbins Papers, Box 4, NJLWV Papers, Ac. 1937, Special Collections, Alexander Library, Rutgers University.

11. *Trenton Evening Times*, November 21, 1927; *University Extension Record* (published monthly during college year by Rutgers University of New Jersey Extension Division), 3 (March 1929): 1.

12. *Bulletin* [of the New Jersey State Division, American Association of University Women] 14 (November 1943): 3, in Robbins Papers.

13. Biographical information is drawn from Edward T. James, ed., *Notable American Women 1607–1950: A Biographical Dictionary* (Cambridge, Mass., 1971), 3 : 638–639; Obituary, *New York Times*, December 5, 1932; *Stute* [of Stevens Tech, Castle Point, Hoboken], December 7, 1932, Ac. 1811, Special Collections, Alexander Library, Rutgers University; *Civic Pilot* 1 (April 1923): 4; "Women of New Jersey," *New Jersey Club Woman* 15 (November 1940): 8. See also Wittpenn as "The Woman of the Month," front page, *Woman's Journal* 14 (May 1929).

14. Reference to Colonel John Stevens quoted from James, *Notable American Women*, p. 638; citation regarding Camden and Amboy line from *Stute*, December 7, 1932, p. 2.

15. *Jersey Journal*, September 27, 1920; *Civic Pilot* 2 (December 1923): 5.

16. Board Minutes, January 20, 1926, Box 1, NJLWV Papers. See also *Manual of the Legislature of New Jersey: One Hundred and Fifty-Fourth Session, 1930* (Trenton, 1930), p. 453.

17. *Stute*, December 7, 1932, p. 2.

18. Obituary, *Camden Courier-Post*, August 1947, in scrapbooks of the Camden Woman's Club, Camden Historical Society. See also "A True Civic Leader: Miriam Lee Early Lippincott," *New Jersey Club Woman* 22 (October 1947): 10.

19. See papers of New Jersey Woman's Committee for Law Enforcement, Robbins Papers; Miriam Lee Early Lippincott, "New Jersey Woman's Committee for Law Enforcement," *Civic Pilot* 2 (June 1924): 13.

20. *Camden Daily Courier*, August 16, 1920.

21. *Camden Courier-Post*, February 1951, in scrapbooks of the Camden Woman's Club. Lippincott also was the Camden Historical Society's only woman president, serving from 1941 to 1945.

22. Mary Philbrook, "Woman's Legal Status: Should It Be Altered?" *New Jersey Law Journal* 20 (November 1897): 324–327.

23. Quotations are from *Bergen Evening Record* (1950), newsclipping in Scrapbook 3, Box 4, Mary Philbrook Papers, New Jersey Historical Society, Newark. See also Autobiographical Notes, Folder 1, Box 1, Philbrook Papers; "Miss Mary Philbrook, 1st N.J. Woman Lawyer," September 3, 1958, newsclipping in Folder 8, Box 2, Federal Writers' Project, New Jersey Women's Archives, 1890–1953, New Jersey Historical Society.

24. *Bergen Evening Record* (1950) (see note 23).

25. "Chairman of Archives Addresses Woman's Party," *Equal Rights*, May 9, 1936, p. 77.

26. Event recounted in ibid.

27. Mary Philbrook to Beatrice Winser, August 7, 1944, Box 1, Folder 5, Philbrook Papers.

28. "Lillian F. Feickert, Candidate for U.S. Senator, a Personal Record," Broadside, Special Collections, Alexander Library, Rutgers University.

29. *New York Times*, May 27, 1923.

30. "Husband Preferred Blond Mrs. Feickert Testifies," *Newark Evening News*, April 28, 1927.

31. "Woman in Race for U.S. Senate," *New York Times*, April 15, 1928.

31. "Women to Recall Old Fight for Vote," ibid., February 20, 1938.

32. Ibid., January 22, 1945.

Chapter 8: Depression Years, 1930–1940

1. See Board Members, 1926–1949, Box 3, NJLWV Papers, Ac. 1937, Special Collections, Alexander Library, Rutgers University.

2. See Programs of Work-State 1929–1940, Box 1, ibid.; Department of Efficiency in Government, Box 2, Box 6, ibid.; Good Government Council, Box 6, ibid.; *Bulletin of the New Jersey League of Women Voters* (hereafter *Bulletin of the NJLWV*), 1931–1940.

3. Civil Service, Box 5, NJLWV Papers; Department of Government and Its Operation, 1934–1940, Box 2, ibid.; Resume of Activities Authorized by Platform Items, 1933–1953," October 13, 1954, Historical Statements, ibid.; Elections—Party Platform, 1929–1940, Box 6, ibid.; *Newark Evening News*,

September 21, 1934; *Laws of New Jersey: Acts of the One Hundred and Fifty-Ninth Legislature of the State of New Jersey and Ninety-First Under the New Constitution* (Trenton, 1935), p. 944.

4. Programs of Work-State 1929–1940; Committee on Women in Industry, Box 2, NJLWV Papers; Candidates Questionnaires, 1932–1938, Box 6, ibid.; Publications, Box 7, ibid.; Lydia Sayer Walker, "Women in Industry," *Civic Pilot* 14 (December 1950): 5; idem, "Department of Women in Industry," ibid. (March 1937): 11. The passage of a minimum wage law in New Jersey at the nadir of the Depression, after more than a decade of effort on the part of reform and labor groups, reflected changing political attitudes in the nation at large. When, in 1923 in the *Adkins* case, the Supreme Court struck down the Washington, D.C., minimum wage law, finding that it violated women's right to contract, it appeared that similar existing and future laws were doomed to failure. But the Depression and ensuing election of the New Deal administration brought a new willingness to pass such laws with the hope that the Supreme Court would ultimately retreat from its earlier judicial interpretation. See William H. Chafe, *The American Woman: Her Changing Social, Economic and Political Roles, 1920–1970* (New York, 1972), pp. 80–82; William L. O'Neill, *Everyone Was Brave; A History of Feminism in America* (Chicago, 1969), p. 293; see also Minutes, May 18, 1933, Box 1, NJLWV Papers.

5. *Newark Evening News*, May 10, 1935; Equal Rights, Box 6, NJLWV Papers.

6. Bills similar to the New Jersey one were being introduced in other state legislatures. "Women in Industry," *Bulletin of the NJLWV* 10 (December 1939) : 5; Annual Report of Department of Government and Economic Welfare, 1937–1938, Box 2, NJLWV Papers.

7. See Publications, Box 7, NJLWV Papers; programs of Work-State, 1929–1949; Legislation, 1930–1940, Box 2, NJLWV Papers.

8. Lena Anthony Robbins, "The Welfare Issue," *New Jersey Club Women* 10 (February 1936) : 11.

9. See, for example, *Bulletin of the NJLWV* 5 (June 1936); ibid. 8 (June 1939) for an elaboration of this point of view.

10. See Committee on the Legal Status of Women, NJLWV Papers; Box 2, Jury Service, Box 6, ibid.; Elizabeth C. Butterfield, "First Federal Jury Commissioner Organizes Jury Schools," *Democratic Digest*, December 1937, pp. 17.

11. See Louise S. Steelman, Statement on Sterilization, April 25, 1932, Department of the Efficiency in Government, Box 6, NJLWV Papers; Elizabeth MacMillan, "Do We Need A Sterilization Bill?" *Bulletin of the NJLWV*, 8 (May 1939) : 14; Louise S. Steelman, "The Case against Common Law Marriage," February 1939, Department of Government and the Legal Status of Women, Box 2, NJLWV Papers; *Laws of New Jersey*, 1939, p. 624.

12. See *Bulletin of the NJLWV*, 1931–1940; Foreign Policy Committee, Box 2, NJLWV Papers; "The League of Women Voters and Neutrality," 1937, Box 6, ibid.; Candidates Questionnaires, 1932–1938, ibid.; J. Stanley Lemons, *The Woman Citizen: Social Feminism in the 1920s* (Urbana, Ill., 1973), p. 231.

13. *Bulletin of the NJLWV* 10 (June 1940), p. 2.

14. Lena Anthony Robbins, "Could Women Rule New Jersey?" *New Jersey Voter*, June 1940, p. 5.

15. *Bulletin of the NJLWV* 8 (June 1939), p. 2.

16. Robbins, "Could Women Rule New Jersey?"

17. See *NJSFWC Year Book*, 1930/1931, 1935/1936, SFWC headquarters, New Brunswick.

18. For the activities of the federation departments, see *NJSFWC Year Book*, 1930–1940. See also Ruth Johnson Keeth, "Department of International Relations," *New Jersey Club Woman* 10 (February 1935): 8, for federation's peace position.

19. See, for example, *NJSFWC Year Book*, 1930/1931.

20. C. L. Reagan, "Noblesse Oblige of the Ballot," *New Jersey Club Woman* 10 (February 1936): n. p.

21. "Party Politics and the Lady," *New Jersey Club Woman* 12 (February 1938): 14.

22. See, for example, *NJSFWC Year Book*, 1938/1939, p. 13.

23. Reagan, "Noblesse Oblige of the Ballot."

24. See *NJSFWC Year Book*, 1950/1951; national membership figures cited in *New York Times*, April 21, 1940.

25. *New Jersey Club Woman*, 15 (May 1941): 7.

26. Corrspondence, Box 2, CLNJ Papers, Ac. 1811, Special Collections, Alexander Library, Rutgers University.

27. See "The Industrial Standards Committee of New Jersey," ibid.

28. "Story of the Year," Report of the Executive Secretary, April 22, 1931, Box 1, ibid.

29. For an account to the CL's legislative program, see Minutes of the Executive Board, Reports of the Executive Secretary, Box 1, ibid.; Correspondence, Box 2, ibid.; Scrapbooks, Box 6, ibid.

30. See Industrial Standards Committee, Box 3, ibid.

31. These comments may be found in Helena Simmons to Senator William Albright, n.d. [probably March 1933], Box 2, ibid. Both old and new arguments are used in this letter. See also Simmons to Albright, March 17, 1933, ibid.; Simmons to Mrs. F. R. Kellogg, March 9, 1933, ibid.

32. See Simmons to Hon. Doyden Kuser, April 26, 1932; Miles's statement about CL bills cited in Simmons to Mrs. George H. Miles, March 17, 1932, ibid. Simmons to Summers, April 15, 1932, ibid.; Miles's statement about 48-hour bill cited in Simmons to Summers, March 17, 1932, ibid.; Simmons to Mary Norton, January 3, 1938, ibid.; Norton to Simmons, Janu-

234 / Notes to Pages 153–157

ary 5, 1938, ibid.; Simmons to Norton, January 28, 1940, ibid.; Simmons to Norton, January 30, 1940, ibid.; Report of the Executive Secretary, February 11, 1938–March 11, 1938, Box 1, ibid.; Report of the Executive Secretary, March 11, 1938–April 8, 1938, ibid.; Simmons to Dorothy Kenyon, February 3, 1938, Box 9, ibid.; "The Industrial Standards Committee of New Jersey," Box 2, ibid.

33. See Minutes of the Executive Board and Reports of the Executive Secretary, Box 1, ibid.; quotation may be found in Minutes of the Executive Board, October 11, 1934, ibid.

34. The CL's financial crises is reported in *Newark Evening News*, September 28, 1932; ibid., October 21, 1932. Membership figures in *Newark Evening News*, September 28, 1932; Minutes of the Executive Board, January 7, 1932, Box 1, CLNJ Papers; Minutes of the Annual Meeting, May 23, 1933, ibid.; Report of the Executive Secretary, May 12, 1936, ibid.; Minutes of the Annual Meeting, May 26, 1939, ibid. For General Federation membership figures see Scrapbooks, Charlotte Williams, General Federation secretary to membership, 1939, CLNJ Papers.

35. President's Report, April 1934, Box 1, ibid.; for a general picture of Simmons's activities, see Reports of the Executive Secretary, especially February 1936 and April 1937, ibid.

36. Quotation in Report of the Executive Secretary, January 27, 1939–February 23, 1938, ibid.

37. Report of the Executive Secretary, May 6, 1938–May 25, 1939, ibid.

38. See *Newark Evening News*, April 13, 1934; ibid., May 1, 1935; ibid., May 13, 1936; ibid., September 20, 1939; Women's International League for Peace and Freedom, State Executive Board, 1936, Box 4, MG 830, Federal Writers' Project, New Jersey Women's Archives, 1890–1953, New Jersey Historical Society (hereafter NJWA). See pamphlet of New Jersey Committee on the Cause and Cure of War, February 8, 9, 10, 1937, New Jersey Broadsides, Special Collections, Alexander Library, Rutgers University.

39. For a survey of international affairs in the 1930s and the response of the Roosevelt administration, see William E. Leuchtenburg, *Franklin D. Roosevelt and the New Deal, 1932–1940* (New York, 1963), pp. 197–230, 275–298.

40. *Jersey Journal*, April 21, 1933.

41. *Newark Evening News*, September 8, 1933; ibid., April 13, 1934; ibid., September 4, 1935; *Jersey Journal*, October 25, 1935; *New Jersey Club Woman* 10 (April 1935): 11. Pamphlets of the New Jersey Committee on the Cause and Cure of War, 1930–1940; *Newark Evening News*, November 3, 1937; Tenth Conference of the New Jersey Committee on the Cause and Cure of War, Foreign Policy Committee, Box 2, NJLWV Papers.

42. Leadership Institute pamphlet "New Jersey Committee on the Cause and Cure of War," Leadership Institute Chairman Mrs. Frederic Beggs, April 6, 1938, New Jersey Broadsides, Special Collections.

43. *Newark Evening News*, September 20, 1939.

44. *New Jersey Club Woman* 13 (February 1939): 3, 14; ibid. (November 1939): 19; *Bulletin of the NJLWV* 10 (February 1940): 6.

45. See New Jersey Committee for Law Enforcement, Lena Anthony Robbins Papers, Box 4, NJLWV Papers, Ac. 1937.

46. Miriam Early Lippincott to "Daughters of the Constitution," January 8, 1931, ibid.

47. Lippincott to "Friend," October 6, 1931, ibid.

48. *Jersey Journal*, October 10, 1931; ibid., May 25, 1932; see CFLE Broadside, "How Can I Vote Against Repeal?" Robbins Papers.

49. "How Can I Vote Against Repeal?"

50. Lippincott to Robbins, October 25, 1932, Robbins Papers. In this correspondence Lippincott notes that there was four dollars in the treasury and thirty-five dollars in debts.

51. Leuchtenberg, *Roosevelt and the New Deal*, pp. 46–47; *Newark Evening News*, November 8, 1933.

52. The number of women running for state and county office as Democrats and Republicans between 1920 and 1929 was as follows:

Year	Number of women running	Year	Number of women running
1920	7	1930	15
1921	7	1931	15
1922	13	1932	16
1923	13	1933	14
1924	15	1934	15
1925	18	1935	17
1926	17	1936	13
1927	18	1937	13
1928	13	1938	12
1929	11	1939	12

Information was gathered from official returns filed with the secretary of state in the State Library, Trenton.

53. The number of women elected to the assembly between 1920 and 1929 was as follows:

Year	Number of women elected	Year	Number of women elected
1920	2	1930	6
1921	2	1931	4
1922	3	1932	6

Year	Number of women elected	Year	Number of women elected
1923	4	1933	5
1924	5	1934	6
1925	7	1935	5
1926	9	1936	5
1927	7	1937	5
1928	6	1938	5
1929	6	1939	5

See *Manual of the Legislature of New Jersey* (Trenton, 1921–1940).

54. Ibid.; see *Manual of the Legislature of New Jersey: One Hundred and Sixty-Third Session, 1939*, pp. 392–393, for biography of Thelma Parkinson.

55. See *Newark Evening News*, October 10, 1927, for 1927 figures; Report of Women in Public Office in New Jersey, 1935, Efficiency in Government Committee, Box 2, NJLWV Papers.

56. Suffragists held the following positions in the party organizations as well as elective and appointive offices in the 1930s:

Lillian Feickert	State Council of Republican Women, president
Margaret Laird	Newark Women's Republican Club, president
Florence Haines	Newark Eighth Ward Women's Republican Club, president; assemblywoman, 1930–1932; State Rehabilitative Commission for Physically Handicapped
Geraldine L. Thompson	Women's State Republican Club, vice chairman; Republican State Committee, 1933–1940; Board of Control of Institutions and Agencies
Edith Hyde Colby	Women's State Republican Club, Board of Governors
Amelia Moorfield	Essex County Women's Republican Club, president
Beatrice Stern	State Board of Children's Guardians
Agnes Cromwell	State Board of Education
Helena Simmons	Democratic Women's Luncheon Club, president; Sanitorium for Tuberculosis Diseases, Glen Gardner
Bertha Shippen Irving	Postmistress, Haddonfield, 1933
Bessie Pope	State Home for Boys, Jamesburg

Caroline Wittpenn   Board of Control of Institutions and
Agencies
Rose Anne Billington   Democratic National Committee,
1930−1940

57. *Jersey Journal*, April 21, 1932; *New York Times*, March 25, 1931.

58. See Georgianna B. Miles to Katherine G. T. Wiley, March 30, 1932, listing Thompson as vice president on letterhead, *Equal Rights*, Box 9, CLNJ Papers; *New York Times*, April 7, 1931.

59. *New York Times*, April 28, 1931. "The committee submitted the following list of positions for which women were considered eligible: women as assistants to attorney general. A woman assistant purchasing agent. At least one woman juvenile court judge and support of legislation to permit this. At least two women on State Board of Health. At least two women on State Highway Commission. At least one woman on State Board of Tax Appeals. One woman at least on every county tax board. At least one woman on every county election board. Two women as motor vehicle agents in each first-class county and one woman agent in the others. At least two women on the Legislative Conference Committee, one woman in the Congressional delegation and two women on the Tenement House Commission. At least two as members of the State Board of Conservation and Development, two on the Public Library Commission and two on the Civil Service Commission."

60. *Jersey Journal*, April 28, 1931.

61. See, for example, Editorial, ibid.; the contents of Baird's letter is reported in *Newark Evening News*, May 18, 1931, and *New York Times*, May 19, 1931.

62. *Newark Evening News*, April 28, 1931; ibid., May 14, 1931.

63. Ibid., May 25, 1931; ibid., May 27, 1931.

64. *New York Times*, June 9, 1931.

65. "Hoover Greets Mrs. Feickert, Glad to Get Her Pledge of New Jersey Support," *Jersey Journal*, April 21, 1932.

66. *Equal Rights*, February 20, 1932; *Manual of the Legislature of New Jersey: 1936*, p. 138; ibid.: *1937*, p. 139; *Newark Evening News*, May 20, 1936.

67. See, for example, *Jersey Journal*, September 21, 1931; *Newark Evening News*, October 9, 1931.

68. Quoted in *Equal Rights*, July 27, 1935, p. 164. Although there was a dramatic increase in the number of women serving in appointive posts in the New Deal administration, national figures on women's electoral performance in the 1930s gave a more accurate accounting of women's political standing in the nation. The number of women elected to Congress had remained stable, ranging from eight to nine from 1929 to 1940. The total of women elected to the state legislatures declined from 149 in 1929 to 130 in 1939. See Louise M. Young, *Understanding Politics: A Practical Guide for Women* (New York, 1950), pp. 206, 305−309.

69. *Newark Evening News*, September 8, 1933; ibid., April 25, 1938. These objectives are those of the National Order of Women Legislators, whose goals were described as "almost identical with those of the OWLs of New Jersey."

70. Ibid., October 25, 1933; ibid., April 9, 1934; ibid., April 17, 1937; ibid., May 10, 1937; ibid., September 20, 1937; ibid., May 25, 1938.

71. Ibid., May 24, 1939; ibid., April 3, 1940.

72. For a description of this view of the 1920s, see Henry F. May, "Shifting Perspectives on the 1920's," *Mississippi Valley Historical Review* 43 (December 1956): 405–427.

73. See, for example, the Democratic platform adopted in 1938 in *Manual of the Legislature of New Jersey: 1939*, p. 137.

74. "Historical Sketch of the National Woman's Party," *National Woman's Party Papers*, 1913–1974, The Guide to the Microform Collection (North Carolina, 1979), pp. 2–3.

75. *Equal Rights*, January 2, 1932, p. 382. See also ibid., November 7, 1931, p. 316; Correspondence, Reel 54, NWP Papers, Alexander Library, Rutgers University.

76. See Leila Enders to Burnita Shelton Mathews, March 24, 1931, Correspondence, Reel 45, NWP Papers; *Equal Rights*, April 4, 1931, p. 71; ibid., September 22, 1934, p. 264; *Newark Evening News*, April 29, 1936.

77. See Enders to Elsie Hill, January 13, 1932, Correspondence, Reel 47, NWP Papers, for listing of New Jersey Woman's Party state officers.

78. Quoted in *Equal Rights*, March 19, 1932, p. 55; see also "New Jersey Introduces Nefarious Legislation," ibid., March 12, 1932, pp. 47–48; ibid., March 26, 1932, p. 62; ibid., July 2, 1932, p. 176.

79. *Newark Evening News*, April 19, 1933.

80. Clara Snell Wolfe to Mary Philbrook, March 13, 1940, Folder 2, Box 2, Philbrook File, NJWA. See also Wolfe to Enders, March 19, 1940, ibid.

81. Nancy F. Cott, "Feminist Politics in the 1920s: The National Woman's Party," *Journal of American History* 71 (June 1984): 43.

82. Mary Philbrook, "New Jersey Women Battle for Equal Rights," *Equal Rights*, May 1, 1938, pp. 253–254.

83. Committee to Eliminate Discriminations Against Women, Folder 4, Box 2, Mary Philbrook Papers, New Jersey Historical Society, Newark.

84. Mary Philbrook to Party Leaders, September 20, 1938, Box 9, CLNJ Papers; *Manual of the Legislature of New Jersey: 1939*, pp. 37, 150; ibid.: *1940*, pp. 134, 141.

85. *Newark Evening News*, May 20, 1939.

86. "New Jersey Bar Studies Status of Women," *Equal Rights*, June 15, 1938, pp. 275–276; Resolution of New Jersey State Federation of Colored Women's Clubs, January 18, 1940, Folder 7, Box 1, Philbrook File, NJWA;

Statement by A. Harry Moore, governor of New Jersey, March 20, 1940, Folder 4, Box 2, Philbrook Papers.

87. See Press Release of National Woman's Party, March 21, 1940, Folder 3, Box 2, NJWA, for reference to Mary Norton's statement to Mary Philbrook, as well as Norton to Simmons, January 30, 1940, Box 9, CLNJ Papers, in which Norton corroborates her statement and notes "that there is much discrimination against women."

88. Reference to the Republican "failure . . . to support their own platform" is in Philbrook to Republican Legislators, April 20, 1940, Folder 2, Box 2, NJWA

Chapter 9: Equal Rights and the State Constitution, 1940–1947

1. See Board of Directors, New Jersey League of Women Voters, 1940, Box 3, NJLWV Papers, Ac. 1937, Special Collections, Alexander Library, Rutgers University; "History of the Movement for Revision of the New Jersey Constitution," Box 5, ibid.; Board Minutes, February 26, 1941, Box 1, ibid.

2. "History of the Movement for Revision"; Minutes, February 24 [1941] Meeting Citizens' State Committee for Constitutional Convention, Box 5, NJLWV Papers; Minutes of March 13 Meeting of Executive Committee Authorized by Meeting of February 24, ibid.; Richard N. Baisden, *Charter for New Jersey: The New Jersey Constitutional Convention of 1947* (Trenton, 1952), p. 6.

3. "Should New Jersey Have a Constitutional Convention?" *Bulletin of the NJLWV* 10 (January 1941); "Has New Jersey a 'Horse and Buggy' Constitution?" ibid. (February 1941); "What Do We Mean—A Good Constitution?" ibid. (March 1941); "New Jersey's State Convention," ibid. (May 1941); "Constitution Primer," *New Jersey Voter*, July 1941; Governor's Edison's statement is quoted in *Asbury Park Evening Press*, November 9, 1940; 1941 Democratic and Republican party platforms are in *Manual of the Legislature of New Jersey: One Hundred and Sixty-Sixth Session, 1941*, (Trenton, 1941), pp. 134, 138.

4. Board Minutes, January 8, 1941, Box 1, NJLWV Papers.

5. "Report of the Commission on Revision of the New Jersey Constitution, 1942," State of New Jersey, Trenton, Box 5, NJLWV Papers.

6. "History of the Movement for Revision"; Richard J. Connors, "The Movement for Constitutional Revision in New Jersey, 1941–1947 (master's thesis, Columbia University, 1955), pp. 60–61.

7. *Bulletin of the NJLWV* 14 (October, 1944).

8. Connors, "Movement for Constitutional Revision," pp. 71–80. Jane

Barus, "Report on Constitutional Revision in New Jersey, 1940–1947," May 1948, p. 7, Box 5, NJLWV Papers.

9. See newsclipping "Women in Politics," *Newark Evening News*, January (n.d.) 1940, Equal Rights, Box 5, CLNJ Papers, Ac. 1811, Special Collections, Alexander Library, Rutgers University; see also Women's Consultative Committee on Constitutional Amendments, Folder 4, Box 2, Mary Philbrook Papers, New Jersey Historical Society, Newark. In her capacity as acting chairman of the New Jersey state branch of the Woman's Party between 1940 and 1942, Philbrook kept the Washington office aware of the drive for a state ERA. During her tenure the NJWP remained an organization in name only. Toward the end of 1942 she was succeeded by Anna B. Hogan, of Jersey City, as the NWP sought to reactivate state support for the federal ERA. See Philbrook to Alice Paul, November 30, 1942, Folder 4, Box 1, Philbrook Papers.

10. See *Laws of New Jersey: Acts of the One Hundred and Sixty-Fifth Legislature of the State of New Jersey and Ninety-Seventh under the New Constitution* (Trenton, 1940), p. 970; see also *Newark Evening News*, December 13, 1941.

11. Mary Philbrook, "The Case for Equal Rights," *New Jersey Club Woman*, February 1942, pp. 12–13, 17; Marion E. Cox to Philbrook, February 2, 1942, Folder 4, Box 1, Philbrook Papers; for CL reaction to SFWC publication of Philbrook's article, see Mary Dyckman [CL vice president] to Mrs. John J. Cox, February 8, 1942, Box 9, Equal Rights, CLNJ Papers; Dyckman to Cox, February 10, 1942, ibid.

12. For a record of the activities of the Committee to Eliminate Discriminations Against Women and the passage of equal rights legislation in the early 1940s, see, for example, *Newark Evening News*, January 27, 1940; ibid., June 11, 1941; ibid., December 3, 1941; ibid., December 13, 1941; ibid., February 4, 1941; ibid., April 29, 1942; ibid., September 19, 1942; ibid., October 10, 1942. The measure to allow a married woman attorney admitted to the bar under her maiden name to continue her practice under that name was proposed to the state legislature at the request of a female Newark attorney. It passed the senate 15–0 and the house 15–1; see *Newark Evening News*, November 19, 1941. *Newark Star Ledger*, May 7, 1940.

13. Philbrook to H. Alexander Smith, June 22, 1942, Folder 4, Box 1, Philbrook Papers; see also Philbrook to Smith, July 21, 1942, ibid.; ibid., July 26, 1942, ibid.; ibid. August 7, 1942, ibid.; Frank Hague to Philbrook, August 31, 1943, ibid.

14. Press Release, August 31, 1941, Folder 4, Box 2, ibid.

15. See the Women's Non-Partisan Committee Against the Proposed Revised Constitution, Folder 2, Box 1, ibid.

16. Edison's statement is quoted in *New York Times*, November 22, 1941; *Newark Evening News*, November 3, 1943; *Jersey Journal*, November 3, 1943.

17. Connors, "Movement for Constitutional Revision," pp. 60–61.

18. See *Manual of the Legislature of New Jersey: 1945*, p. 142; Mary Phil-

brook's autobiographical notes entitled "Equal Rights," Folder 1, Box 1, Philbrook Papers; editorial "N.J. Women Organize to Beat New Constitution," *Jersey Journal*, July 27, 1944.

19. "History of the Movement for Revision"; *NJSFWC Year Book*, 1940–1941 (in the NJSFWC headquarters, New Brunswick), p. 29; Minutes of Annual Meeting, May 3, 1944, Box 1, CLNJ Papers; *Bulletin of the NJLWV* 14 (October 1944).

20. See broadside "Women's Rights Are Not in Danger!" in *Bulletin of the NJLWV* 14 (September 1944); see also broadside "Women's Rights Are Protected!" in Box 5, NJLWV Papers; CLNJ *News Letter*, October 14, 1944, Box 4, Scrapbooks, CLNJ Papers.

21. Connors, "Movement for Constitutional Revision," pp. 83–85. Edge quoted in *Jersey Journal*, November 6, 1944; see also ibid., November 8, 1944; editorial "An Outrageous Campaign," *Newark Evening News*, November 6, 1944; ibid., November 8, 1944.

22. Connors, "Movement for Constitutional Revision," pp. 88–89; Baisden, *Charter for New Jersey*, pp. 7, 149; *Bulletin of the NJLWV* 14 (November 1944).

23. Emma Dillon to Philbrook, November 8, 1944, Folder 5, Box 1; Philbrook Papers; Philbrook to Beatrice Winser, December 26, 1944, Women's Rights, Folder 2, Box 1, ibid.

24. *Manual of the Legislature of New Jersey: 1947*, pp. 704–707; "New Jersey Constitutional Revision, 1944–1947 and the Part Played by the League of Women Voters," Box 5, NJLWV Papers; *Bulletin of the NJLWV* 16 (February 1947).

25. "New Jersey Constitutional Revision"; Papers of Women's Alliance for Equal Status, Folders 1, 4, Box 2, and Folder 5, Box 1, Philbrook Papers. It is not clear if the New Jersey Education Association was a member of the alliance. In 1953 Gussie Vickers wrote a summary of the activities of the Alliance for Equal Status to the members of the council of the NWP: "Miss Mary Philbrook, a brilliant and able lawyer had organized these women into the Alliance of which I was made President. One of the constituent groups, she tells me, consisted of 28,000 teachers and educators." See Gussie Vickers to the Members of the Council of the National Woman's Party, November 9, 1953, Folder 5, Box 1, ibid. But, when representatives of the New Jersey Education Association appeared before the Committee on Rights and Privileges, no mention was made of support for the alliance or for the ERA. For Simmons's obituary see *Newark Evening News*, October 12, 1942.

26. Barus, "Report on Constitutional Revision."

27. *State of New Jersey, Constitutional Convention of 1947*, vol. 3: *Committee on Rights, Privileges, Amendments and Miscellaneous Provisions and Committee on the Legislative Record* (Trenton, 1947), pp. 356–361, 462–464. "New Jersey Constitutional Revision"; Vickers to the Members of the Council of the Na-

tional Woman's Party, November 9, 1953, Folder 5, Box 1, Philbrook Papers.

28. *NJSFWC Year Book*, 1944–1945, p. 29; "Action Taken by Board of Trustees re Equal Rights Amendment," November 9, 1943, NJSFWC, in Box 9, Equal Rights, CLNJ Papers; Mary Barbehenn to Philbrook, August 27, 1947, Folder 5, Box 1, Philbrook Papers; "Statement made by the President of the New Jersey State Federation of Women's Clubs, Mrs. Robert W. Cornelison, at a hearing on Rights, Privileges and Amendments, of the Constitutional Convention of the State of New Jersey, New Brunswick, N.J.," ibid.; *New Jersey, Constitutional Convention of 1947*, pp. 404–405.

29. "State Bar Committee Reports," Committee to Study the Status of Women, adopted by the N.J. State Bar Association, Atlantic City, June 13, 1947; *New Jersey Law Journal*, June 12, 1947; *New Jersey, Constitutional Convention of 1947*, pp. 412–413, 438.

30. *New Jersey, Constitutional Convention of 1947*, pp. 356–361, 325–328; Vickers to Members of the Council (see n. 27). Minimum wages orders had been issued for the laundry, restaurant, beauty shop, and cleaning and dyeing trades.

31. *New Jersey, Constitutional Convention of 1947*, pp. 418–419. J. Margaret Warner, "It Has Happened in New Jersey," *Independent Woman* 26 (December 1947): 362–363.

32. Warner, "It Has Happened in New Jersey," p. 362.

33. Ibid.

34. *Bulletin of the NJLWV* 17 (October 1947): "The Most Important Changes Made in the Present Constitution of New Jersey by the Proposed Revision," October 1947, Box 10, CLNJ Papers.

35. Vickers to Members of the Council (see n. 27).

36. *Newark Evening News*, November 5, 1947; for official returns see *Manual of the Legislature of New Jersey: 1949*, p. 54.

37. "What the Proposed New Constitution Means to You," a report to the people of New Jersey by their elected delegates to the Constitutional Convention, New Brunswick, 1947, Box 5, NJLWV Papers.

38. For evidence of women's static political status in the 1940s in terms of state elective and appointive office, see *Manual of the Legislature of New Jersey*, 1940–1947; see also, for example, *Newark Evening News*, December 10, 1941; ibid., January 13, 1943; ibid., January 27, 1943, for OWLs continuing failure to achieve a greater number of gubernatorial appointments of women to state boards and commissions; Warner, "It Has Happened in New Jersey," pp. 362–363.

Chapter 10: The New Jersey Suffragists in Retrospect

1. William H. Chafe, *The American Woman: Her Changing Social, Economic and Political Roles, 1920–1970* (New York, 1972), pp. 55–56; Carl N. Degler, *At Odds: Women and the Family in America from the Revolution to the Present* (New York, 1980), p. 391.

2. William L. O'Neill, *Everyone Was Brave: A History of Feminism in America* (Chicago, 1969), pp. 3–76, quotation on p. 21.

3. Degler, *At Odds*, pp. 328–361, quotation on p. 357.

4. Aileen Kraditor, *The Ideas of the Woman Suffrage Movement, 1890–1920* (New York, 1965), pp. 38–57, quotation on p. 44.

5. Mary Philbrook, "Suffrage Movement," "Early Women Leaders," Autobiographical Notes, Folder 1, Box 1, Mary Philbrook Papers, New Jersey Historical Society, Newark; *Bergen Evening Record*, 1949 (n.d.), Scrapbooks, Box 4, ibid.

6. The passage of the Industrial Home Work Act is cited in *Laws of New Jersey: Acts of the One Hundred and Sixty-Fifth Legislature of the State of New Jersey and Ninety-Seventh under the New Constitution* (Trenton, 1941), p. 843. See also chaps. 3, 4, 8 in this book.

7. The act making a married woman "solely responsible for her torts" is cited in *Laws of New Jersey*, 1929, p. 205. A summary of laws passed owing to NJWP efforts may be found in n. 25 in the notes to chap. 6 in this book.

8. See this book, chaps. 6, 9.

9. U.S. Department of Commerce, Bureau of the Census, *Provisional Estimates of Social, Economic, and Housing Characteristics, 1980 Census of Population and Housing* (Washington, D.C.: U.S. Government Printing Office, 1982); U.S. Department of Labor, Bureau of Labor Statistics, *Perspectives on Working Women: A Data Book*, Bulletin 2080 (Washington, D.C.: U.S. Government Printing Office, 1980); Mary Eastwood, "Feminism and the Law," in Jo Freeman, ed., *Women: A Feminist Perspective* (New York, 1975); Ruth B. Mandel, *In the Running: The New Woman Candidate* (New Haven, Conn., 1981), pp. 3, 15–17.

10. These surveys are cited in Irene Frieze, Jacquelynne E. Parsons, Paula B. Johnson, Diane N. Ruble, and Gail L. Zellman, *Women and Sex Roles: A Social Psychological Perspective* (New York, 1978), p. 349, and Mandel, *In the Running*, p. 14.

11. For the impact of World War II on women's economic status and the postwar mood of normalcy, see Chafe, *American Woman*, chaps. 6–8; the reference to an average woman worker as "married and over thirty-five" is on p. 144. For an excellent exposition of the concerns and demands of the woman's movement, see Freeman, *Women*.

12. U.S. Department of Labor, Employment and Training Administration, *Women and Work*, R and D Monograph 46 (Washington, D.C.: U.S.

Government Printing Office, 1977), pp. 3–12, 23; U.S. Department of Labor, Bureau of Labor Statistics, *News*, Press Release, USDL 82-86, March 7, 1982; Mandel, *In the Running*, pp. 98–123.

13. Mandel, *In the Running*, pp. 252–253.

14. Jean Bethke Elshtain, *Public Man, Private Woman: Women in Social and Political Thought* (Princeton, 1981), pp. 335–336, 348.

15. Mandel, *In the Running*, p. 255.

Bibliography

Bibliographies

Stanwick, Kathy, and Li, Christine. *The Political Participation of Women in the United States: A Selected Bibliography, 1950–1976*. New Brunswick: Rutgers University, Eagleton Institute of Politics, 1974.
Steiner-Scott, Elizabeth, and Wagle, Elizabeth Pearce. *New Jersey Women 1770–1970: A Bibliography*. Madison, N.J.: Fairleigh Dickinson University Press, 1978.

Manuscript Collections

Camden Woman's Club Papers. Camden Historical Society.
Consumers' League of New Jersey Papers. Special Collections, Alexander Library, Rutgers University.
Federal Writers' Project, New Jersey Women's Archives, 1890–1953. New Jersey Historical Society, Newark.
Moorfield, Amelia Berndt, Papers. New Jersey Historical Society, Newark.
National Woman's Party Papers. Alexander Library, Rutgers University.
New Jersey League of Women Voters Papers. Special Collections, Alexander Library, Rutgers University.
New Jersey State Federation of Women's Clubs Papers. New Jersey State Federation of Women's Clubs Headquarters, New Brunswick.
New Jersey Woman Suffrage Association Papers. New Jersey Historical Society, Newark.
Norton, Mary T., Papers. Special Collections, Alexander Library, Rutgers University.
Philbrook, Mary, Papers. New Jersey Historical Society, Newark.
Pope, Elizabeth, Scrapbook. New Jersey Historical Society, Newark.
Robbins, Lena Anthony, Papers. In New Jersey League of Women Voters Papers, Special Collections, Alexander Library, Rutgers University.

Other Unpublished Sources

Connors, Richard J. "The Movement for Constitutional Revision in New Jersey, 1941–1947." Master's thesis, Columbia University, 1955.

Gammage, Judie Karen Walton. "Quest for Equality: An Historical Over-
view of Women's Rights Activism in Texas, 1890–1975." Ph.D. diss.,
North Texas State University, 1982.
Gordon, Felice. "Women in New Jersey Politics: Running for Elective
Office, 1920–1934." Rutgers University, 1978. Mimeo.
Jackson, Emma Louise Moyer. "Petticoat Politics: Political Activism among
Texas Women in the 1920s." Ph.D. diss., University of Texas at Austin,
1980.
Roydhouse, Marian. "The Universal Sisterhood of Women: Women and
Labor Reform in North Carolina, 1900–1932." Ph.D. diss., Duke Uni-
versity, 1980.
Schrom, Nancy. "The Women's Trade Union League of New York, 1903–
1920." Ph.D. diss., University of Wisconsin, 1974.
Stickle, Warren Edward. "New Jersey Democracy and the Urban Coalition:
1919–1932." Ph.D. diss., Georgetown University, 1971.
Taylor, Paul. "The Entrance of Women into Party Politics: The 1920s." Ph.D.
diss., Harvard University, 1966.

Public Documents and Government Publications

Laws of New Jersey. Acts of the legislature of the state of New Jersey.
Camden, Paterson, or Trenton, 1895–1947.
Manual of the Legislature of New Jersey. Trenton, 1914–1947.
New Jersey Minutes of Assembly (New Jersey Legislative General Assembly).
Minutes of votes and proceedings of the 81st General Assembly of the
state of New Jersey, convened at Trenton, January 13, 1857.
State of New Jersey, Constitutional Convention of 1947. Vol. 3: Committee on
Rights, Privileges, Amendments and Miscellaneous Provisions and Commit-
tee on the Legislative Record, Trenton, State of New Jersey, 1947.
U.S. Department of Commerce. Bureau of the Census. Provisional Estimates
of Social, Economic, and Housing Characteristics, 1980 Census of Population
and Housing, Washington, D.C., U.S. Government Printing Office,
1982.
U.S. Department of Labor. Bureau of Labor Statistics. Perspectives on Work-
ing Women: A Data Book. Bulletin 2080. Washington, D.C., U.S. Government Printing Office, 1980.
———. News. Press Release, USDL 82-86, March 7, 1982.
———. Employment and Training Administration. Women and Work. R and
D Monograph 46. Washington, D.C., U.S. Government Printing
Office, 1977.

Books

Anthony, Susan B. *History of Woman Suffrage, 1885–1900*. Vol. 4. Rochester, N.Y.: Susan B. Anthony, 1902.

Baisden, Richard N. *Charter for New Jersey: The New Jersey Constitutional Convention of 1947*. Trenton: New Jersey Department of Education, 1952.

Banner, Lois W. *Women in Modern America: A Brief History*. New York: Harcourt Brace Jovanovich, 1974.

Becker, Susan D. *The Origins of the Equal Rights Amendment: American Feminism between the Wars*. Westport, Conn.: Greenwood, 1981.

Breckinridge, Sophinisba. *Women in the Twentieth Century: A Study of Their Political, Social and Economic Activities*. New York: McGraw-Hill, 1933.

Bussey, Gertrude Carman. *Women's International League for Peace and Freedom, 1915–1965*. London: Allen and Unwin, 1965.

Chafe, William H. *The American Woman: Her Changing Social, Economic and Political Roles, 1920–1970*. New York: Oxford University Press, 1972.

Commager, Henry Steele, ed. *Documents of American History*. 9th ed. New York: Appleton, Century, Crofts, 1973.

Cott, Nancy F. *The Bonds of Womanhood: "Woman's Sphere" in New England, 1780–1835*. New Haven, Conn.: Yale University Press, 1977.

Degler, Carl N. *At Odds: Women and the Family in America from the Revolution to the Present*. New York: Oxford University Press, 1980.

Dubois, Ellen Carol. *Feminism and Suffrage: The Emergence of an Independent Women's Movement in America, 1848–1869*. Ithaca, N.Y.: Cornell University Press, 1978.

Duster, Alfreda M., ed. *Crusade for Justice: The Autobiography of Ida B. Wells*. Chicago: University of Chicago Press, 1970.

Elshtain, Jean Bethke. *Public Man, Private Woman: Women in Social and Political Thought*. Princeton: Princeton University Press, 1981.

Erdman, Charles R., Jr. *The New Jersey Constitution of 1776*. Princeton: Princeton University Press, 1929.

Fass, Paula. *The Damned and the Beautiful: American Youth in the 1920s*. New York: Oxford University Press, 1977.

Flexner, Eleanor. *Century of Struggle: The Woman's Rights Movement in the United States*. Rev. ed. Cambridge, Mass.: Harvard University Press, Belknap Press, 1975.

Freeman, Jo, ed. *Women: A Feminist Perspective*. New York: McKay, 1975.

Frieze, Irene; Parsons, Jacquelynne E.; Johnson, Paula B.; Ruble, Diane N.; and Zellman, Gail L. *Women and Sex Roles: A Social Psychological Perspective*. New York: Norton, 1978.

Gusfield, Joseph R. *Symbolic Crusade: Status Politics and the American Temperance Movement*. Urbana: University of Illinois Press, 1963.

Harper, Ida Husted. *History of Woman Suffrage*, 1900–1920. Vols. 5–6. New York: National American Woman Suffrage Association, 1922.

Hartman, Mary; and Banner, Lois W., eds. *Clio's Consciousness Raised: New Perspectives on the History of Women*. New York: Harper and Row, 1974.

Irwin, Inez Haynes. *The Story of the Woman's Party*. New York: Harcourt Brace, 1921.

Kessler-Harris, Alice. *Out to Work: A History of Wage-Earning Women in the United States*. New York: Oxford University Press, 1982.

Kraditor, Aileen. *The Ideas of the Woman Suffrage Movement, 1890–1920*. New York: Columbia University Press, 1965.

League of Women Voters of New Jersey. *Spotlight on Government*. New Brunswick: Rutgers University Press, 1969.

Lemons, J. Stanley. *The Woman Citizen: Social Feminism in the 1920s*. Urbana: University of Illinois Press, 1973.

Lerner, Gerda. *Black Women in White America*. New York: Pantheon, 1972.

Leuchtenburg, William E. *Franklin D. Roosevelt and the New Deal, 1932–1940*. New York: Harper and Row, 1963.

———. *The Perils of Prosperity, 1914–1932*. Chicago: University of Chicago Press, 1958.

Mandel, Ruth B. *In the Running: The New Woman Candidate*. New Haven, Conn.: Ticknor and Fields, 1981.

Nichols, Carole. *Votes and More for Women: Suffrage and After in Connecticut*. New York: Haworth, 1983.

O'Neill, William L. *Everyone Was Brave: A History of Feminism in America*. Chicago: Quadrangle, 1969.

Rosenberg, Rosalind. *Beyond Separate Spheres: Intellectual Roots of Modern Feminism*. New Haven, Conn.: Yale University Press, 1982.

Rosenthal, Alan; and Blydenburgh, John, eds. *Politics in New Jersey*. New Brunswick: Rutgers University Press, 1975.

Scott, Anne Firor. *The Southern Lady: From Pedestal to Politics, 1830–1930*. Chicago: University of Chicago Press, 1970.

Stanton, Elizabeth Cady; Anthony, Susan B.; and Gage, Matilda Joslyn, eds. *History of Woman Suffrage, 1848–1861*. Vol. 1. New York: Fowler and Wells, 1881.

———. *History of Woman Suffrage, 1876–1885*. Vol. 3. Rochester, N.Y.: Susan B. Anthony, 1887.

Young, Louise M. *Understanding Politics: A Practical Guide for Women*. New York: Pellegrini and Cudahy, 1950.

Articles

Allen, Florence E. "The First Ten Years," *Woman's Journal* 15 (August 1930): 5–7, 30–32.

Blackwell, Alice Stone. "Lucy Stone: New Jersey Pioneer Suffragist." *Civic Pilot* 2 (September 1923): 8, 21–24.

Blair, Emily Newell. "Why I Am Discouraged about Women in Politics." *Woman's Journal* 16 (January 1931): 21.

———. "Women in the Political Parties." *Annals of the American Academy* 143 (May 1929): 218.

Bromley, Dorothy Dunbar. "Feminist—New Style." *Harper's* 155 (October 1927): 554–562.

Brown, Gertrude Foster. "Are Women Voters Making Good?" *Woman Citizen* 11 (August 1926): 5–7.

Buenker, John D. "The Urban Political Machine and Woman Suffrage: A Study in Political Adaptability." *Historian* 33 (1970–1971): 264–279.

Butterfield, Elizabeth C. "First Federal Jury Commissioner Organizes Jury Schools." *Democratic Digest*, December 1937, p. 17.

"'Carpenter vs. Cornish': Harriet F. Carpenter Petitions for Right to Register to Vote. Miss Mary Philbrook for Relator. New Jersey Supreme Court, April 11, 1912." *New Jersey Law Journal* 35 (July 1912): 212–216.

Cott, Nancy F. "Feminist Politics in the 1920s: The National Woman's Party." *Journal of American History* 71 (June 1984): 43–68.

[Douglas], Ann Douglas Wood. "'The Fashionable Diseases': Woman's Complaints and Their Treatment in Nineteenth-Century America." In Mary Hartman and Lois W. Banner, eds., *Clio's Consciousness Raised: New Perspectives in the History of Women*, pp. 1–22. New York: Harper and Row, 1974.

Fischer, Marguerite J. "Women in the Political Parties." *Annals of the American Academy* 251 (May 1947): 90.

Freedman, Estelle B. "The New Woman: Changing Views of Women in the 1920s." *Journal of American History* 61 (September 1974): 372–393.

———. "Separatism as Strategy: Female Institution Building and American Feminism, 1870–1930." *Feminist Studies* 5 (Fall 1979): 512–529.

Hyde, Anne Rogers. "Women Walking on Their Hind Legs." *Harper's* 162 (May 1931): 680–690.

"In the Matter of the Application of Mary Philbrook to an Examination as an Attorney at Law." *New Jersey Law Journal* 17 (1894): 202–203. See also "A Woman Asks Leave to Practise Law," p. 93 in the same volume.

Lerner, Gerda. "Early Community Work of Black Club Women." *Journal of Negro History* 59 (April 1974): 158–167.

Mahoney, Joseph F. "Woman Suffrage and the Urban Masses." *New Jersey History* 87 (1969): 151–172.

May, Henry F. "Shifting Perspectives on the 1920s." *Mississippi Valley Histori-cal Review* 43 (December 1956): 405–427.
McKee, Oliver, Jr. "Ten Years of Woman Suffrage." *Commonwealth* 12 (July 16, 1930): 298–300.
Mussey, Henry Raymond. "Law and a Living for Women." *Survey Graphic* 61 (November 1, 1928): 156–158, 194–195.
Philbrook, Mary. "Woman's Legal Status: Should It Be Altered?" *New Jersey Law Journal* 20 (November 1897): 324–327.
Smith-Rosenberg, Carroll. "Beauty, the Beast and the Militant Woman: A Case Study in Sex Roles and Social Stress in Jacksonian America." *American Quarterly* 23 (1971): 562–584.
———. "Puberty to Menopause: The Cycle of Femininity in Nineteenth-Century America." In Mary Hartman and Lois W. Banner, eds., *Clio's Consciousness Raised: New Perspectives in the History of Women*, pp. 23–37. New York: Harper and Row, 1974.
Swift, M. E. "Suffrage for Women a Handicap in Civic Work." *New Jersey Bulletin* 1 (October 1916): 3. Published in the interests of the State Federation of Women's Clubs.
"Ten Years of Suffrage." *Survey* 63 (January 15, 1930): 454.
Turner, Edward Raymond. "Woman Suffrage in New Jersey, 1790–1807." *Smith College Studies in History* 1 (July 1916): 165–187.
Warner, Margaret J. "It Has Happened in New Jersey." *Independent Woman* 26 (December 1947): 362–363.
Welter, Barbara. "The Cult of True Womanhood: 1820–1860." *American Quarterly* 18 (Summer 1966): 151–174.

Pamphlets

"Five Reasons Why Believers in Prohibition Should Vote for Lillian F. Feickert for United States Senator in the Republican Primary May 15, 1928"; "Lillian F. Feickert, Candidate for U.S. Senator: A Personal Record"; "Why You Should Vote for Lillian F. Feickert for United States Senator in the Republican Primary May 15, 1928." New Jersey Political Broadsides, Special Collections, Alexander Library, Rutgers University (hereafter cited as SCAL).
"How New Jersey Laws Discriminate against Women." National Woman's Party, New Jersey, 1926. Catalogued in New Jersey Collection, SCAL.
Lawrence, M. E., New Jersey Woman's Christian Temperance Union State Superintendent of Franchise. "A Suffrage Quiz." New Jersey Pamphlets (uncatalogued), SCAL.
"New Jersey State Federation of Colored Women's Clubs, Incorporated."

Available from the New Jersey State Federation of Colored Women's Clubs Carver Center, Trenton.

Pamphlets of the New Jersey Committee on the Cause and Cure of War, 1930–1940. New Jersey Broadsides, in SCAL.

"Pilgrimage to the Home of Lucy Stone, Orange, New Jersey, August 13, 1915. New Jersey Broadsides, in SCAL.

"Report of the Conference on the Cause and Cure of War, Held in Washington, D.C. January 18, 1925." New York. SCAL.

Stone, Lucy. "Reasons Why the Women of New Jersey Should Vote, as Shown from the Constitution and Statutes of New Jersey." Caption title "Approved by the Executive Committee of the New Jersey Woman Suffrage Association, Vineland, New Jersey, March 1, 1868." SCAL.

Stone, Lucy, and Blackwell, H. B. "Woman Suffrage in New Jersey." [1867]. New Jersey pamphlets (uncatalogued), SCAL.

"The New Jersey Republican." New Jersey Women's Republican Club, 1923–1927. Lena Anthony Robbins Papers, in New Jersey League of Women Voters Papers, SCAL.

Index